AF361365

BEASTLY POSSESSIONS

Animals in Victorian Consumer Culture

Beastly Possessions

Animals in Victorian Consumer Culture

SARAH AMATO

UNIVERSITY OF TORONTO PRESS
Toronto Buffalo London

ISBN 978-1-4426-4874-6

Library and Archives Canada Cataloguing in Publication

Amato, Sarah, 1977–, author
Beastly possessions : animals in Victorian consumer culture / Sarah Amato.

Includes bibliographical references and index.
ISBN 978-1-4426-4874-6 (bound)

1. Consumption (Economics) – Social aspects – Great Britain – History – 19th century.   2. Animals and civilization – Great Britain – History – 19th century.   3. Human-animal relationships – Great Britain – History – 19th century.   4. Pets – Social aspects – Great Britain – History – 19th century.   5. Great Britain – Social life and customs – 19th century. I. Title.

HC79.C6A438 2015   306.3094109'034   C2015-903241-5

University of Toronto Press acknowledges the financial assistance to its publishing program of the Canada Council for the Arts and the Ontario Arts Council, an agency of the Government of Ontario.

Contents

Illustrations

Acknowledgments

So many people have kindly supported me and this project along the way. I thank the many archivists, curators, and collectors who provided me with access to materials: Jeremy Adams at the Brighton & Hove Council Booth Museum of Natural History; Beverly Cook at the Museum of London; Joanne Hatton and Vicky Pearce at the Horniman Museum & Gardens; Julie Anne Lambert from the John Johnson Collection of Printed Ephemera at Oxford; Brad Millen at the Royal Ontario Museum; Michael Palmer at Zoological Society of London Library; Martha Scott at the Osborne Collection of Early Children's Books, Toronto Public Library; Alexis Turner at London Taxidermy, and Sebastian Wormell at Harrods Ltd, Knightsbridge. Thanks additionally to the helpful staff at the British Newspaper Library – an amazing resource.

I received generous funding from the University of Toronto, in the form of travel grants from the Department of History and the School of Graduate Studies; from the Social Sciences and Humanities Research Council of Canada; from Victoria College, in the form of a George C. Metcalf Research Fellowship and a Victoria College Research Publication Grant; from the Ontario Student Assistance Program, in the form of an Ontario Graduate Scholarship; from the Huntington Library, in the form of a Huntington-British Academy Grant; and from Wilfrid Laurier University, in the form of a Short Term Research Grant.

For their generous friendship, hospitality, and knowledge about and enthusiasm for London, I thank Isobel, Stephanie, and Victor Aptaker, and Amelia and David Lasserson.

For their encouragement, mentorship, direction, and friendship – well beyond graduation – I thank Adrienne Hood and Lori Loeb, as well as Eric Jennings and Derek Penslar. Ariel Beaujot, Max Bergholz, Jeff Bowersox, Liz Burns, Kathy Cawsey, Geoff Hamm, Tomaz Jardim, Steve Maddox, Amy Milne-Smith, Ruth Percy, Mike Pettit, and Nathan Smith made the initial phases of research and writing great fun – and also provided ideas along the way.

In its transformation to a book, this project benefited from conversations with colleagues and friends, as well as the careful attention of reviewers. Thanks to Asher Alkoby, Nadine Attewell, Scott Bohaker, John Christopolous, Angela Fernandez and the Animals in the Law and Humanities group at the Jackman Humanities Institute, Carla Hustak, and Lori Loeb for reading (and rereading) and commenting on chapters, and providing suggestions. I am grateful to Richard Ratzlaff, Judith Williams, and the University of Toronto Press for guiding me and this project through publication; and thank the two anonymous reviewers who engaged with the manuscript and suggested revisions in such thoughtful and thought-provoking ways. This book is much better for your efforts; its shortcomings are very much my own.

I am forever indebted to those who brought me to and across the finish line (with humour, encouragement, and a shove): Asher Alkoby, Nadine Attewell, John Christopolous, Adrienne Hood, Carla Hustak, Franca Iacovetta, Sonya Jampolsky, Sheldon Levitt, Lori Loeb, Bridgette Lord, Maureen Shandling, and Lionel Nguyen Van Thé. This book is dedicated to Naomi and Victor Amato, as well as Becky and Hym Shandling.

BEASTLY POSSESSIONS

Animals in Victorian Consumer Culture

Introduction

It is early in the morning on a crisp December day in Christchurch, Hampshire, at the turn of the twentieth century. The taxidermist eagerly approaches the bird trap and is overcome by the beauty of the scene: next to the trap and ignoring it sits a robin redbreast, its bold colours bright against the snow. He returns to his workshop inspired (figure 0.1).

In London, a census enumerator reviewing returned papers laughs over the impudence of one respondent. A cat has been listed as a member of a household: "Jim," of the male sex, aged one, is described as a "lodger," and his occupation as "mouse-catcher, worker on his own account."[1]

In her cage the canary sings and heralds the day to come; the artisan will soon rise and tend to his pet rabbits before carrying on with the day. Meanwhile, across town, a Scotch terrier jumps into a chair, curls up, and goes to sleep. The chair is upholstered with the skin of a baby giraffe, and the long neck and head form the back and headrest (figure 5.7).[2]

In the London Zoological Gardens, the keepers are already at work loading duplicate animals onto a horse-drawn van bound for the docks to be shipped on to zoological collections in Calcutta.[3] One of the keepers considers the day ahead. He wonders if the old lady will visit the Gardens. She likes to poke the lion with her parasol and watch the crowd.

For Marion in Market Deeping, Lincolnshire, times are hard; she is in need of an income, and cannot sew fast enough. Sensing Marion's worries, Flo, the retriever, wags her tail and licks Marion's hand. Marion hesitates and then pens the following classified: "Will anyone give me

0.1. Edward Hart case, NH.83.3/91. © Horniman Museum and Gardens

a sewing machine for my beautiful, faithful, fascinating young retrieving Flo?"[4]

And the suffragette peruses her morning mail. She has received a postcard with a picture of an angry cat; the image is offensive and distinctly anti-suffragist, but the sender has a sense of humour and good wishes for the feminist cause. Written on the back is a message: "Wishing you a merry Xmas time and most Happy New Year + may it bring you what you want [the vote], + what I want too."[5]

In each of these stories, the biographies of animals and people have collided and intertwined at the very heart of British consumer culture.

In the pages that follow we travel with animals through a variety of households, and accompany middle-class observers into working-class dwellings. As Victorian Britons go about their daily routines, we watch them fuss over pets and express concern about the arrangement of taxidermy. Peering over shoulders, we read newspaper articles, postcards, and advertisements. We escort animals on railway journeys and accompany a humbug into the London Zoological Gardens. *Beastly Possessions: Animals in Victorian Consumer Culture* examines the ways Britons used animals as animate possessions and mass commodities between 1820 and 1914, a time of social upheaval and imperial expansion. It argues that pet keeping, zoo visiting, and taxidermic decoration became mass phenomena in the nineteenth and early twentieth centuries, during which Britons explored the human/animal boundary, tested socially acceptable behaviours, and participated in consumer culture. In each chapter, we experience the joys and anxieties of Victorian relations to animals – and not just living animals, but also representations of animals (in pictures, novels, sculptures, toys, advertisements, ornaments, postcards, guidebooks) and preserved animals (taxidermy). We witness how animals shaped and disrupted daily life and could bring into sharp relief the contested nature of consumer processes as well as social values and identities. This is a history of Victorian social life told through an examination of human-animal relations.

Because I am charting a constellation of attitudes and practices that reached their apogee in the nineteenth century, I refer to the people who populate this book as Victorians, even when describing occurrences before the reign of Victoria (1837–1901) and after the turn of the twentieth century. This book excludes discussion of livestock and labouring animals, except to note that working animals lived and roamed alongside people in Victorian cities, where horses, dogs, pigs, poultry, and cattle served as sources of food, transport, and labour. Over half of the British population lived in cities by 1851, but urbanization did not bring a separation from the animals that were constituent parts of agricultural life. Animals were so ubiquitous that Victorians sought to accommodate some of their needs, providing, for example, drinking fountains along the routes of drovers and in certain parks in London.[6] At the same time, and of great significance to this book, animals were being turned into commodities and decorative objects in new ways. They were incorporated into urban life and assigned purposes that were increasingly social, as pets, zoo-dwelling creatures, representations, taxidermic ornaments, and museum exhibitions. The social function of these creatures was not entirely separate from economic and productive priorities. Victorians emphasized the commercial and utilitarian nature of their relationships to these animals, which continued to provide opportunities for profit, acclaim, morality, and erudition. At the same time, they were keenly aware of the diverse social lives of the animals in their midst.

The Social Lives of Animals

As animals were subject to different managements, manipulations, and interpretations, they took on different social roles, and this irrevocably changed the lives of both animals and humans.[7] An animal fulfils multiple functions in human society, and sometimes takes on the same role more than once. For example, a creature could be captured and sold as a commodity and transformed into a pet. As a pet, the animal could serve as a companion as well as a living parlour decoration and evidence of household social and moral status; it could be eventually donated to the Zoo as well as preserved as taxidermy. In the Zoo, the animal could become a public pet, moral exemplar, object of science, source of erudition, object of curiosity, symbol of empire, and, later, consumer mascot. Surplus zoo creatures could be sold to individuals and later kept as pets. At any point, an animal could be illustrated or painted by an artist and transformed into a representation, sometimes with political repercussions. As this trajectory suggests, the same animal could re-enter commodity chains and be exchanged from hand to hand at various stages of its life course, whenever sold, traded, bred, donated, or preserved as taxidermy. In these moments, the animal slowly acquired meaning, took on new social significance, and had different impacts on human society.[8]

Then as now, animals thwarted the intentions of the humans with whom they came into contact. Victorians tried to curb beastly behaviours and reform animality, sometimes to no avail. The disciplining of animals in order to make them trustful, compliant, and orderly became especially important because animals were understood to signal the characteristics of the people who owned and kept company with them. In and around the home, for example, pets were understood as harbingers of household harmony – indicating social status. It even became important to "civilize" the animals in the care of the London Zoological

Gardens, since reforming previously "wild" animals signalled the power of the Zoo and was believed to have beneficial effects on certain Zoo visitors. Representations of animals in pictures, paintings, and novels also made evident the extent to which animal behaviours were understood as exemplars for human conduct. In this book, I show how Victorians used animals to signal and enforce appropriate and polite behaviours in humans.

When Victorians interacted with living animals, representations of animals, and parts of animals (taxidermy), their lives changed profoundly and subtly. To be a pet keeper in nineteenth-century Britain, for example, necessitated certain responsibilities, affinities, and types of sociality. Pet keeping often, though not always, involved bringing animals inside homes, which were places already imbued with symbolic and moral meaning. Pets were special possessions, contributing to the atmosphere of the home and signalling to outsiders the domestic harmony of its inhabitants. Similarly, the London Zoological Gardens facilitated particular encounters with animals that had ramifications for norms of behaviour. Encountering representations of animals in visual, literary, and material culture informed the Victorian world view and dictated, often unconsciously, codes of conduct. Very often the limits of polite behaviours were tested through interactions with living and representational animals. Representations were not unconnected to real animals, since they drew attention to characteristics of and beliefs about animals that Victorians considered fascinating and problematic. Human-animal encounters became forums for exploring and expressing Victorian social hierarchies and intersections of class, gender, and race, as well as human and animal.

Animals were often perceived as models for human propriety and were prominently featured in discussions of gender roles and relations between the sexes. Since the 1860s, Victorian society was galvanized by campaigns mounted by middle-class women for access to higher education, the professions, the franchise, and the repeal of the Contagious Diseases Acts. (The Contagious Diseases Acts were intended to regulate prostitution and reduce the incidence of venereal disease in garrison towns. They gave police the authority to arrest any woman suspected of being a prostitute and subject her to a medical examination. The feminist campaign against the CDA made prostitution a public issue.)[9] These demands inspired debates about ideologies that stipulated separate roles for men and women in all areas of Victorian life, including in leisure activities.[10] In this context, representations of animals became implicated in high-stakes gender politics. As I show, representations of cats and dogs, in particular, were used to regulate women's participation in public life, and became important in women's attempt to access the franchise.

Victorian relationships to animals were fraught with tension and offered a means of exploring ideas about human kinship with animals, at a time when this was a pressing issue and a subject of widespread interest, made increasingly prescient by Darwinian science. The publication of Charles Darwin's *The Origin of Species by Means of Natural Selection* (1859), *Descent of Man and Selection in Relation to Sex* (1871), and *The Expression of the Emotions in Man and Animals* (1872) bolstered long-standing debates about the nature of human-animal kinship by suggesting evolutionary linkages between people and animals. Many of the incidents and representations that I discuss demonstrate the pervasive obsession with the natural order that informed the context in which Darwin and others worked. As Kenneth Ames puts it, this context was "alive with questions and assertions about hierarchy, dominance, progress, and relationship of humankind to the rest of the world, past and present."[11] While I share with some scholars the concern that notions of a "Darwinian Revolution" have been overemphasized, references to Darwin's discoveries abound in Victorian popular culture after 1859.[12] Darwin provided Victorians with a narrative about human evolution that was both liberating and unsettling. On the one hand, Darwinism justified the kinds of affinities and affections Victorians could feel towards animals, since animals were now acknowledged to be linked to humans by ancestry; and on the other, it intensified anxieties about the possibility of the animal lurking in the human. In this context, the imperative to curb animal-like behaviours became pressing, and was something of a two-way street affecting interactions both among people and between people and animals. In the chapters that follow, I discuss efforts to reform beastliness and change animal behaviours so that they were more in line with human codes of civility. In some cases, efforts to discipline animals extended beyond death and were completed only when the animal was resurrected as taxidermy in a pose that demonstrated its compliance to human wishes. While interacting with animals, Victorians considered what it meant to be human, alive and wilful, middle-class, working-class, male, female, and white in a stratified and imperial society.

By the twentieth century Britain had become the largest European empire, having added, over the course of the nineteenth century, four hundred million people and ten million square miles to its imperial holdings.[13] Exchanges and representations of animals became ways to negotiate imperial relationships between colonies and metropole. Sometimes imperial subjects catered to the British proclivity for pet keeping in an attempt to express gratitude or seek favour. For example, in 1869 Sir Cowasjee Jehangir of Bombay funded the building of an elaborate drinking fountain for dogs in Regent's Park.[14] Colonial administrators and indigenous rulers often gifted animals to prominent zoological institutions, and animal dealers sold exotic animals to pet owners. These gifts and commodities were understood to be representatives of territories under British control, and their incorporation into metropolitan life suggests the acceptance of a certain form of intimate colonial relation, via the animal as proxy. Animals, like other goods, were transported across vast distances and through domestic and imperial commodity chains to inhabit urban and domestic spaces, as well as menageries and zoos.

As living beings, animals were animate possessions and unique commodities. Unlike other consumer goods, they were not produced by human craftsmanship, but they were subject to various manipulations. Like other goods, animals could take on and express social and cultural meaning through acquisition, use, and other consumer processes. They became commodities and possessions at a particularly significant moment in the development of consumer society.

Mass Commodities and Animate Possessions

Most of the interactions with animals that I discuss in this book involved consumer processes. Consumerism in the nineteenth century entailed more than shopping for goods or moments of purchase and became a means to solidify or transform identities and relationships.[15] As much a social as an economic process, consumerism involved the movement of goods through networks of retail, exchange, acquisition, use, and divestment.[16] Though the origins of consumer society in Great Britain remain a subject of debate, many historians agree that it began to arise in the eighteenth century.[17] By the late nineteenth century, a marked increase in the goods, services, and leisure opportunities available for consumption, as well as new methods of retailing and an expanding empire, created a thriving consumer society.[18]

According to John Benson, a consumer society is one "in which choice and credit are readily available, in which social value is defined in terms of purchasing power and material possessions and in which there is a desire above all for that which is new, modern, exciting and fashionable."[19] In an important article, Peter Stearns discusses the difficulty of locating the moment in which these conditions are met and a majority of the population can partake in consumer processes. According to Stearns, there can only be a consumer society when a large portion of the population has enough disposable income "at least from time to time to purchase beyond immediate necessities" and must stake "a real portion of their personal identity and quest for meaning – even their emotional satisfaction on the search for and acquisition of goods." By the late nineteenth century, he suggests, the conditions were in place for a thriving consumer culture: there was an increase in the goods, services, and leisure opportunities available for consumption; new methods of retailing; and an expanding market for these services.[20] Moreover, as Paul Johnson shows, even very poor families between 1870 and 1914 participated in these new consumption patterns, "not just to meet their basic needs for food, clothing and shelter, but also to define their social position" within their own communities.[21] Diets comprising meat and tea, Sunday dress, and tablecloths, ornaments, and cheap lithographs signified self-sufficiency and respectability to neighbours.[22] To this list, I would add the ownership of pets and participation in certain leisure activities, including the animal fancies as well as visits to zoos and museums. (The animal fancies were activities that involved breeding animals for points of beauty.) Zoos and museums were part of a thriving entertainment market in Victorian cities that included other forms of commercial leisure, such as exhibitions of living foreign peoples, tea gardens, galleries, music halls, and sporting venues.[23]

Through their engagements with animals, Victorians participated in consumer society. Animals were among the goods that could be acquired, purchased, and exchanged as mass commodities in the second half of the nineteenth century alongside other possessions. The diverse possessions that cluttered the lives of middle-class Victorians have been a subject of interest ever since Asa Briggs published his groundbreaking book *Victorian Things*,[24] but none have located Victorian relations with animals in the broader context of Victorian consumer and material culture more generally, as this study intends to do.[25] Other scholars have shown how Victorians of all social classes placed great value in their possessions as indicators of status and sources of financial security, especially in times of need when they could be pawned or sold as second-hand goods.[26] Pets and pet-keeping accoutrements may well have been among the articles that were exchanged. The historian

Melanie Tubbett, for example, notes that in 1932 one working-class woman pawned her pet canary before she went to work and redeemed it each evening upon her return.[27] We can speculate that such occurrences also took place in the nineteenth century.

Victorians used new consumer amenities to complete transactions involving animals, including railway systems, which revolutionized possibilities of domestic transport, travel, and retail within Britain, allowing for everyone and everything to be put in motion.[28] Sometimes the sight of animals on the railway caused quite a stir, especially in the early days of this transport. In 1832 the *Liverpool Times* published a report of people flocking to witness circus animals passing through the city under the headline "PASSENGERS EXTRAORDINARY BY THE RAIL-ROAD."[29] The shipment of animals by rail soon became commonplace.

Victorian consumer culture provided multiple opportunities to purchase, show, and care for animals, many of which are discussed in the pages that follow. The ownership of animals often entailed the purchase of new objects and services to care for pets, and exhibitions of prized animals were forums which made available the latest products. Exhibitions took place across the country, mostly in humble country pubs, but more illustrious venues, such as the Crystal Palace, which had been the site of the Great Exhibition of the Art and Industry of All Nations (1851), also hosted these events. The Great Exhibition has been examined as a consumer venue that permitted Victorians to contemplate displayed goods as things they might like to own.[30] It was therefore fitting that in the Crystal Palace, after it had been moved to Sydenham in 1854 and turned into a popular exhibition venue, and at other animal exhibitions, vendors made available the latest cages, transport baskets, medicines, and collars that might adorn animals and assist in their management. Zoological gardens, menageries, and museums also offered Victorians the leisure to learn about animals, often at a low cost. These institutions were part of a network of rational recreations that offered educational amusements – that is, entertainments that were morally uplifting and instructive as well as entertaining. Pictorial advertisements, which were produced more cheaply in the late nineteenth century, increasingly figured animals, sometimes to sell goods that had nothing to do with animal care.[31] Though in the early twentieth century department stores increasingly offered for sale collars and equipment for making taxidermy, the sale of pets remained predominantly an open-air and marketplace activity. In London, through the early twentieth century, dogs could be purchased on the streets in the East End (figure 2.5).[32] The trade in animals via classified advertisements was also thriving by the late 1870s, when a number of cheap newspapers circulated throughout the country.[33] In these ways, and many others that I will discuss, animals were fully implicated in burgeoning Victorian consumer culture and entered social history.

Animals in History

This book contributes to a growing literature on the subject of how animals play a role in the histories of human societies and affect human social structures. Over the past three decades, historians have shown how human relationships to and understandings of animals are historically and culturally contingent.[34] The basic premise of this scholarship is that human relations with and attitudes towards animals change over time and shed light on the components and complexities of human culture. As Erica Fudge puts it, this scholarship aims to "trace the many ways in which humans construct *and are constructed by* animals in the past," and *Beastly Possessions* contributes to this discussion.[35]

The books that have inspired investigations of the place of animals in human histories are Keith Thomas's *Man and the Natural World: A History of the Modern Sensibility* and Harriet Ritvo's *The Animal Estate: The English and Other Creatures in the Victorian Age*. Thomas argues that it "is impossible to disentangle what the people of the past thought about plants and animals from what they thought about themselves" and examines the evolution of attitudes towards plants and animals from the sixteenth through to the nineteenth century.[36] Focusing on nineteenth-century Britain, Ritvo argues that human-animal interactions "illuminate the history not only of the relations between people and other species, but also of relations among other human groups," and her work has been integral to historians exploring this field.[37] Ritvo's examination of specific institutions and moments of crisis, such as networks of high stockbreeders, dog shows, animal fights, the Royal Society for the Prevention of Cruelty to Animals, zoological gardens, anti-vivisection societies, and rabies outbreaks, has set the agenda for subsequent studies of human-animal relations in the nineteenth century, which have focused on similar topics.

Most studies of human relations to animals in Victorian and Edwardian Britain have investigated changing attitudes towards animal welfare, sometimes focusing on a single humanitarian institution or campaign. Taken together, these books have shown how attitudes towards animals changed over the course of the eighteenth and nineteenth centuries as middle-class humanitarians campaigned against animal cruelty and promoted kindly treatment of animals.[38] Some of this scholarship has located the origins of twenty-first-century preoccupations with animal rights and environmental destruction in Victorian culture.[39] Hilda Kean, in particular, has traced the genealogies of these organizations, showing how the Royal Society for the Prevention of Cruelty to Animals was just one of a number of institutions advocating for animal rights and welfare, and that the most unlikely individuals, from across the political spectrum, made common cause when it came to anti-cruelty campaigns. As part of their efforts, humanitarians encouraged their contemporaries to consider animals as fellow beings with capacities to experience pain, but also as moral exemplars for human conduct. Kean shows how these attitudes proliferated in Victorian middle-class culture and gave rise to new relationships and ideas about kinship with animals.[40]

The Anglo-Western European middle classes and their interactions with animals have received much attention in the scholarly literature. Kathleen Kete's work on nineteenth-century Paris, for example, investigates taxes imposed on the ownership of dogs, middle-class domestic relations with animals, and the "phobic imagination" of rabies infection. Kete suggests that relations with pet animals were fundamental to the ways the bourgeoisie experienced modernity.[41] In her work on dog breeding Harriet Ritvo focuses on the Victorian-British middle-class, showing how they used dog shows to promote a vision of middle-class ascendency and dominance.[42] Similarly, Katherine Grier, examining the American context, has also focused on the middle class and located twenty-first-century American concerns for the well-being of pets in middle-class Victorian attitudes towards their animals, as well as in burgeoning American consumer culture.[43] Nigel Rothfels's study on nineteenth-century Germany looks at the exploits of Carl Hagenbeck, a renowned animal dealer and founder the Tierpark Hagenbeck in Hamburg, as a window onto bourgeois German culture, imperial attitudes, and networks.[44] Together, these scholars argue convincingly that examining human-animal relations provides a window onto the complexities of middle-class culture and experience in the nineteenth century.

In contrast, the people that appear in the pages that follow represent a cross-section of British society, encompassing all social ranks, though most are middle class. These individuals were not particularly concerned about the welfare of the animals they encountered on a daily basis. I have no evidence that kindness was their primary concern or the basis of their sentiments towards animals. Most of these individuals were not animal welfare activists, vegetarians, anti-vivisectionists, or other humanitarians of any demonstrable stripe; their interactions with animals were often mediated by Victorian consumer culture and the possibilities for acclaim, companionship, moral enhancement, income, and erudition that it offered. Some did not even keep animal companions, but images of animals affected the ways in which they understood their world; others went to the London Zoological Gardens, not to look at animals, but to socialize and flirt. For pet owners, keeping pets provided opportunities for intimate interactions with animals as part of daily routines, even as these same pets were treated as living commodities and later dead ornaments that could signal status and impart moral lessons. Interactions with animals and representations of animals affected the ways Victorians of all classes understood their place in the world.

In the period under discussion, the middle class was an amorphous group, and, when defined by income, evinced considerable disparity, ranging between £150 and £1000 per family per annum.[45] This means that many individuals who aspired to middle-class status – associated with education, refinement, high standards of morality, freedom from manual labour, and the employment of at least one domestic servant – were only nominally middle class, and their status was precarious. Ownership of certain animals and ornaments figuring animals became one way to assert membership in the middling ranks.

Yet the rising middle classes remained a relatively small segment of the population compared with those who were considered working class, whose annual income per family could fall well below the £150 mark. Because small animals, such as birds, mice, and rats, could be easily captured and elevated to the status of pets, people of minimal economic resources became pet keepers, acquiring animals for companionship, household décor, entertainment, and supplemental income. Canaries and other animals were kept in even in the poorest homes – and the meaning of these animals as commodities was similar in lower-class and middle-class culture. Pets were objects of conspicuous consumption for working people and a means of proclaiming higher status among neighbours within working-class communities. In the second half of the nineteenth century, these same people visited zoos and museums that offered reduced entrance fees on specific days of the week. This scheduling prevented mingling between classes, but provided labourers with opportunities to enjoy some of the same entertainments and opportunities for education as their social superiors. Where possible, this book shows working-class engagement with animals as pets and zoo captives.

The most recent scholarship on the history of human-animal relations has attended to the material traces of animals in order to recover animals as historical actors in their own right. This has involved the difficult project of trying to access the experience(s) of being animal in certain historical moments, places, and conditions.[46] Another approach explores the way animals and representations of animal have affected people – and this book proceeds in a similar manner.[47] For Victorians, the materiality of living animals was a matter of common sense and sometimes problematic. Their relationships to pets and zoo animals were tangible, smelly, messy, disconcerting, comforting, and sometimes tasty; representations could be equally troubling. Where possible, I have tried to recover these experiences and describe the lives of animals.

The Structure of This Book

To discuss interactions with animals and the lives of animals in the Victorian era, I examine a variety of sources. In addition to the newspaper reports, social investigations, manuals, guidebooks, printed ephemera, lithographic images, and photographs that are increasingly the cultural historian's stock in trade, I draw on novels, and museum collections of advertisements, postcards, toys, art, ornaments, and taxidermy. These sources indicate the pervasiveness of Victorian interest in and engagement with animals – and draw our attention to the material and linguistic qualities of these relationships. Katherine Grier, in particular, has encouraged scholars of history and material culture to consider animals and various representations of them in pictures, postcards, and ornaments as important sources which enrich understandings of Victorian culture in general.[48] Grier's work on American pet keeping in the nineteenth and twentieth centuries also provides a model for examining the various products and amenities that were designed for and used by animals in the past.[49] Following her example, I deliberately use a variety of visual and material sources to tell the history that follows. These sources make visible and tangible past perspectives and also challenge us to reconsider longstanding periodization.[50] Some of the cultural phenomena discussed in the pages that follow endure for a long time and give rise to both our relationships with animals and certain cultural constructs involving animals – not in a teleological way, but in a way that is complex, halting, and multifaceted.

In the tradition of material culture analyses, a particular artefact inspired this book. Some years ago I received a postcard showing "The Kittens' Wedding," a diorama of taxidermy produced circa 1890 by the amateur taxidermist Walter Potter (1835–1918).[51] In the tableau eighteen kittens are dressed and standing upright to enact a wedding (figure 0.2). The scene piqued my interest and I wanted to know what Potter's creation signified to his contemporaries. Since I received the postcard, a number of scholars and writers have been similarly intrigued by "The Kittens' Wedding" and have offered rich interpretations, situating it in the context of Victorian animal stories and other taxidermy.[52] Potter's work has also become the subject of widespread interest.[53] My own route to understanding this artefact took me to the rituals of Victorian pet keeping, gendered depictions of cats and dogs, and the company of female animal fanciers, into the Zoo, through several museums, and into Victorian consumer culture. I return to "The Kittens' Wedding" in the last chapter of the book.

The chapters that follow move from intimate to distant and abstract relationships with animals as pets, illustrations, zoo creatures, advertisements, and museum exhibitions. This ordering can also be viewed sequentially as a narrative about the lives of certain animals after they enter human society through to their after-death embodiment as taxidermy. Each chapter stands on its own or can be read as part of the broader whole.

I start with the question "What was a pet?" In search of an answer, the first chapter describes the practices of keeping pets and foregrounds the discussion of consumerism that underpins the subsequent chapters. Here we see that pet keeping involved all sorts of emotional and economic transactions. Animals became pets when they were so designated, and any animal could be captured in the local environs and made into a pet. Pet keeping was a multifaceted endeavour; there were so many ways of being a pet and pet keeper that Victorians were divided on these matters, and these divisions were often manifested across class lines. The first part of the chapter discusses the range of animals that were kept as pets, and the different meanings ascribed to these animals by working-class pet keepers and middle-class commentators. Turning

0.2. "The Kittens' Wedding," taxidermy by Walter Potter, circa 1890.
© Marc Hill/APEX

to consumer culture, I show how pet keeping involved full participation in the expanding marketplace, paving the way for treatments of animals discussed in the following chapters as acquisitions, collectibles, and advertisements, as well as sources of entertainment, profit, acclaim, utility, moral erudition, and contemplation. As animals were incorporated into daily routines, pet keeping became a process of reforming animals into compliant pets, and this required the use of new consumer amenities. Finally, I turn to the animal fancies and the show circuit as the most commercial of all pet keeping activities that fully involved Victorians in the marketplace of things, but could have dire consequences for animals.

The second chapter discusses cats and dogs as "Sexy Beasts" and shows how the activities of pet keeping, discussed in the first chapter, had a bearing on Victorian and Edwardian society writ large by influencing popular notions of middle-class masculinity and femininity.

In theatrical performances, sculptures, paintings, illustrated supplements, sentimental narratives, and pet-keeping manuals, dogs were ascribed with masculine heroism and sincerity, while cats were considered emblems of female sexuality and perfidy. The first part of the chapter explores the figure of the fallen feline, the cat described as a model of feminine virtue, likened to middle-class women and easily led into vice. Turning to "man's best friend," the second part discusses the dog as a masculine hero, epitomizing the chivalrous, guileless, and loyal aspects of middle-class manhood. Gender trouble was provoked when women asserted themselves as owners and breeders of dogs. Female fanciers seemed unnatural in the order of things – unwomanly creatures with emasculated dogs. Women's participation in the dog fancies was directly correlated to women's struggle for the franchise and considered destructive to the Edwardian gender order. Just before the First World War, militant suffragettes attempted to turn this iconography on its head by dissociating women from cats. Their activities forced a reconsideration of ideologies that posited men as masters of nature and defined men and women as being as different as cats and dogs.

Turning to the London Zoological Gardens in the third chapter, we see how the Zoo was a site for comparing humans and animals in ways that involved the civilizing of animals and the displaying of people. Like the cat and dog fancies, the Zoo became a site for policing socially aberrant behaviour, especially flirtation between men and women. Those who entered the London Zoo could directly interact with the living artefacts on display. The architectural style of the enclosures resembled human dwellings and made the animals appear tame. In this seemingly benign setting, Victorians seized opportunities to poke fierce creatures, feed buns to bears, give snuff to monkeys, and administer gin to badgers. As attempts were made to reform the eating habits of certain parrots, pythons, and apes, these feeding rituals became highly symbolic and connected to the imperial rhetoric of the civilizing mission. At the same time, Victorians and Edwardians drew attention to perceived human aberrance by likening some visitors to zoo-dwelling animals. This was a means of regulating human behaviours, and any visitor could fall prey to censuring humour and allegations of beastliness. Keepers were similarly conflated with beasts. The presence of European keepers in colonial drag or foreign keepers in their native costumes authenticated exhibitions of animals, while all keepers provided a spectacle of working-class industry. Humans and human behaviours were thus on display in the London Zoo. The Zoo was a site for encounter and reflection, encouraging Britons to contemplate what it meant to be human, white, and British in a fluidly stratified society.

The fourth chapter continues the discussion of the Zoo as a significant forum for encounter and contemplation; it shows how a white elephant exhibited in the London Zoological Gardens in 1884 materialized late nineteenth-century theories of scientific racism and had a lasting impact on the history of advertising. The animal was the showpiece of Phineas Taylor Barnum, the American showman and trickster, who set out to exploit the mythology of white elephants in a period of mounting Anglo-Burmese tension. White elephants had been described in memoirs and travelogues recounting voyages to Siam and Burma. These accounts articulated orientalist fantasies by implying that the Siamese and Burmese worshipped these animals because they were white. When Barnum's elephant arrived in the London Zoo, disappointment with its appearance provoked a fierce debate. Visitors, scientists, newspaper editorialists, and many others expressed dissatisfaction with the creature's splotchy colouration and questioned the authenticity of the animal. Pears' Soap exploited these anxieties and used the image of the elephant to advertise their product. This was the beginning of a longstanding advertising campaign that drew on imperialist anxieties and promoted racist humour, while promising the ability of soap to regenerate whiteness. In the episode of the white elephant in London, human whiteness was acknowledged as an artificial construct and a status of the most superficial kind.

In their interactions with living animals, and especially pets, Britons struggled to control and discipline beastliness, but dead animals could serve their human masters in more ingenious ways. As taxidermy, the subject of the fifth chapter, stuffed animals were integrated into human society and subjected to the imagination in ways not possible with living animals. When dead animals were transformed into household furnishings, they were reintegrated into the routines of the living as material memories, moral embodiments, and household ornaments. Similar purposes were assigned to taxidermy in Victorian museums, where animals were also used for education. This chapter demonstrates the various uses Victorians assigned to taxidermy and argues that posthumous treatments marked the limit of any perceived connection between humans and animals. Animal corpses were easily treated as objects, stuffed for posterity and turned into articles for daily use and contemplation. In contrast, the dissection and dismemberment of the human corpse remained a source of fear and opprobrium through the nineteenth century. I trace attitudes towards after-death treatments of humans and animals by examining the exceptional case of the utilitarian philosopher Jeremy Bentham, who had his remains dissected and displayed. Bentham aspired to a future in which all human corpses would serve science and remain present among the living. His vision was realized by taxidermy, through which Victorians granted animals a paradoxically animated and provocative afterlife as dead things. In the final part of the chapter I return to the Kittens' Wedding and the taxidermy of Walter Potter, situating it in the context of Victorian taxidermy, as well as the diverse manifestations of human-animal relations discussed in this book.

Chapter One

The Social Lives of Pets

Portraits

The pale light creeps through windows and under doors, then the neighbourhoods erupt in song. From every country house, town lodging, and mean hovel, caged birds signal the coming dawn. For the moment, the pet canaries, titmice, skylarks, blue jays, and magpies are well fed, as are their owners, and times are good.

Across town, the gentleman emerges from sleep. He stretches and opens his eyes. Next to him, under a fold of the bed-cover, curled up and content, is Billy the squirrel. Today the companions will journey across country, catching the train. Billy will sleep in his master's pocket. The gentleman will compose an article about Billy for a popular magazine. He will be elegiac in praise of his pet.[1]

Meanwhile, standing in a kitchen, the maid surveys the mess: pots and utensils strewn about and a pile of shredded house flannels lies in the corner. The cause of this mayhem, Peter the hedgehog, is asleep in the nest of cloth. Peter has been drunk again, fed with "stiff whiskey-and-water" to render him tame. For a time, Peter was such "an amusing and instructive pet" and well worth the price paid for him in Covent Garden. But now, as a "dissipated hedgehog," he no longer catches beetles and cockroaches and has become rather useless.[2] The maid sighs, knowing her mistress will be displeased.

On a train, the ticket collector spots a monkey in a basket. When he requests fare for the creature, its owner becomes irate. A young girl pays the charge for her dog without comment. Other animals, including dogs, cats, canaries, and rabbits, are jostled about with the luggage. Some are in wicker hampers, others in margarine boxes, and still others are chained to posts. In their fear, the pets make a ruckus. Another railway employee surveys the scene. He has an idea for a carriage to improve the transport of dogs. The carriage will run on the London and North Western lines in the late 1890s.[3]

These stories evoke the rich textures of life with pets in late nineteenth- and early twentieth-century Britain. I have added fictional embellishments, but the main substance of each narrative is lifted directly from primary sources. Read together, these situations tell us much about the variety of emotional and economic interactions that were associated with pet keeping. In these stories, pets are "wild" and tame, existing between these binaries. They are also commodities that journey in and out of households and through commodity chains alongside other goods. The commodity state is just one phase of the animal's biography; the animal becomes a commodity when it is intended for exchange. In moments of exchange, commodities circulate the beliefs and values that have accrued to them through production, ownership, and use.[4] A pet, in the nineteenth century, was alternately and sometimes simultaneously perceived as an object and possession, a subject and a commodity – that is, a thing, a singular being, a moral exemplar, and an object of exchange. Animals that became pets existed between these classifications and had diverse social lives.

This chapter details life with pets in the nineteenth and early twentieth centuries. Where possible, I refer to the lives of specific pets and their owners so that I am not merely describing pet keeping in the abstract. I devote particular attention to working-class pet keepers, since their activities are crucial to my argument that pet keeping became a *mass* consumerist enterprise by the end of the nineteenth century, and in this my analysis differs from that of other historians who have focused on pet keeping in the nineteenth century as a bourgeois pastime. As we will see, working-class individuals also kept pets, but treated some pets differently from their middle-class counterparts; these differences vexed middle-class observers, whose voices dominate the historical record. Most sources on pet keeping – manuals, newspaper articles, novels, and social investigations – were written by upper- and middle-class commentators who proclaimed themselves experts in these matters, and I rely on these materials to glean information about working-class pet keepers. My conclusions about working-class pet keeping are therefore tentative, and suggest that poorer people engaged in many of the same practices as their social superiors, albeit in less costly ways. In general, animals became pets when they were so designated. This designation, entailing rituals of possession and regimens of training, affected both pet keeper and pet, changing domestic routines and enrolling both in consumer culture. Pet keeping was a multifaceted endeavour, and there were different ways of keeping pets and becoming a pet keeper – so many, in fact, that contemporaries often disagreed about these matters. For some commentators, rabbits, cats, and hedgehogs, for example, were strictly utilitarian animals, kept for a specific purpose. Others argued that they were amusing, instructive, and affectionate pets. Pets served different purposes, and were even sometimes believed to confer morality on their owners. Some activities associated with pet keeping were enacted in the privacy of the household and others were performed for the purposes of public exhibition and acclaim.

My understanding of nineteenth-century pet keeping practices encompasses these multiple facets, and therefore differs from that of other historians. Keith Thomas, for example, offers a tripartite definition of a pet in eighteenth- and nineteenth-century Britain, suggesting that they were allowed into the house, individualized and granted personal names, and never eaten.[5] Katherine Grier argues that nineteenth-century pet keeping (in America) became a sentimental activity that involved increasing concern for the well-being of pet animals.[6] In contrast, I show that the possession of a pet involved simultaneous imperatives of love, companionship, moral enhancement, utility, discipline, abuse, investment, and profit. Not all animals that were considered pets lived indoors. Through its lifespan and beyond, the pet had latent value and could be sold for cash or wages, possibly eaten, refurbished and enhanced (painted, cropped, and dyed, for example, by a duffer or zealous pet keeper), exchanged for other goods, and recrafted as a taxidermic furnishing – a posthumous treatment that will be discussed in the last chapter. A domesticated, affectionate, and useful animal was worth *something*, and it, its reproductive capacity, offspring, or preserved remains could fetch a price, a romance, another commodity, or a commendation. Unlike most other commodities, pets were alive and mischievous, both accommodating and thwarting the intentions of their owners. This made relationships between pets and pet keepers potentially fraught, but always interesting and highly revealing.

To elaborate on these points, this chapter is composed of several parts. In the first section, I discuss the variety of creatures kept as pets, and the often contradictory purposes and meanings assigned to each animal by working-class and middle-class pet keepers. I then turn to the processes by which a pet was acquired, and here we witness the complex ways pet keeping became a consumer enterprise and involved pet keepers in nascent consumer society. Once an animal was acquired, owners went to considerable lengths to reform their animals into compliant pets. The third section describes methods of maintaining and training pet animals, and the extent to which this involved strict regimens, permissible forms of cruelty, and new consumer products. Finally I turn to the show circuit as the most commercial of all pet-keeping activities and demonstrate the ways a pet could initiate owners in new consumer amenities and offer possibilities for prestige and profit.

A Variety of Pets

Throughout the nineteenth century, people kept a variety of creatures and considered them to be pets. An animal became a pet when it was so designated, and the transformation into a pet was at first a matter of appellation and then extensive training. To understand the diversity of creatures that were kept as pets, consider that by 1862, when the *Book of Home Pets* was published, it provided instruction on the maintenance of fifty-seven different types of animals. The list is striking for a number of reasons: first, it suggests that as of 1862, the most common pets were birds. Most of the birds discussed in the book were indigenous to the British Isles, and the manual gives instructions on methods of "snaring" these creatures, transforming this small part of nature into a singularized pet and living commodity. Some of these birds, such as falcons and hawks, required outdoor space to be used effectively, and it is worth noting that such space was available in the countryside, but also on the outskirts of cities. Second, the inclusion of donkeys, goats, ponies, silkworms, and poultry suggests that utilitarian and agricultural animals could also be kept as pets. As late as 1901, one commentator wrote, "The goat is the pet of the children of the poor, and may be said to be in some degree their playmate. It has also another character – it is their draught animal."[7] Third, with the exception of goats and donkeys, it seems that many of the animals were fairly small, and size may have been a factor in recommending animals to keep. For example, baboons and bears were often (though not always) considered too large, expensive, and fierce to domesticate. Badgers were suggested as suitable alternatives, since they were "very reasonably bearish, if not a true bear, and can be depended upon not to outgrow a manageable size."[8] Fourth, though parrots and monkeys are conspicuously absent from this list, these creatures were frequently classified as "domestic pets" in other manuals, such as *Notes on Pet Monkeys and How to Manage Them* and *Parrots and Monkeys*.[9] Their exclusion from the *Book of Home Pets* might have had something to do with the expense of acquiring them.[10]

The *Book of Home Pets* was only one of a number of books providing advice on the management of pets. Other books and newspapers reveal diverse attitudes about the creatures and activities associated with pet keeping. Pet animals could be singularized and cherished companions, or the focus of sustained attention, even if they were not particularly individualized. Some pets lived indoors, others did not. Some were potential food and valued for their culinary merit; others were sources of moral edification and profit, often reared as fancy animals for the purposes of exchange, exhibition, and competition in animal shows. The term "fancy animal" was used frequently in the nineteenth century to denote animals that exemplified certain unique physical characteristics of which their owners were proud. Owners of these animals considered themselves to be "fanciers" – that is, men and women who believed they possessed critical judgment in matters relating to breeding animals. The term "fancy" also connotes whimsy, fantasticalness, and arbitrary capriciousness[11] – all of which were also evident in the animal fancies. Fanciers bred animals in order to propagate unique characteristics and create lines of pedigree. Almost any pet could be considered a fancy animal. The most common were dogs, pigeons, canaries, and rabbits, but by the end of the century there were clubs and associations devoted to the breeding of almost any pet including guinea pigs, cats, magpies, mice, and rats.

Dogs were the most celebrated pets and provided the standard against which all others were measured. Victorians liked to extol the virtues of their dogs, and some commentators argued that there was something particularly English about keeping canines. The social investigator Henry Mayhew (1812–1887), for example, remarked in passing, "I need not dwell on the general fondness of the English for dogs," and certain breeds, such as bulldogs and greyhounds, were believed to epitomize the loyalty, strength, and nobility of the English character.[12] Dogs were a source of national pride, and newspapers proclaimed that in "no other country save England are such beautiful dogs to be seen as those we meet with on our bench-shows and occasionally in the street."[13] The keeping of dogs suggests the extent to which pet keeping could be a prestigious activity which enhanced the social reputation of pet owners. Dogs were objects of conspicuous consumption, and if one had social pretensions, it was considered important to keep a dog of known lineage.[14] Though the aristocracy had long kept lapdogs as well as hunting and sporting dogs, most modern dog breeds were inventions of the nineteenth century and associated with middle-class status. When middle-class pet keepers bred and exhibited their dogs, they asserted aspirations for bourgeois ascendency. These efforts were institutionalized by the Kennel Club, created in 1873, which regulated dog breeding by maintaining the exclusive lineages of dogs owned by middle-class pet keepers.[15]

For the upper classes, pedigreed dogs reflected the high status of their owners, whereas mongrels were linked to owners of ill repute. Dogs were owned as pets by individuals of all classes, but the treatment of dogs by the working poor was a cause of concern for middle-class commentators. Henry Mayhew was particularly scathing about the treatment of dogs by slaughterers, drovers, coachmen, and cabmen in London in the middle of the nineteenth century. Mayhew could not acknowledge these "varmint" dogs as pets, though they may well have served as work animals and companions. In Mayhew's view, the owners of these dogs "have no feeling" and were as rough, brutish, and debased as their dogs.[16] Similarly, the naturalist W.H. Hudson found the condition of urban dogs a source of curiosity and opprobrium. He offered the following description of dogs that wandered the streets of London at the end of the nineteenth century:

> One thing that was a cause of surprise to me in those days was the large number of dogs, mostly mongrels and curs, to be seen roaming masterless about the streets … Many of these London pariahs were wretched-looking objects, full of sores and old scars, some like skeletons and others with half their hair off from mange and other skin diseases. They were to be seen all over London, always hunting for food, hanging about the areas, like the bone-and bottle-buyers looking for an open dust-bin where something might be found to comfort their stomachs … Most, if not all, of these poor dogs had owners who gave them shelter but no food or very little, and probably in most cases succeeded in evading the license duty.[17]

Dogs were treated differently by the urban poor who had less food to spare for these creatures. Since at night these dogs slept indoors, they may well have been considered pets by those who offered them shelter. Hudson's observations indicate that he found fault with the ways these dogs were kept.

Though middle-class commentators heaped scorn on the ways work-folk maintained their dogs, they generously praised those who kept birds. The breeding of pigeons and canaries had long been an organized pastime in working-class communities.[18] Canaries were much-loved animals, kept inside cages that decorated the parlours or main rooms of most homes; the elaborateness of the cage depended on the wealth of the household.[19] One authority, a Reverend Francis Smith, claimed in 1868 that the artisans of Manchester were particularly avid canary fanciers who thought "nothing of giving one, two and three pounds for a single bird." So widespread was canary keeping in Manchester that "when cottage-doors were open, you might see breeding cages hanging on the walls, and hear the occupants enlivening the gloomy desolation around."[20] According to Smith, canary keeping appealed to large numbers of people because these birds were believed to be ornamental and moral creatures, epitomizing domestic bliss and enhancing household harmony. He describes the canary as a model husband and master of his own household:

> In sunshine gay, in winter dull, in spring-time full of life and vigour, in autumn moulting, and sick and weak; when courting the most ardent of lovers, when married the most dutiful and affectionate of husbands, helping their wives with the most assiduous attention when making their nest, and superintending the bringing up and education of their family with exemplary regularity and care, now receiving some delicate morsel from their owner's hand, and then showing gratitude by repaying him with a song.[21]

These euphemisms anthropomorphized canaries, implying that they might serve as moral exemplars to their human owners.

Other birds were similarly believed by middle-class commentators to create industrious workers and loving working-class families.[22] Henry Mayhew, for example, recorded the following observation about London workers who kept birds as pets:

> The readers who have perused this work from its first appearance will have noticed how frequently I have had to comment on the always realized indication of good conduct, and of a superior taste and generally superior intelligence, when I have found the rooms of working people contain flowers and birds. I could adduce many instances. I have seen and heard birds in the rooms of tailors, shoemakers, coopers, cabinet-makers,

hatters, dressmakers, curriers, and street-sellers, all people of the best class. One of the most striking, indeed, was the room of a street-confectioner. His family attended to the sale of the sweets, and he was greatly occupied at home in their manufacture, and worked away at his peppermint-rock, in the very heart of one of the thickest populated parts of London, surrounded by the song of thrushes, linnets, and gold-finches, all kept, not for profit, but because he "loved" to have them about him. I have seldom met a man who impressed me more favourably.[23]

Characterizing this bird lover as "generally a more domestic, and perhaps consequently, a more prosperous and contented man," Mayhew described bird keeping as an elevating pursuit linked to domesticity.[24] A bird, no matter how feral or common, could also be considered a fancy animal, as the existence of the Magpie Fanciers' Association, active in the 1890s, demonstrates.[25]

Working-class and middle-class bird keepers did not always agree about the morally elevating possibilities of domesticating birds, and their opinions were clearly divergent when it came to the domestication of the robin redbreast. The robin was a favoured pet among the middle classes and believed to be a model for human conduct and "Christian" values – possibly because according to folklore a robin landed on the shoulder of Christ and plucked thorns from his brow. As a "Christian" animal, the robin was considered "a respectable member of society," and had been a popular subject of instructive children's literature since the late eighteenth century.[26] Yet the "Christianity" of the robin also made it an object of contention among the working classes, who considered its caging unlucky and refused to offer this bird for sale.[27] Instead, labourers tamed robins by offering them food out of doors, and even fixing silver rings to their legs as symbols of ownership; yet these birds were allowed to roam free.[28] Middle-class commentators heaped scorn on the workers who refused to cage robins, arguing that the robin should be thoroughly domesticated.[29] Differences in beliefs and superstitions may therefore have had an impact on the keeping of some animals as pets. These moments of disagreement are illuminating because they complicate the tendency to make generalizations about pet keeping across class lines.

Though middle-class commentators agreed about the morally elevating possibilities of bird keeping, they expressed considerable ambivalence about the cat.[30] Street cats, in particular, faced great cruelty, and were sometimes stolen, stoned, and skinned alive.[31] While some middle-class pet owners kept cats as pets and defended their virtues, others regarded them as utilitarian animals that should be brought inside only during the day to rid the house of mice. Many cats were underfed, since people made "the cruel mistake of supposing that a cat will be a keener and better mouser if not sufficiently fed in other ways."[32] Consequently, when owners attempted to sell their cats, they sometimes emphasized the animal's utility. One ad, for example, read: "Angora cats. Several very handsome ones, splendid mousers, sweet-tempered, quite lovely in appearance, and scrupulously clean. Wanted, a hunting saddle. Open to offers."[33] (Angora cats were expensive to acquire, and this perhaps explains why this advertiser valued the cat as equivalent to a hunting saddle.)[34] Other advertisements referred to characteristics that made the cat a good household companion: "Quiet, well-behaved tabby cat (owner leaving England), 12 s. To good home, if sold by 5th."[35] Cats and kittens were generally treated differently; as one newspaper asserted, "people who like the playful and amusing ways of kittens refuse to keep the unfortunate animals when they are fully grown."[36] For most of the nineteenth century, cat breeding was not considered prestigious, and cats were often classed with rabbits and cavies (guinea pigs) as lesser fancy animals and pets of the working man.[37] Cats were often judged too independent and promiscuous to be reliable pets of the middle class, and it was not until the founding of the National Cat Club (NCC) in 1887, an institution made up of middle-class fanciers, that the social status of cat keeping began to change. By seeking respectability for their fancy, NCC members used their shows as a way to assert themselves in the Victorian social order. NCC shows enshrined the Victorian social hierarchy by exhibiting working men's cats in a distinct category. Working men were permitted to show their animals, but their cats were judged separately from the other animals in the competition.[38] Apparently there was something inherently different about working-class cats, and these differences were obvious to those in the know. As one reporter opined about an NCC show in 1899, "I am sorry to see that some cats entered in the working-men's classes are also entered in the ordinary classes; these, to my mind are only bogus working-men's cats, and have no right to compete in the working-men's classes."[39]

Middle-class Victorians expressed their opinion about other working-class pets in similarly snobbish ways. In reference to the keeping of mice, a very common practice among middle-class schoolboys and working-class men, the *Book of Home Pets* made the following incredulous comment: "What next? Pray, Sir, have you not this time made a slight mistake and substituted a pest for a pet; or are we to have in due course instructions how to make the black-beetle happy, how the domestic spider may be fattened and fondled, and the cockroach rendered comfortable?"[40] One can only speculate how the same author would have responded to the keeping of rats, which became popular in the early twentieth century. Though pet mice and rats were usually feral animals that had been captured by their keepers, some manuals insisted that it was better to purchase these creatures.[41] This advice was an attempt to endow the keeping of these pets with social pretensions. Anyone could capture a mouse or rat and transform it into a pet, but, if purchased from a vendor, the animal was already commodified and singularized. Some mouse keepers may even have believed that there was an intrinsic difference between the common mouse and the purchased pet, though by the first decades of the twentieth century experts were admitting "that domesticated mice are descended from the Common House Mouse, which is a familiar object."[42] The fancy rat was also endowed with social pretensions, described as a high-bred creature and worthy of a Latinized appellation. One manual, for example, referred to "Rattus" as "one of the most graceful of existing quadrupeds, a thorough aristocrat."[43] The keeping of rats was first commended in 1901, when a rat, owned by a Miss M. Douglas, competed for a prize under the supervision of the Mouse Club at Aylesbury. Shortly thereafter, rat keeping became an institutionalized hobby supported by a network of clubs and shows, often affiliated with the National Mouse Club, which was founded in 1895.[44] The keeping of mice and rats as fancy animals suggests the extent to which pet keeping involved social emulation by the end of the nineteenth century and a pervasive obsession with pedigree. These animals were inexpensive (if not free) to acquire and maintain, and so they appealed to working-class pet keepers.[45] Middle-class schoolboys could also use the opportunity of keeping these creatures as an initiation into the animal fancies, before they graduated to the keeping of more prestigious animals. The keeping and breeding of mice and rats therefore maintained class distinctions.

Middle-class commentators considered some animals to be pets only if they were expensively acquired and carefully distinguished from agricultural stock and working-class associations. For example, fancy fowls and pigeons, though also kept in outdoor aviaries by people of all classes, were often recommended as pets, especially for middle-class girls in a column titled "Girls' Pets and How to Manage

Them."[46] An article in the *Ladies' Kennel Journal* also suggested "poultry keeping as an interesting hobby for a lady who could not compose her peace of mind upon the subject of pets." According to the article, poultry keeping was a hobby taken up by duchesses and middle-class ladies alike, who "testify strongly to the thoroughly reputable state of the poultry fancy." Such assertions assure upper-class ladies that in keeping chickens they would not be confused with agricultural labourers, since apparently "a pure-bred bird is a very different creature to the wretched be-draggled hen that haunts the lanes of our villages" – though this was surely in the eye of the beholder.[47] The class dimension in poultry keeping was emphasized by one manual which likened the pet hen to a servant.[48]

As the example of chickens suggests, the sharp distinction between keeping an animal as fancy, pet, and food had not yet been established, and this was most obvious when it came to the keeping of rabbits. Rabbit keeping had a complex institutional aspect, with clubs dedicated to the hobby located all over the country by the end of the nineteenth century. As one writer to *Fur and Feather*, signing himself "One who Will be a Member," commented in 1890, "There seem to be rabbit clubs for almost all the towns, not to mention counties, in the North, and some parts of the South, while we poor isolated fanciers in Dorset have not, to my knowledge a single club amongst us."[49] Each club published minute specifications outlining the standard for judging different breeds in the hopes that fanciers would produce these special characteristics. Rabbits were also judged by the domestic habits which made them good pets. In 1907 one manual claimed that the Dutch rabbit was the most popular breed because of "their unique style of marking and their devotion to their young." The lop-eared rabbit was considered a fashionable children's pet, while the long-haired angora rabbit was judged appropriate for ladies.[50] Since the costs of feeding rabbits were estimated to be as low as one penny a week, men, women, and children of all social ranks kept these animals, but rabbits were especially associated with working men. (This remained true through the first half of the twentieth century.)[51] As one manual noted, "Prize-rabbit keeping is essentially a poor man's hobby, and the hobby pays many a man's rent; at the same time, every section of society is found rubbing shoulders in the attempt to become successful exhibitors."[52] The rabbit bred for the show circuit was to be thoroughly domesticated so that it would not appear "wild or fretful in the show pen" and could be handled like any well-trained pet.[53] At the same time, the rabbit could be "sold for killing, or killed for home consumption." Experts recommended that "[w]eeds [any rabbit that was weak or undesirable] from a good strain" of high-bred rabbit "be made to afford an agreeable dish for the table."[54] Even the *Girl's Empire*, in its column on "Girls' Pets," gave directions on how to kill rabbits for food, advising novices on which to select for this purpose and which to breed for show and profit.[55]

Like rabbits, guinea pigs (also known as cavies) were valued as potential foodstuff, excellent companions, and fancy animals. Writing a series of articles on the creatures in 1885, one authority, Charles Cumberland, told his readers, "When there is no intention of using the cavies otherwise than as pets, the treatment becomes somewhat different from that described. Those kept as agricultural stock are better not to be petted."[56] Yet, in the last article, when Cumberland wrote specifically about the guinea pig as pet, he explained that though the "cavy is always pretty and gentle as a pet," it is also "quite good to eat."[57] In a manual giving more lengthy directions on keeping and breeding cavies, Cumberland lists the gastronomic merits of a recipe he endows with social pretensions and titles "Cavy au Fine Herbes [*sic*]." He states explicitly, "I do not wish it supposed that I recommend Cavy as a cheap food, but rather for its delicious flavour and recherché quality."[58] (There was no consensus on the culinary merit of the cavy, however, and another author classed its flesh "unfit for food.")[59] As a dependent and endearing creature, the cavy was additionally suggested as a pet for children. Anecdotes from other cavy owners attested to the intelligence and affection displayed by guinea pigs, even towards other pets. One book, for example, describes the ways guinea pigs wait for masters and mistresses, jump onto laps, and are particularly friendly towards cats.[60] Guinea pigs additionally appealed as fancy animals because they were considered relatively easy to breed. As one newspaper noted, the cavy "gives the breeder such excellent opportunities for selection and experiment, that no other fancy can hold a candle to them."[61] Initially, cavy keeping was considered a hobby of working men, but by the 1890s people of all classes were participants in this activity, though usually with different roles. As one article in the *Fur Fanciers' Journal* stated, "Exhibitors have formed themselves into societies which are holding shows almost daily. The societies are not composed entirely of the working classes for some of the most wealthy and honourable personages in the land can be seen acting as either Patrons or Presidents of them."[62] Cavy keeping therefore maintained class distinctions, allowing patrons to serve as benefactors to working-class amusements.

Acquiring a Pet

Through the nineteenth century a pet could be acquired in a number of ways: purchased from street vendors or shop owners, obtained through classified advertisements, or found in local environs. As such, pet animals offered easy opportunities for participation in nineteenth-century consumer culture. Squirrels, toads, grass snakes, and mice captured in the surrounding countryside were the most affordable, especially for those of lesser means, since they cost "next to nothing to get, nothing to keep, and yet [afford] endless amusement and interest."[63] Birds were often trapped by bird catchers, and then sold as living commodities.[64] On any given Saturday afternoon and night in Manchester, "the market and shops, as well as the public-houses used for the purpose [were] crowded with men and lads, having either birds to sell, or looking on and watching what is going on around them."[65] If sales were low, live birds could be painted brilliant hues by men called "duffers" to attract customers, since "the more outlandish a bird is made to look the more chance there is of selling it." For example, an old canary, "faded and worn out with age, is re-dyed with queen's yellow; blackbirds are imbued with a deeper tint by using the soot off the frying-pan, a common parrot is painted in marvellous hues, and its legs and beak varnished."[66]

Pets could be acquired in the streets and marketplaces of major cities, where there was a particularly thriving trade in birds, dogs, mice, fancy rabbits, squirrels, and hedgehogs.[67] In his study of London street life, Henry Mayhew described street vendors selling to gentlefolk, tradespeople, and working-class animal lovers; they also supplied shopkeepers with various pets.[68] This trade was still thriving at the turn of the twentieth century, when another commentator made note of the "perambulating dealer[s]" of birds on the streets of London (figure 1.1), some of whom transported their wares on horse-drawn carts.[69] By this time, other pets, including monkeys, mongooses, Persian cats, armadillos, snakes, and mice, could be purchased from shops which served a clientele of diverse economic means (figure 1.2).[70] By mid-century, the railway was particularly important for the success of these ventures. Individuals could go bird catching in the environs of Oxford, for example, and send their merchandise to London by train for sale.[71] Newspapers and manuals additionally offered opportunities for individuals to cast themselves as experts and dealers and advertise animals for sale.[72] Interested buyers would respond to the ad and, in cases of distance, have their new pets sent by railway.

1.1. "A Street Bird Stall." From Henry Scherren,
"Bird-Land and Pet-Land in London," 329

Starting in 1868, the *Exchange and Mart* (after 1872 titled *Bazaar, Exchange and Mart*) was one of the more popular forums for the trade in pets. In the pages of this newspaper, animal enthusiasts with diverse economic means offered to buy, sell, breed, and exchange pets of every variety alongside other second-hand goods. By 1890 this trade was prolific and included all sorts of birds, aquarium fish, cats, ferrets, foxes, guinea pigs, mice, silkworms, squirrels, and sometimes more exotic animals. The most numerous listings were for poultry (eleven columns), dogs (eight columns), pigeons (two columns), and rabbits (one column).[73] These ads are fascinating because they invite readers to imagine the circumstances of the sellers and their relationships with pets. Consider the following sampling of ads, most from the *Exchange and Mart*:

1.2. "In a Bird and Animal Shop, Great Portland Street."
From Henry Scherren, "Bird-Land and Pet-Land in London," 327

I have two pair of white fantail pigeons to part with, quite young, and of very pure breed. My wants are strong, useful inkstand and bookcase, need not be ornamental, and some looking glasses to hang against the wall, suited for servant's bedroom.[74]

A very handsome cameo brooch (cost £10) will be given for a good parrot or parakeets. State kind and particulars.[75]

Several perfectly tame piebald Chinese rats. Price 2s. 6d. each, charming docile pets package 3d. Messrs C. and H. Gardener II Victoria road, Leicester.[76]

> Charming Persian kittens, old china. Want winter dress material. Ditto for
> handsome mantle, long cloth, for cape or cash.[77]

> Require new clothing for cutting up for children. Poultry, pigeons, canar-
> ies, and cash given in exchange.[78]

Feral creatures, also considered pets, were offered for larger sums or
more expensive goods:

> Very tame and large mongoose, perfectly harmless, a great pet, runs loose.
> Price only 25s. E. Webber, 63 Windsor-road, N.[79]

> A very handsome pet dappled fallow deer, 6 months old, female. Price 5
> pound 5 s. – Mrs. Nash, Wroxall, Isle of Wight.[80]

> Australian native bear for sale, tame pet. Price £10, or exchange furniture.
> 65 Bensham Manor-rd. Thornton Heath, Surrey.[81]

These ads are tantalizing for the glimpses they provide into anonymous
lives. The ads dare readers to imagine the circumstances of their authors and their relationships to pets, which come across as tenuous and
dependent on economic circumstances. In these ads, animals can pass
in and out of any number of categories, and emotional attachment to
pets seems less important than material concerns and desires for economic or social advancement. According to these ads, pet cats, birds,
dogs, mice, and koalas were considered equivalent to furniture, fabric,
hunting equipment, sewing machines, cash, jewellery, and other animals. What had transformed the pet from subject to object and from
singular being to mere thing? Were these animals unloved or unruly?
Were the advertisers financially strapped or moving house? At any moment, it seems, a newly captured or a long-kept pet could be transformed into a commodity and exchanged for cash or other goods.

As might be expected, the trade in pets was full of misleading ventures. In 1895 the newspaper *Fur and Feather* issued a disclaimer asserting, "We cannot be responsible for the statements made in Advertisements or for the trustworthiness of either buyers or sellers."[82] Even so,
a disgruntled owner of caged birds, identified as S.D., wrote to the
newspaper in 1896 asking for legal advice. S.D. had answered an advertisement for birds "properly paired for breeding, sent on seven days
approval," but when they arrived, all were hens. The paper counselled

S.D. to seek financial restitution in the county court.[83] Despite the occasional fraud, the sheer number of advertisements suggests a thriving trade, so much so that occasionally sellers posted ads to prevent further inquiries about the animals they had offered for sale. For example, one ad proclaimed, "Ferret advertised last week sold, no more letters or orders please, have already spent about its value returning orders & c."[84] Such statements suggest that the occasional swindle did not dampen enthusiasm for these transactions, which provided fierce competition for pet stores.

Pet stores were not numerous before the turn of the twentieth century, and owners of these shops resorted to innovative means to provide customer service, advertising in the back of pet-keeping manuals. In 1896, for example, one store on Great Portland Street (London) suggested that fanciers send letters stating their "requirements"; the store would then provide any type of pet. It claimed to stock the most popular domestic animals, including fancy mice and their houses, fancy rats, fancy rabbits, cavies, cats, kittens, puppies, monkeys, frogs, birds, reptiles, fish, and tortoises. Pets for show, home, and children could also be provided, as could "lovely tame squirrels."[85]

Interest in pets was so widespread that, starting in the second half of the nineteenth century, there was a proliferation of books and newspapers discussing matters relating to pet keeping. The existence of these print materials suggests the extent to which pet keeping became a profitable and consumerist enterprise as the century progressed. For example, the *Book of Home Pets*, discussed above, was a lengthy manual (over eight hundred pages) and divided into twenty-six parts, each priced at three pence. Since it was affiliated with the *Beeton Book of Household Management*, a popular resource for middle-class wives (and those aspiring to middle-class status) seeking advice on matters related to domestic etiquette, the *Book of Home Pets* may have been widely consulted. It was originally released in weekly pamphlet form and then as a compendium in two editions in 1861 and 1862. Other manuals, on the breeding and care of dogs, cats, mice, rabbits, cavies, and birds, were also available. In addition, mainstream newspapers aimed at middle-class audiences, such as the *Illustrated London News* and the *Illustrated Sporting and Dramatic News*, published content related to pet keeping. By the 1880s, a number of cheaply available newspapers, accessible to working-class readers, were devoted exclusively to pet keeping and gave instructions on managing various animals and information on exhibiting prized pets. These newspapers catered to those who kept a variety of animals, but other papers, such as *Canary and Cage Bird Life* and *Our Cats*, were more specialized in focus. Most of these papers were published in London and circulated throughout the country, but several were produced in northern England. Editions cost one or two pennies and were therefore affordable to anyone interested in keeping up with the latest trends. The exceptions were the more expensive *Kennel Gazette* and the *Ladies' Kennel Journal*, two newspapers that went to great lengths to give the impression that dog keeping was a socially exclusive and expensive recreation.

Via these media, pet keepers sought advice and offered information; they traded pets and advertised stud animals; they lobbied, complained, gossiped, and formed communities with similar interests. The *Bazaar, Exchange and Mart* and the *Fancier's Chronicle: A Journal for Poultry, Pigeon, Dog, Pet Stock and Bee Fanciers* even published the results of post-mortems for owners anxious to determine what caused the death of their pets.[86] Animal corpses could be sent by mail, "as soon after death as death as possible," to an expert who would later report the results of examinations in the newspaper, addressing owners directly. Presumably others could learn better techniques of pet care through this column. Consider the following reports about dead birds:

F.E.W. – *Dead Cordon Bleu:* The cause of death was constipation.

H.B.S. – *Dead Canary:* Consumption was the cause of death. The bird was almost a perfect skeleton. Moving a bird about from one part of a warm room to another is most dangerous, and worse still changing the cage. Give your birds a little inga [*sic?*] or pinch of maw seed sometimes, and be sure all the seed is good.[87]

Pet keepers seeking other guidance could write to newspapers and soon receive an answer. Often the original questions were never published. Under a column titled "Answers to Correspondents" in *Fur and Feather*, each correspondent was addressed directly. For example, "A.H.B. – In either a box or hamper. The matter you refer to was unfortunately crowded out last week."[88] Experienced individuals could additionally give advice to novices, even on the keeping of exotic animals. In 1910, for example, Mademoiselle Juilliette, a "clever trainer and exhibitor," recommended sea-lions as excellent pets, but with the following caveat: "I should not describe the sea-lion as a poor man's pet, for a young untrained one costs £60 … Again a good-sized tank and a warm, dry sleeping place are necessary, while the bill for food is alarming."[89] These newspapers give the impression of widespread fascination with pet keeping and the formation of communities of animal enthusiasts in which individuals keeping the same type of pet might come to know each other and exchange advice on the maintenance and training of their animals.

Training and Maintaining Pets

The training of any animal involved the adaptation of both owner and pet to a series of expectations; this process was symbiotic as pet and owner developed new routines of coexistence and participation in consumer culture. Often training made obvious the extent to which pets straddled the divide between wild and tame – divisions that were never entirely resolved in the process of trying to make animals more docile. When animals were granted (or denied) access to the house, caged, cleaned, fed, entertained, trained, and disciplined, human routines were also transformed – many thought for the better, since, as we have seen, pet keeping was considered a morally elevating activity. The transformation of animals into pets thus transformed the animal into a potential exemplar for human conduct, as we shall see. In fact, the "longing to protect and care" for animals was regarded as one of the "healthiest instincts" of Victorian English men and women.[90] As one expert proclaimed, the "love of Pets is one of the flowers of civilization" and "on the whole there is something humanizing in a Pet, which makes the heart open to genial warmth of kindness."[91] The pet's liberty was restricted, even as it was ostensibly protected and improved. By meeting expectations of behaviour, the pet became "civilized" – and so too did its keeper. The sentimentality fostered by pet keeping ran the gauntlet from gestures of care and expressions of love to permissible forms of extreme disciplining. Through the processes of training and maintenance, an animal was elevated to the status of "pet" while its owner became a "pet keeper." As a pet, the animal could become a companion, foodstuff, and fancy animal, as well as a source of status, profit, moral righteousness, and social mobility, but since animals were not always obedient, their status as pets had to be continually reaffirmed through ongoing discipline.

The establishment of new routines began at the moment a pet was acquired. Some pets were allowed to roam about the house; others, like the robins "owned" by labourers, remained out of doors, while other pets were caged. Cages allowed owners to interact with their pets in restricted conditions and made some animals more compliant and seemingly civilized. For songbirds, small cages without gadgets were considered necessities: the limitation on space was believed to induce them to perform. According to one expert, "the larger the dwelling, the less music you will in all probability get out of its occupant. He will think more of skipping and jumping than singing – in short, he will pay more attention to his own amusement than to yours."[92] Monkeys also required caging as part of their domestication. One manual made clear that the "right place for a monkey, in civilized society is in a cage; here the once pest of everybody becomes everyone's pet."[93] Pigeons were kept in outdoor aviaries, while rabbits could be caged in or out of doors. Cats were mainly outdoor animals and the construction of catteries was only recommended if they were being bred for show.[94] Dogs, both pedigreed and mongrel, were allowed to wander the house, but if they were pedigreed and kept outside, experts advised that kennels be built or purchased for them, presumably to keep them from mating with mongrels.[95]

Cages were an integral part of the process by which common animals were transformed into domesticated, singularized, and ornamental pets. Cages could be acquired from animal shows, street vendors, or shops.[96] At dog shows, kennels and kennel runs could be purchased which had been partially prefabricated.[97] Some cages were so architecturally elaborate that they transformed the pet into an ornamental furnishing and household accessory. One catalogue sold all manner of cages for canaries, parrots, dormice, and squirrels. Some were made of riveted brass and ruby glass. The most intricate cages were made for squirrels; these were described as the "Best Squirrel Cages with Bells, polished mahogany and tinned wire."[98] Apparently the more common the pet, the more lavish the cage. Consider the following observation by one fancier:

> I have seen cages of almost every conceivable pattern, representing cottages, abbeys, castles, cathedrals, and palaces, with fine fluted columns, porticoes with pediments, stained glass windows & c., rich and varied in design and in every conceivable style of architecture including Gothic, Doric and Ionic, and displaying great taste and mechanical skill.[99]

Such cages were household decorations as well as dwellings for pets, and they could be fitted with all sorts of appliances, such as trapezes, wheel perches, rings, bells, and looking glasses. Bird cages adorning windows on the outside of dwellings were also "characteristic ... of London homes, especially in the suburbs."[100] Figure 1.3 shows birds living in twenty-five small cages, which frame and adorn the window on the *outside* of a building – and not in the parlour or main room. Caging birds outside and in full view of the street served a similar function to keeping them indoors; it proclaimed the morality and harmony of the household. The dwelling looks bleak, possibly inhabited by individuals aspiring to more solid middle-class status. The birds provide song on streets that were perhaps not lined with trees. In support of this assumption, the author of the article accompanying the photograph complimented "the brightness these petted little prisoners bring into dull, grey human lives."[101] The title of the photograph, "Caged," seems to allude to the home's animal and human inhabitants. A woman, who is possibly a servant, leans out the window to feed the creatures, a duty that is presumably one of her chores. We are thus presented with an interesting hierarchy in which women and animals are presented as lesser creatures. Both are used to shore up the social position of those who live behind the window – proclaiming to the outside world (and to anyone who passes by) that this is a respectable household.

Pet keepers unable to afford cages could alternatively purchase more utilitarian hampers, made by Spratt's, specifically designed to contain animals inside the home or to transport them by rail.[102] In some cases, a much cheaper alternative, in the form of a margarine box, was recommended to do the job.[103] If pet keepers wanted to build cages, some manuals and advice columns provided step-by-step directions on fabrication. The most complex directions were for the construction of an aquarium, which had to be functional as well as picturesque.[104] A pet in a cage had to be a satisfying, ornamental, and entertaining spectacle because only then could it create the elevated domestic atmosphere associated with pet keeping.

Other accoutrements could also be purchased to pamper pets and their owners. A number of objects were available for dogs in particular, including all sorts of collars, muzzles, and chains. Some of these were electroplated or made of fancy leather, studs, and fittings.[105] These goods were available through advertisements, hawked on the street, and even sold in department stores by the turn of the twentieth century. Henry Mayhew, for example, counted twelve street vendors of dog collars in London and records that brass collars were most in demand.[106] By 1910, Harrod's, the department store, even had an entire department

1.3. "Caged." From Henry Scherren,
"Bird-Land and Pet-Land in London," 328

dedicated to dog's collars which sold all sorts of collars made from leather with brass studs or metal bells. Very light collars were available for toy dogs, and dog owners could additionally purchase an assortment of whips, chains, leads, chain collars, bells, medallions, muzzles, brushes, combs, hound gloves, poodle clippers, and dog whistles.[107] The availability of these items in department stores suggests the extent to which dog care had become a commercial enterprise as shopping became increasingly institutionalized.

Maintaining and training an animal could additionally involve strict feeding regimens, and most manuals provided advice on food preparation.[108] Alcohol, as we have seen, was given to hedgehogs to make them docile, though this impaired the efficiency with which they hunted cockroaches and beetles. Some experts advised pet owners to prepare various homemade concoctions of meat, fish, bread, milk, and sometimes vegetables for their pets, making specially purchased food unnecessary.[109] Dogs owned by poorer people, as we have seen, were often left to their own devices, scrounging for food in city streets. Dogs kept by middle- and upper-class owners were often fed from the table and ate the same food as their owners. In 1892 *Punch* published a cartoon poking fun at these rituals (figure 1.4). The image shows two upper-class ladies walking dogs; the pets resemble their mistresses. The plumper lady inquires of her more slender friend, "May I ask you how you manage to keep your little pet so sleek and thin?" The other replies, "I don't know. It has its lunch and dinner with me every day." The inquirer retorts, "Well, so does mine!" Both dogs are clearly spoiled, but in different ways.

Towards the end of the century, brands of manufactured pet food came on the market, and each company attempted advertising gimmicks to encourage the purchasing of their products. All sorts of images and testimonials were used to advertise these products from bird seed to dog food. Since there were no laws regulating the truth in advertisements, entrepreneurs could provide fictional testimonials by actresses, politicians, and royalty.[110] One company selling Clarke's Buffalo Biscuits for dogs, for example, associated itself with Queen Victoria, adding to its advertisements the statement "By Special Appointment to Her Majesty the Queen." Other companies connected their products with domestic harmony, such as Melox, which was endorsed by the statement "Every Happy Family Owns a Happy Dog if Fed on Melox and Mixed Marvel."[111] Many manuals additionally advertised dog food, which suggests that it was becoming an increasingly

1.4. "Q.E.D.," *Punch*, 27 February 1892

lucrative business. For example, an ad for Spratt's Patent Dog Cakes could be found in the back of a manual about fancy mice.[112] Mellin's (also a manufacturer of food for babies) sold gruel for puppies by picturing bulldogs alongside small children and stating, "nothing better for young puppies."[113] These ads presented pet owners with numerous options for feeding their pets, and associated the feeding of animals with the raising of healthy children.

The analogy to child rearing was not coincidental: pets were trained, much like children, to adopt habits of cleanliness, politeness, and dependency. The point of such efforts was to make pets dutiful, compliant, and moral members of the household. The other analogy for Victorians was empire. Like the civilizing mission which subjected the colonized to restricted liberty and foreign habits in return for a paternalistic elevation, pets were confined and disciplined, but also raised up, sometimes literally. Through repeated cajoling, canaries, for example, were taught to stand on fingertips and to fly out of doors and return. They were also trained to ring for their food, control their appetites, and take baths first thing in the morning.[114] Such routines personified the animal, making its habits similar to those of a Victorian lady. Regimens for other animals involved similar objectives. According to one expert, a house dog was to "be clean, well-behaved and obedient; he must not worry visitors, scratch their clothes or rush barking to the door every time it is opened. He must only bark at burglars, or growl at suspicious characters ... Good manners are a matter of training." To establish this behaviour, dogs were "taken to the scene of action and sharply scolded and smacked."[115] Eager pet owners looking for advice on how best to train dogs could consult columns in newspapers, as well as manuals, with titles such as *Hints to Beginners (Dogs)* and *Training Dogs; and How to Make Them Good Companions.*[116] These sources gave advice on how to impart good canine behaviour, teaching dogs to fetch, carry, retrieve, swim, dive, and save life, so that they could best serve their owners in every possible situation. A well-behaved dog was considered a credit to its keeper; conversely, as one commentator in the *Bazaar, Exchange and Mart* proclaimed, "a quarrelsome dog is a public nuisance and a danger, as well as a disgrace to himself and his owner."[117] Given the accolades that could be received for a well-behaved pet, owners prided themselves on their abilities to make their animals perform all sorts of tricks.

An animal became a good pet when it submitted to human ministrations, but this was sometimes the result of extreme measures. Animals of nasty temperament that were resistant to human control had to be disciplined in radical ways that could involve permissible forms of abuse. Though monkeys, for example, were touted as fun-loving pranksters and affectionate creatures, their behaviour often got out of hand. To tame monkeys, one manual suggested that owners let a friend go up to the cage with a stick and frighten the animal. The owner of the monkey should then pretend to "take the part of your pet and thrash your friend to within an inch of his life with the very stick he has been using, and put him out."[118] This would gain the confidence of the monkey and simultaneously demonstrate the owner's authority. In the event that the monkey became too unruly, owners were advised to sell it to a passing menagerie or itinerant, since "the said few shillings are better in your pocket than treble the amount in the doctor's for sundry patches ... to fingers lacerated and bitten."[119] The beating and banishing of the monkey was so common that it was frequently satirized in the illustrated press.[120]

Cruelty was condoned when it came to pets that were resistant to human management – and all pets could be unmanageable at times. For example, to make dogs good companions, it was thought "best to come to an understanding when the first act of disobedience is committed." A "thorough good whipping" was considered better than "a series of minor corrections."[121] Violence to pets was a common phenomenon and could take many forms, from the killing of unwanted offspring to cropping, painting, and dyeing for sale or the show circuit, and to various forms of neglect. By 1910, this mistreatment was increasingly noticed. Pet-keeping newspapers published lists titled "Some Don'ts for Pet Lovers," which indicate the type and frequency of abuse. One included such maxims as

> Don't hang your canary in the broiling sun.
> Don't make your dog run for miles after your bicycle.
> Don't leave your cats to starve while you go for an enjoyable holiday.
> Don't omit to give your pets fresh water every day.
> Don't give your cat sour milk or food.
> Don't punish your pets because you lose your temper.
> Don't let your dog's collar be too tight.
> Don't forget that your cat may creep to a terrible death if the kitchen oven
>   is left open overnight …
> Don't keep pets if you are not an animal lover.[122]

The very existence of such lists indicates the pervasiveness of these problems.

Despite permissible cruelties, the exercise of kindness was considered an important component of stewarding pets, and advocated by most authors of pet-keeping manuals. If animals were being cultivated through pet keeping, so were human beings, as one author wrote: "Every lesson, as it is given [to pets], reacts happily on the teacher in the way of increased patience and a new loving-kindness toward all weak and defenceless creatures."[123] Since the late eighteenth century, children, in particular, were encouraged to keep pets in order to foster their softer emotions. Learning kindness to animals during the childhood years was believed to develop character, leading to moral righteousness in adulthood.[124] Developing an interest in the breeding of fancy livestock during boyhood, for example, was believed to create a lifelong passion for pet keeping and prevent the squandering of money on less savoury pursuits, such as drink, in the adult years. The effect of keeping animals on "rough uncultured men" was similarly extolled.[125] Pet keeping additionally cultivated humanitarian feelings in girls, teaching them "to exercise care, to be observant and thorough, to be thoughtful and kind for other [*sic*] than herself, and to be independent of others for the carrying out of little everyday necessary duties."[126] These demonstrations of kindness and emotional attachment to animals were taken as indices of civilization. Consider the following quotation:

> For some time past civilized communities have recognized their responsibility towards domesticated animals. The principle is universally accepted, but it is impossible to convince some callous owners of dogs and cats that to abandon their pets to starvation and the tender mercies of the street ruffian is as deserving of censure as cruelty of a more obvious nature.[127]

Civilized societies, according to this logic, evinced emotional attachment to animals and protected them against cruelty.[128] As the quotation also makes clear, the discussion of kindness was often prejudicial against the poor: middle-class owners of dogs and cats are urged to protect their pets from street ruffians.[129]

The middle class liked to blame their social inferiors for brutality to animals. For example, cruelty against canaries was frequently blamed on servants and children, who were regarded as equally untrustworthy. According to one manual, "Birds should never be left to the sole care of a domestic, or entrusted entirely to children, however attached or affectionate they may appear to be. They have not the necessary judgment, and are quite as likely to kill their pets with over-kindness as with neglect."[130] Middle-class adults were rarely faulted for harming their pets. Indeed, the link between the humanitarian treatment of animals and class control has been noted in the actions of Victorian animal welfare organizations. The Society for the Prevention of Cruelty to Animals, perhaps the most famous of all such institutions, was founded in 1824 (and made Royal by the patronage of Queen Victoria in 1840). Animal welfare organizations, according to several historians, demonstrated an obsession with restricting the pleasures and work habits of the urban poor, while turning a blind eye to the cruel practices of the middle and upper classes.[131] These attitudes were adopted and proliferated by pet-keeping manuals and suggest the extent to which the arguments of animal welfare activists had become mainstream.[132]

In return for confinement and discipline, the animal received sustenance and love. Some Victorians went to great lengths to care for their pets as cherished possessions. This ownership could be experienced as reciprocal; so much so, in fact, that one author described his pets as "creatures that have taken possession of us – of my wife and myself."[133] Books were frequently published that documented sentimental and inspiring stories of life with pets.[134] One book related such remarkable tales that its author included the names and addresses of his sources so that readers could verify the stories.[135] Proud owners wrote letters to newspapers sharing information about beloved pets. One woman, for example, sent a photograph of her "tame sparrow" to *Household Pets* and described the tricks it could perform. It was civilized: the "wild" made tame. The bird offered a foot to shake hands, kissed, and wiped its nose: "you would laugh to see her put her beak in my handkerchief," she proudly proclaimed.[136] This owner was clearly fond of her animal.

The extent to which some keepers were attached to their pets was demonstrated by the lengths to which they would go to ensure the health and comfort of their animals. Towards the end of the nineteenth century, pet care was increasingly big business, and treatments for various ailments could be purchased alongside pet food and medicines for people. Many treatments were similar to the patent medicines and remedies that were available to humans. Pet keepers could purchase, for example, a range of soaps, pills, powders, tonic condition balls, distemper balls, worm balls, and carbolic smoke balls that promised to maintain or improve the health of their pets.[137] Sometimes the same medicines were advertised for people and pets simultaneously. One advertisement for St Jacob's Oil promised cures for "Sprains Headaches Neuralgia and all Aches and Pains." The image showing a bandaged puppy alongside an unhappy child suggested that the product would conquer the pain of both creatures.[138] Other products were advertised as preventive measures and cure-alls for dogs, such as Calvert's Carbolic Acid Dog Soap. The advertisement for this product read as follows:

> The active principle of This Soap is Carbolic Acid, which is a thorough preventive of infectious diseases, and destroyer of all insect life, such as Fleas or other Parasites, on domestic Animals; it is not poisonous, and may be relied on for the cure of Mange and other Skin diseases; it also gives a healthy tone to the skin and improves the appearance of the coat.[139]

One can imagine an eager dog owner rushing out to purchase this product in the hopes that it would keep his pet in fine condition and improve its appearance. Dogs were not the only pets to experience such treatments, and a strikingly similar advertisement for Condion, endorsing a cure-all for birds, was published in the newspaper *Fur and*

Feather.[140] Even dog hospitals advertised in language similar to endorsements for human services. For example, one establishment in Halifax advertised "Splendid Accommodation for In-Patients."[141] Through the use of consumer goods and services, pets were increasingly personified while their owners were caught up in the latest consumer trends. Care for animals was increasingly a consumerist enterprise.

Pets on Show

The most commercial of all pet-keeping activities was perhaps the show circuit; it was here that a pet could garner significant prestige and profit for its owner. Since the eighteenth century, proud dog owners had competed for prizes in coffee houses and small taverns across the country.[142] Pigeon societies originated in similar contexts, and the most famous of these, the Columbarian Society, was founded in 1750.[143] In the late nineteenth century many of these activities became centrally coordinated under the auspices of umbrella organizations with mandates to direct the breeding of companion animals. The Kennel Club remains the most famous of these institutions, all of which developed increasingly high profiles as the passion to breed pets became something of a mania. The Kennel Club sponsored an average of fifty shows a year between 1885 and 1900, with a record number of sixty-four shows in 1899.[144] The *Fur Fanciers' Journal* gave notice for the occurrence of thirty-five shows devoted to the exhibition of rabbits, cats, and cavies in the south of England for July 1891 alone,[145] and by 1907 one manual claimed that there was a rabbit show every day in the United Kingdom, at which three or four hundred rabbits came upon the judging table.[146] There were additionally shows exhibiting all manner of cage birds, poultry, mice, and later rats, as well as cats. Judges at each show examined animals for their physical attributes and awarded prizes for points of beauty. Obsessions with the lineage of pet animals suggest the extent to which pet keeping replicated the stratified Victorian social order. No less a venue than the Crystal Palace, which was moved to Sydenham in 1854, hosted some of these shows. By providing opportunities for competition, business transaction, trade, entertainment, and conspicuous display, these events garnered attention in the local and national press, which published lists of champions and their keepers.[147] There were even collectible cards, available with the purchase of chocolates and cigarettes, featuring prize-winning birds and dogs. Chocolate and cigarette companies may have been copying the marketing techniques of

Spratt's, which sold a variety of products for animal care and also produced collectible cards of prize-winning canines.[148]

These various accolades were financially beneficial to pet keepers. Those whose animals succeeded on the show circuit could profit from pet keeping and were continually lauded. In 1892, for example, the *Fur Fanciers' Journal* reported on the success of a Mr Wilson of Hull who bred two red cavies, "Reliance" and "Defiance," and sold them to Mr T. Hewson "for the modest sum of £30. Besides I know that he has bred and sold pigeons that have realized from £40 to £60 each."[149] In addition to selling their champions, owners could charge hefty fees for mating their animals. The ownership of male champions was especially profitable, as would-be entrepreneurs advertised the "stud" services of their animals in a variety of classifieds.[150] These ads provided information on the best attributes of the stud, describing size, colouration, pedigree, and prize-winning capacity. Some advertisements included illustrations or photographs and family trees. Witness, for example, a typical advertisement for a stud bulldog:

> Moston King
>   (K.C.S.B. 838g.)
>   Colour, Brindle Pied; weight, 45lbs.; born May 22nd, 1902. Sire – Champion Prince Albert, dam – Gyp, by Champion Portland. A long and broad skulled dog, with good under jaw, turn-up and lay-back, good shoulders, short body, well sprung ribs, deep brisket, nice tucked-up loin, splendid roach, low-set tail, immense bone, and a big winner.
>   Fee, £4 4s.[151]

The impregnating services of less prestigious animals, such as rabbits and mice, were marketed in similar ways.[152] In response, owners of female pets, often euphemistically referred to as "queens," would pay the stipulated fee and send their animals by rail to mate with the stud. After "servicing" was complete, the queen would be sent back to its owner, who hoped to breed prize-winning animals of known pedigree.

The return of the queen to the show circuit could be expedited by using a foster mother to nurse offspring. Manuals provided information on how to go about this task, advising keepers to acquire these animals "from either private persons who advertise in the … journals, or from one or other of several firms who make the supply of foster-mothers their business."[153] The foster mother was usually a mongrel; her progeny were treated as inconsequential and disposable. Foster mothers were animals that were considered working class and functioned like wet nurses. Using female animals in this way recapitulated and reinforced the Victorian social structure. An author of a manual on cats made the class privileges associated with this practice explicit by claiming that when "the nurse Cat appears on the scene, [it] undertakes the duties that belong to its sex in a much higher order in society."[154] The acquisition of foster mothers could be expensive. According to an article published in 1895, an "average price paid for the use of a foster-dam may be put down to a guinea."[155] By 1905 there were firms specializing in the trade of these creatures. One such establishment claimed that it was "prepared to supply foster-mothers for anything from toy puppies to lion cubs at a moment's notice, and a wire to this firm will generally result in the arrival of a foster-mother as fast as steam can bring her."[156] Indeed, any animal could be fostered, including fancy poultry, but the most common were cats and dogs.[157]

Individuals wanting to send animals to foster, mate, or show relied on the railway to transport their pets. These animals were treated much like other goods, and the railway facilitated the transport of pets alongside other freight. The railway created the possibility for everyone and everything to be put in motion, and it joined once disparate groups of pet keepers into communities. One pet-keeping manual even attributed the existence of "modern pigeon shows" to the invention of railroad transport, which drew together birds and their owners from all parts of the country.[158] Pets accompanied by owners were a familiar spectacle at train stations, so much so that a painting dating from 1893 depicts the wealthy and their dogs boarding the train at King's Cross station.[159] Use of the railway was so widespread that one newspaper estimated in 1895 that over a hundred thousand dogs were transported annually in this way.[160] Animals travelling alone to be mated or exhibited were an equally a common sight. Owners expected show officials, railway attendants, or servants to look after unaccompanied pets, even if they were sent with only "collar, chain and muzzle." This could result in all sorts of mishaps as animals were lost amid the chaotic transport of goods or arrived "in a highly nervous, tired out condition."[161] Even the transport of animals could be inflected with class prejudice, and the *Bazaar, Exchange and Mart*, for example, sympathized with one dog owner and blamed a servant for a mishap in transport, stating, "We think you are entitled to compensation for loss of bitch [*sic*], as there was in our opinion great carelessness on the part of the servant of the owner of the stud dog."[162] Disgruntled owners often had different animals returned from the ones they had sent, and show managers were faulted for the mistake.[163] Railway companies were also accused of mishandling animals.[164] A typical complaint read as follows: "I think railway arrangements simply shocking. My Cat arrived in London at 11:30 a.m., and reached her destination, some six miles out at 7:30 p.m."[165] A more serious grievance was launched by a pet owner whose animal arrived some ten days after it was sent, "by which time it was quite ill." She took the matter to county court, suing for damages.[166] Other animals died en route, but it was sometimes difficult to establish fault. The number of unaccompanied pets suggests that pet owners were learning to use the railway – and testing the possibilities this type of transport offered.

At the end of the century, some railway companies went to great lengths to facilitate the comfort of pets travelling alone, especially dogs, suggesting the extent to which the transport of unaccompanied dogs had become a priority. To this end, the *Dog Owners' Supplement* reported on and celebrated an invention of the London and North Western Company's carriage superintendent, Mr C.A. Park. Park had designed a carriage that was "lofty, spacious, well ventilated, well drained and contains separate compartments for no less than twenty-six dogs; while there is additional space on shelves set apart for baskets, boxes and the like." Each compartment had an enamel drinking trough and was sectioned off by iron railings. The floors were zinc-lined and covered in straw. There were troughs for drainage so that the carriage conformed to standards of hygiene. Such efforts were a response to repeated calls for "more comfortable and safe travelling for dogs unaccompanied by owners."[167] The transit of dogs was a serious concern – and efforts were expended to ensure their safe passage.

Manuals instructed owners on how to send pets by rail. This advice indicates that some pet keepers were unfamiliar with railway travel, and pet keeping initiated them in the ways of mass transport. Consider the following instructions offered to a fancier sending an unaccompanied cat:

> Before sending off a Cat make every enquiry as to route, always selecting the more expeditious, and of course find out what day it should be sent and advise the owner of the stud Cat accordingly. Use very distinctive labels, and words "Live Cat" should find a place; while in the case of valuable animals insurance should be effected.[168]

Even if they labelled their animals, fanciers sometimes sent their pets to the wrong location. To counter this tendency, *Fur and Feather* suggested that show organizers specify the location of their exhibitions, stating, "It is all right for local exhibitors, they know well enough, but the great majority do not, and we have not always a map of England by us to which we can refer and search out the locality of the different shows, neither do we want to be going continually to the post office or the railway station to enquire."[169] Not surprisingly, animals travelling by train could become agitated and even sick. The concern for unaccompanied dogs, in particular, was frequently vented in pet-keeping newspapers, and two novels dramatizing the lives of show dogs attempted to educate readers about the unaccompanied transit of animals, describing the terror, hunger, and thirst animals experienced during these journeys.[170] Another manual, giving hints on the transport of birds, stated emphatically,

> The great secret is to keep them dark and left in peace … Some persons when traveling with birds, always make a point of poking at, and peeking, and talking to their pets (already sufficiently alarmed by the noise of the train, with the intention of "making them cheerful and look alive,") and so additionally terrify the birds, that they expire ere the end of the journey. If you value their comfort pray let them alone.[171]

Transport by rail, though widespread, could be perilous for animals.

Despite these hazards, pet keepers who joined the ranks of fanciers found the exhibiting and breeding of their pets an exciting and conflicting experience. One fancier, for example, described the thrill of exhibiting her cats as addictive, though detrimental to her animal: "when in the second year I had been at it, I bred a very promising blue male, of which, of course, I was inordinately proud; after showing him at most of the north country shows and generally getting first with him, in an evil moment I sent him to Bristol Show, where he contracted distemper."[172] The breeding of prized pets was equally fraught, and there were frequent complaints against profiteering owners who were accused of sexually exhausting their studs. Fanciers seeking to impregnate queen cats were advised to "see if possible the kind of Cat offered. Stud cats that are run as mere money-making machines are likely to be overtaxed."[173] Bad experiences notwithstanding, pet keepers were tempted to show and breed their animals at every opportunity, and they were encouraged to do so by reports of success on the show circuit.[174]

Such reports were carefully crafted to promote fancy matters among novices needing encouragement to persist in the hobby. Accordingly, *Our Cats* reported that "Mrs. Slingsby kindly allows us to publish a list of the wins of her cats at Manchester as encouragement to beginners ... Mrs. Slingsby's first purchase was Daisy Nita in 1900, and until then she knew nothing about Persian cats."[175] By 1910, dedicated fanciers were suspicious of beginners, accusing them of excessive greed or faddishness. As one veteran fancier remarked in *Canary and Cage Bird Life*, "one not infrequently hears remarks of this sort when the topic is touched on: 'Oh, I am very fond of birds. I tried Canary-breeding once, but I could not get on with it, so had to give it up.'"[176] Most experts claimed that breeding was rarely lucrative and required extensive financial commitment and patience. One manual on the rearing of bulldogs suggested "that every man should ask himself before he enters the ranks of Bulldog fanciers ... Is he sufficiently interested in the breed to put up with many and many a disappointment, to face a certain amount of financial loss, and to devote such time as he can give to the welfare of his dog?"[177] Some enthusiasts were uneasy about the commodification of pet keeping. Though many kept pets for profit, there was no guarantee of financial success, and those who sought revenue by these means risked the scorn of their peers and the death of their pets. Though they may have been companions, pets could also be sources of accolade and profit – possibly leading to the demise of the pet. Yet for many pet keepers the potential excitement of the show circuit was too much to resist.

Conclusion

In nineteenth- and early twentieth-century Britain, pet keeping involved all sorts of domestic routines and consumer activities. When Victorians cared for their pets, they strove to reform the animal, making it obey and conform to human needs and etiquettes. As pet keeping became a mass phenomenon, more and more pets were kept, including animals that could be caught in the local environment and maintained fairly cheaply. This allowed everyone – from poor to rich and young to old – to keep animals, but not all pets were considered equal. Pedigreed dogs made celebrated pets for those able to acquire them; canaries enhanced household harmony of working folk; fancy chickens were objects of conspicuous consumption for upper-class ladies; guinea pigs, pigeons, and rabbits, though kept by people of all classes, were less prestigious and sometimes food; mice and rats were the pets of children and working men; squirrels could be kept by individuals of all classes; cats and hedgehogs were mainly utilitarian creatures, but also sometimes loved pets; and mongrel females could be captured and sold as foster-mothers. Both middle- and working-class individuals kept pets, but these animals differed in prestige and expense required for their upkeep. Some animals, such as mice and rats, were exclusively associated with poorer pet keepers, yet they also provided opportunities to reap all the benefits of love, companionship, investment, profit, and acclaim derived from more prominent pets. There was an emulative aspect to pet-keeping activities, which transformed pets into objects of conspicuous consumption. At the same time, obsessions with pet lineage suggest the extent to which pet-keeping activities imitated and reinforced the stratified Victorian social order. Since those in the know could presumably distinguish a working man's pets from those of his social superiors, pet keeping offered few opportunities for social mobility, but it did shore up social status within working-class and middle-class communities, and involve all participants in nascent consumer culture. By the last quarter of the nineteenth century, pet keeping had become a consumerist enterprise, and all sorts of accessories, foods, and services were available on the market to assist with pet care.

At any moment the pet could be transformed into a commodity. To acquire a pet, nineteenth- and twentieth-century Britons engaged in diverse consumer practices, either capturing the animal or purchasing it from street vendors, shops, or classified ads. As an object of exchange, pets were used to participate in certain consuming practices – advertised in classified newspapers, sent by rail, and bred and shown for profit. Many men and women loved their pets, but they also regarded them as objects and commodities. Individuals in need of cash or other goods could offer their pets for sale, exchange, exhibition, or breeding. From the moment an animal was designated a pet through to its death, it served its owner by providing loyalty, companionship, instruction, utility, revenue, food, and fame. Pet keeping was potentially emotionally satisfying, lucrative, and prestigious for all participants. Victorians were passionate about their pets.

Chapter Two

Sexy Beasts, Fallen Felines, and Pampered Pomeranians

For five weeks in the summer of 1899, *Vanity Fair* published a series of satirical letters on a phenomenon it termed "Poodledom."[1] The letters used pet-keeping practices to lampoon late Victorian gender relations and marriage. The first letter, ostensibly penned by a "Looker On," introduced the cast of characters that would appear throughout the saga. The first to be described was the Poodle – an obsequious lover likened to a poodle dog:

> Few really smart women in Society are smart enough to do without the necessary adjunct to their household, a Poodle. With the demand has risen a supply; and now in both the upper-middle and the very smartest sets there are to be found many animals of this much-sought-after species. They are *generally young men* with more money and good looks than brains.[2]

The "duties of a Poodle" were "devotion absolute" and the regular giving of flowers, chocolates, dinners, and bijouterie. The Poodle must always be at his mistress's beck and call, "always good-tempered and obliging." In return, she "rewards him with sweet smiles, kind words, and occasional pats." The Poodle is a welcome presence in the family and he enjoys being kept, especially in "cases where the lady is particularly pretty or smart" and he "has the satisfaction of knowing that he is envied by all other Poodles; and so he loves to be seen dancing attendance on her." The husband also enjoys the Poodle's company and gives him "choice cigars and a general invitation to fish in his rivers and shoot his coverts. This is one of the strangest things about it." The only objection to poodle keeping comes from the lone moralist, Mrs

Grundy, who is representative of "women who morally purse up their lips at the idea of keeping a Poodle."[3] According to Mrs Grundy, the pampering of the lapdog signalled nothing less than the end of masculine authority and its long history:

> No man could possibly respect himself … who puts himself in the position of your last correspondent [the Poodle] … Fancy any one of the men who have made History, either Ancient or Modern, being any woman's Poodle – Alexander the Great, Peter of Russia, Oliver Cromwell, Nelson, Robespierre, Gordon or Kitchener! No, you are a degenerate race, you men, the product of an over-refined and false age.[4]

No other character in Poodledom agrees with this assessment, and *Vanity Fair*, partially taking the side of Mrs Grundy, implies that that the keeping of poodles might destroy the late Victorian gender order.

These letters are an example of a phenomenon that recurred in the latter half of the nineteenth century in a variety of popular media as diverse as satire, didactic narrative, illustration, painting, and scientific text: a discussion of human gender differences and relations using the figure of the pet. It was also frequently argued that the gender order was threatened by the activities of female fanciers who lavished attention on their pet animals. This chapter will show how the pet-keeping enterprise was important for the production of middle-class gender identities in the late nineteenth century.[5]

This chapter describes the ways cat and dog keeping was discussed outside the pet-keeping enterprise. I draw on Harriet Ritvo's argument that the Victorian discourse on animal breeding was shaped by masculinist understandings of human gender stereotypes, and by ideas about female sexuality in particular. Ritvo is interested in why breeders and fanciers were guided by older ideas about human sexuality, despite experiences managing and mating animals that should have proved these ideas false. Their beliefs were all the more remarkable, she suggests, when viewed in light of the advances made by Victorian science in explaining the mechanisms of sexual reproduction.[6] In contrast, I show that the gender stereotypes rehearsed and perpetuated by fanciers had bearing beyond the world of the animal fancies for all Victorian bourgeois men and women. This was a two-way street: ideas about human gender influenced the discourse on how to care for cats and dogs, and ideas about pet keeping shaped notions of how men and women should behave. Cats and dogs were connected to prescriptive ideas about feminine and masculine behaviour in middle-class society. Cats, irrespective of the actual gender of the animal, were believed to exemplify certain characteristics of bourgeois womanhood. They were perceived as innately sexual animals and far too promiscuous and independent to be good pets. Opinions of the cat affected perceptions of middle-class women, and discussions of feline habits became forums to consider the social possibilities available to women in late Victorian society. Dogs, in contrast, were associated with idealized middle-class masculinity. They were perceived as masculine creatures, innately heroic, loyal, and honest. As men's pets, they were believed to share characteristics with their owners, including patriarchal relations with women.

Victorian perceptions of cats and dogs were used to theorize the proper roles men and women should fulfil in Victorian society. The figure of the pet influenced ideas of how women and men should behave; or, to paraphrase Judith Butler, should perform as gendered persons.[7] This became increasingly apparent in the late nineteenth century when women asserted themselves alongside men as pet fanciers. Pet keeping had previously been considered a masculine pursuit, part of the male prerogative to control and interpret nature. Female pet keepers challenged these views and forced a reconsideration of the relationship between men and nature. In so doing, they also disputed assumptions about the differences between men and women that the pet-keeping enterprise had helped to enshrine. The activities of female fanciers were noticed and used to discredit women's struggle for the franchise.

In late nineteenth-century Britain, Victorians were obsessed by gender ideologies and the setting out of what was expected of men and women. Pet keeping became a forum for debating gender ideologies at a time when female participation in public life was a highly controversial issue as middle-class women campaigned for access to higher education, the professions, and the franchise and for the repeal of the Contagious Diseases Acts.[8] The participation of women in leisure activities that had previously been exclusively male preoccupations also contested ideas about the proper place of middle-class women, who were assigned separate spheres from men. In this context, the activities of women in the animal fancies as pet keepers and breeders of prize-winning animals were considered groundbreaking and also threatening. Female fanciers challenged male control in society vis-à-vis pets, and their actions garnered notice outside the fancies. They forced a reconsideration of commonly held views about the male prerogative to control and interpret nature and also notions about what women could accomplish in the public sphere.[9]

Pet keeping may seem far removed from political discussions of female and male participation in public life, but because so many of the arguments for and against women's suffrage and higher education were based on assumptions of the innate differences between the sexes, pets appeared in some popular discussions of the issue.[10] As representatives of nature within the household, pets could have influence on what was thought of as "natural," including the differences between men and women. Of all pets kept by the Victorians, cats and dogs were particularly significant in the formulation of ideas about gender, and the subjects of popular representations that articulated categories having to do with gender and sexuality, as well as race. Depictions of cats and dogs were symbolic and instructive, and available in all sorts of media, widely consumed, which influenced middle-class understandings of the social roles of men and women.

The following discussion will be composed of three parts. First I will examine how cats were associated with femininity and the implications this had for prescriptions of how women should behave. I will also discuss how fanciers tried to overcome the negative perceptions of their cats as perfidious creatures and terrible pets. I will then turn to the dog fancy and examine the ways dogs were thought of as masculine creatures. The dog too, I will show, was used for didactic purposes to model proper masculine and feminine comportment. Finally, I will discuss the reception women received when they asserted themselves as pet fanciers. The case of the Ladies' Kennel Association, which attempted to advance the activities of female dog fanciers, will be examined at length. The activities of women pet keepers and images of cats and dogs resonated far beyond the narrow world of the fancies and influenced women's struggle for the franchise.

Fallen Felines

Towards the end of the nineteenth century, cat keeping became an increasingly popular pastime. In England and Ireland it was estimated that nearly every household had a cat and that the costs of maintaining these animals could be as high as £3 a year.[11] Cats had been kept as domesticates since the earliest times, but considerations of felines as pets and fancy animals occurred quite late, and did not become widely accepted until the twentieth century. Most cats were outdoor creatures, only brought inside on occasion to hunt for mice. The first organized show devoted exclusively to cats occurred at the Crystal Palace in 1871; before this event, cats were usually exhibited alongside rabbits and guinea pigs, which were less prestigious fancy animals, considered by many to be working men's pets because they were relatively inexpensive to maintain. The National Cat Club, founded in 1887, was a middle-class institution that attempted to improve the reputation of the cat and encourage the development of various breeds.[12] Nevertheless, despite the efforts of fanciers, cats were often mistreated and abandoned on the grounds that they did not make very good pets. Viewed as highly independent creatures, cats were disdained because they seemed to resist human management and were often associated with femininity.

Cats in the nineteenth century were regarded as women's pets and the two were popularly believed to have much in common. Often in discussions of cat keeping, women and cats were made analogous (no matter the sex of the animal), despite the fact that middle-class women, especially, were understood as domestic and indoor creatures – unlike cats, which were primarily outdoor animals. Beliefs about femininity informed perceptions of cats and interactions with cats helped produce ideas of how women should behave. Victorians viewed the cat as an essentially female creature and generated a large quantity of literature on the feminine attributes of the feline. This connection tended to relate cats and women in negative and often contradictory ways. The cat was understood as a strong-willed, independent, and promiscuous as well as a feeble and self-destructive creature that could somehow be reformed into a more ideal and dependent pet. This made the cat an exemplar for womanly conduct since it could be held up as a model of feminine virtue, likened to the idealized middle-class wife who was either viewed as the model of sexual propriety and the hallmark of the Victorian gender order or condemned as an incarnation of female vice, much like the archetypal Victorian prostitute. Women were not merely passive and domestic beings; they could also be sexual like cats. When fanciers attempted to rescue the reputation of their pets, they dissociated cats and women in order to assert the respectability of the cat fancy.

Discussions relating felines to femininity circulated widely and were rarely complimentary. Often in pet-keeping manuals, cats were gendered female and chapters devoted to the maintenance of cats were written by women.[13] The connection between women and cats was believed to be very strong in both positive and negative ways. In particular the feline habit of repetitive self-grooming seemed to correspond to perceptions of female vanity. It was therefore asserted that a "cat is very like a woman; her toilet is the most important business of the day."[14]

Cats were additionally believed to adopt the "exquisite manners" of their mistresses and eat regular meals at the table with their female owners.[15] At the same time, cats were accused of feminine disloyalty, and fans of the cat went to great lengths to dispel this perception. One fancier, for example, dedicated her manual "To the 'Pretty Lady' Who Never Betrayed a Secret, Broke a Promise, or Proved an Unfaithful Friend; Who had all the Virtue and None of the Failings of her Sex."[16] As the inscription implies, the association between cats and women was riddled with assumptions about the weaknesses of the female character.

Many Victorians viewed the cat as an inferior pet because it eschewed human control and was associated with devious femininity and aggressive sexuality.[17] Observations of the cat – and its fierce independence – informed and confirmed perceptions of human women as unreliable, much like their feline friends. Descriptions of the feline character likened cats to women who were eager to escape domesticity and vulnerable to the seductions of outside forces. As one fancier asserted, though cats "are the embodiment of elegance, grace and agility … Very little, in fact, is needed to make the Cat stray from the paths of domesticity and return again to the happier hunting-grounds of its remote ancestors."[18] Many viewed the cat as a perfidious creature that could easily flee the ministrations of its owner and often did. Because they were viewed as highly independent, likely to choose their own mates and breed out of sight of their owners, cats were accused of erratic behaviour. This resistance to human management led to the widespread belief that cats were "unbreedable [sic] and unstable."[19] Such ideas were current even outside the animal fancies in the mainstream press. The *Illustrated London News*, for example, expressed nothing but contempt for "the contemptuous reserve of the sly and calculating cat," which was personified as female.[20]

Instability was believed to manifest itself strongly in female cats, which were notorious for shirking their maternal duties. Felines were frequently accused of murdering their offspring after giving birth.[21] This behaviour was considered innate to the cat, though other pets were believed to display similar habits.[22] Some fanciers defended the loyalty of the feline to her offspring, even claiming to have witnessed instances when she nursed the progeny of other animals, including dogs, rats, chickens, hares, hedgehogs, and squirrels.[23] Nevertheless, there was no consensus on the nurturing instincts of the cat. Cat breeders consequently advised each other to be highly involved in the selection and management of kittens lest the mother cat kill her offspring and destroy a potentially prize-winning litter.[24] Since, as we have seen in the previous chapter, many pet keepers went to considerable lengths to mate their pets, these actions contributed to opinions of feline duplicity and strengthened beliefs in the connection between cats and women; indeed pregnant cats were once referred to as "women enceinte."[25]

Perceptions of the cat as an innately emotive animal given to bouts of passion and mischief also suggested a correlation between cats and women. Since the Middle Ages, cats had been associated with voracious and sensual female sexuality, and these ideas persisted in the Victorian era alongside views of cats (and women) as innately passive non-sexual beings. (These contradictions are implied by the word "pussy," which entered the English language in the sixteenth century to connote a sweet girl or woman exhibiting characteristics of a cat. The term became coarse slang for female genitals in the seventeenth century.)[26] Discipline was considered the best method to reform the cat. For example, Victorian pet keepers who kept cats as companions and not mousers were advised to chastise their cats when they ate birds, rabbits, or mice. Gordon Stables, an authority on cats, in fact argued that catching mice should be regarded as "a mere pastime, only to be resorted to on rainy days."[27] Cats who gave in to these impulses were described as immoral and impious beings. They could nevertheless be reformed from rapacious creatures into models of feline innocence, as Stables argued in language which made clear the personification of cats as women:

> there is no animal that lives and breathes on God's fair earth but is susceptible of improvement, both physically and morally, for, remember, a cat, little as you may think of her, has a mind and a soul, as well as you have. She has thought, and memory, and reasoning powers; she can love and she can fear, can be happy and gay, or sad and sorrowful; and she knows something too of the mystery of death.
>
> With all these qualities will you tell me that she cannot be improved? I say she can; even as to race; for what can be accomplished with individual cats, may be accomplished with the whole race. I can introduce you to dozens of cat-fanciers in this country, who have made the peculiarities of pussy's nature their study, and who find that they can, at will, not only improve the physical condition of their cats; but even, by careful training, occasional gentle correction, kindness, good-feeding, raise them from good to better, and wean them from the ways which are so objectionable in other, or merely half-domesticated cats.[28]

Through careful management, the character of the cat could be transformed into a paragon of domestic innocence. These prescriptions were also directed at human women. Moreover, the quotation demonstrates the conflation of animal keeping and ideas of race. Even through the keeping of cats, Victorians enacted imperial prerogatives of civilization, attempting to reform animals as they might civilize imperial subjects. The intellectual historian James Turner has argued that the language of "race" was more frequently applied to animals in the second half of the nineteenth century than in the first. Employing language which acknowledged kinship between people and animals was part of the way in which Darwinism was employed in popular culture.[29]

By vigilant supervision it was believed that feline nature could be somewhat tempered and the cat reformed into a more compliant pet. Similarly women could be guided in the ways of the world so as not to stray from domestic obligations. Since the two were believed to be similar, the actions of the cat could be used to instruct women on proper comportment. Pictorial representations of women and cats published in the Victorian illustrated press fulfilled this purpose. The images drew upon the comparisons between women and cats that were prominent in pet-keeping manuals and newspapers. Most of the images featured kittens or sleeping cats, portrayed as demure creatures, symbols of the innocent and passive women with whom they were pictured. Both cats and women were shown as childlike creatures whose sexual inclinations were (momentarily) suppressed. In the *Illustrated London News*, in particular, pictures of women and cats were accompanied by short narratives interpreting the image for readers and informing them of its meaning. These narratives allow us to recapture the ways Victorians were intended to understand these pictures. Readers were supposed to relate to the images and learn appropriate modes of feminine conduct.

Grown men were not pictured with cats, though in a few images young boys and kittens were shown together. The narratives accompanying these illustrations made clear that the relationship between the two was unequal; the boy mastered the feline and claimed dominance of nature by ruling his cat. One poem, for example, made this explicit, stating that the child is "Like a boy-King on his throne, / Claiming nature as his own." In popular images, cats were depicted as women's pets.[30]

When girls were figured with cats, the two were often pictured conversing companionably or playing some game (figure 2.1).[31] Often the narratives accompanying the images advised girls to use interactions with cats to prepare for adulthood. For example, the story accompanying one image, titled "Pussy's Perquisite," showing a girl pouring milk for her cat, stated, "As she grows up the little lady will still have a pet, be sure – to tend and love." The girl's attitude towards the cat was maternal, suggesting that these interactions were practice for motherhood.[32] Other images cast girls already as adults. For example, a picture titled "The Stranger within Thy Gates" showed two young girls dolled up and watching a kitten climb towards a saucer at their feet (figure 2.2). When considered carefully, the image invites questions: who is the stranger here? Is it their sexuality, which is being invited in prematurely? There is a dog sitting beside them. The dog seems to be the family member; the cat is the stranger. The narrative suggests that this is a portrait of childhood innocence intended to provide feelings of "gladsomeness." The image is similar to "Cherry Ripe" (1879), a famous portrait, most certainly known to readers of the *Illustrated London News*, by Sir John Everett Millais, which showed a young girl, eyes downcast, lavishly dressed, sitting with her hands clasped in her lap. Interpreters of this and similar images have suggested that such representations show the complexity of Victorian conceptions of childhood, since the children seem anything but innocent. The children in such portraits were clearly involved in the world of adults yet were supposedly unconscious of adult desires.[33] Their passivity is suggestive of what they should become – modest women, with only sublimated passions. This conceit is suggested less subtly in "The Stranger within Thy Gates" by the figure of the kitten and the innocent, yet potentially insatiable, sexuality it represents. The image was intended to warm the heart, even as it reinforced the idea that girls and cats were somehow similar, and potentially very sexual.

These associations proliferated in late Victorian popular culture and appeared in all sorts of literary productions. For example, in the first chapter of Lewis Carroll's *Through the Looking Glass, and What Alice Found There* (1871), Alice is playing with a kitten, talking to it and declaiming its faults as if it were a naughty child. She compares the kitten's faults to her own:

"Do you know, I was so angry, Kitty," Alice went on as soon as they were comfortably settled again, "when I saw all the mischief you had been doing, I was very nearly opening the window, and putting you out into the snow! And you'd have deserved it, you little mischievous darling! What have you got to say for yourself? Now don't interrupt me!" she went on,

2.1. "A Garden Party," *Illustrated London News*, 19 July 1884

holding up one finger. "I'm going to tell you all your faults. Number one: you squeaked twice while Dinah [mother cat] was washing your face this morning. Now you can't deny it, Kitty: I heard you! What's that you say?" (pretending that the kitten was speaking.) "Her paw went into your eye? Well, that's YOUR fault, for keeping your eyes open – if you'd shut them tight up, it wouldn't have happened. Now don't make any more excuses, but listen! Number two: you pulled Snowdrop away by the tail just as I had put down the saucer of milk before her! What, you were thirsty, were you? How do you know she wasn't thirsty too? Now for number three: you unwound every bit of the worsted while I wasn't looking!

"That's three faults, Kitty, and you've not been punished for any of them yet. You know I'm saving up all your punishments for Wednesday week – Suppose they had saved up all MY punishments!" she went on, talking more to herself than the kitten. "What WOULD they do at the end

2.2. "The Stranger within Thy Gates," *Illustrated London News*,
27 December 1884

of a year? I should be sent to prison, I suppose, when the day came. Or –
let me see – suppose each punishment was to be going without a dinner:
then, when the miserable day came, I should have to go without fifty dinners at once! Well, I shouldn't mind THAT much! I'd far rather go without
them than eat them!"[34]

Like the images in the Victorian illustrated press, Carroll's story is in
part about the imaginative romps of childhood and a lesson in the
propriety of children and adults. Given the popularity of comparisons
between girls and cats, it is perhaps not accidental, then, that readers
are introduced to Alice in a scene which also features a mischievous
kitten.

Pictures of adult women and cats were intended to present a portrait
of ideal womanhood by showing the middle-class angel in the house, a
childlike and passive woman almost without personality. The women
in these pictures were shown as innocent, entirely devoid of agency,
and the cats that accompany them confirm this impression by their passive posturing. For example, an image titled "Le Favori," dating from
1872, showed a woman embroidering with a cat asleep in her lap. The
narrative inferred the character of the seamstress from the benign posture of her cat: "She must be as gentle as she is pretty, or her favourite
would not be sleeping in such perfect contentment in her lap." The attitude of the cat reinforced perceptions of the woman's placidity and
beauty (figure 2.3). The narrative accompanying another picture with
the same title, appearing in 1881, took this one step further, making the
woman and cat objects of desire but still essentially passive. The kitten
in this picture also proves the woman's innocence, but both are regarded as possessions of the viewer. The poem narrating the image made
the meaning plain: "see, even the very kitten here, / Her pet, is to *our*
Favourite dear." The woman is directly likened to her cat; she is a pet
and a possession, just like her sleeping friend. The two are passive and
available: the woman is completely unaware of the sexual possibilities
lurking in her own nature and lying asleep in her lap.[35]

These representations provided a view of the similarities between
women and cats as either models of virtue or creatures of vice. The two
characteristics were interrelated, since slippage from innocence to corruption was believed to be an ever-present possibility for both women
and cats, especially if they were left to their own devices. This likeli-
hood inspired melodramatic warnings about the dangers that might
befall a cat should she be abandoned by her owner. Such stories were

2.3. "La Favori" by Jourdan, *Illustrated London News*, 18 May 1872

essentially narratives of sexual danger and proliferated so widely in the 1880s that they even found their way into discussions of pet keeping. Judith Walkowitz has defined narratives of sexual danger as cautionary tales for women, "a warning that the city was a dangerous place when they transgressed the narrow boundary of home and hearth to enter the public space."[36] These stories were predicated on the assumption that when women became involved in the public life of a metropolis, in any capacity, as workers, shoppers, or even charity collectors, they could become victims of sexual solicitation or compelled into a life of prostitution. Following melodramatic conventions, these stories related the plight of the "fallen woman" who had followed her passions and been seduced into a life of vice. The stories about cats used similar themes and rhetorical conventions; they functioned as cautionary tales for women, warning them of their fate should they abandon their domestic duties. Published in pet-keeping manuals and newspaper reports, these narratives had a wide circulation and suggest the extent to which concerns about cats generated fantasies about human women.

The inspiration for these fantasies was a common occurrence: pet keepers, it seems, having little attachment to their cats, frequently deserted these animals when they went on holiday or moved house. Starting in the 1880s, newspaper reports and pet-keeping manuals condemned this practice with increasing vehemence, repeating again and again the imperative, "Don't leave your cats to starve while you go for an enjoyable holiday."[37] Concern about the abandoned cat was based on beliefs that felines were essentially feminine creatures and unable to care for themselves without human protection. An abandoned cat, it was feared, would fall victim to all sorts of temptations by giving in to her feminine inclinations. For example, Gordon Stables, an authority on cat keeping, suggested that a starving cat left to its own devices might catch mice, cannibalize her young, or eat part of her own body.[38] These actions were deemed morally opprobrious because they were atavistic and signalled a return to primitive feline (read feminine) proclivities. In resorting to its own means for survival, the abandoned cat was imagined to undo its domestication. Cats that strayed in these ways were considered beyond redemption and could never be recovered either as pets or prize-winning animals. Such behaviour would even destroy chances of success on the show circuit. This possibility was frequently presented to owners as a consequence of abandonment.

Yet owners were not blamed for deserting their cats; instead the cat was held responsible for yielding to her impulses and held up as model for women, instructing them on proper comportment. For example, one article, accompanied by an illustration, titled "Cats: A Domestic History," argued for more conscientious care of cats by describing the fate of one abandoned pet. The forsaken cat hunts to survive and "does not think it can be very wrong." Her actions are deemed disastrous, and though the narrator "plead[s] for some consideration of the weaknesses and fallibility of the feline [read feminine] nature," the cat is ultimately judged deserving of her misfortune. The narrative begins by recriminating owners who abandon their cats and ends by disapproving of the cat for satisfying her impulse to feed. As the image makes clear, this cat will never again compete on the show circuit, and for satisfying itself, it apparently deserves its fate as a stray animal (figure 2.4).

Stray cats were imagined to be damaged and irredeemable, rather like the archetypal Victorian prostitute. One writer explained the distinction between the house cat and the stray as follows: "The one is placid, purring, and well-fed; the other is stealthy, suspicious and fugitive. It is the pariah of its race, conscious that its only purpose in life is to serve as a target for the missiles of boys or the bait of goaded terriers."[39] The problem of the stray cat was believed to be so acute that one cat shelter estimated that it received over two thousand cats in 1903 alone.[40] Many cat owners felt strongly that one way to control the problem would be through legal measures enforcing the taxation and collaring of the cat, and giving authorities impunity to kill the stray animals.[41] When a cat strayed from domesticity its nature was believed to irrevocably change. Left to fend for itself, the cat could easily be corrupted by its own impulses or killed in an encounter with outcasts of the metropolis. Gangs of street boys, cat-skin collectors, vivisectors, gamekeepers, and men with dogs all apparently delighted in menacing feline victims.[42] In them the spectre of sexual danger to women was made apparent. The stray cat in the Victorian imagination was directly analogous to the prostitute, who was so betrayed and degraded that she could never return to her former life. The only solution to her fall from grace in many of these narratives was death.

During the 1890s, the death of the cat became a popular trope in narratives of feline abandonment. In one story, "Frowned Upon by Fortune: A Tale of Feline Love and Suicide," published in *Vanity Fair*, a typical "well-bred" cat is left without food when her wealthy family goes holidaying in the country. Luckily she has one friend, Franz, the black cat next door whom she "keep[s] in the background" because he is a mongrel and not so high-born. Franz can fend for himself and he helps her

2.4. "Our Cats: A Domestic History," *Illustrated London News*,
18 October 1884

catch birds. They survive together. Over the course of the month she becomes increasingly filthy and scraggly. Franz is killed by boys who tie up his legs and throw stones at him. The abandoned cat vows to "enter upon a career of crime," but before she can fulfil her plans, she is picked up by a poor spinster who lives in a lodging house. Being utterly destitute, the cat and spinster commit suicide (thus eliminating the problems of abandoned cat and unmarried woman).[43] In another version of the same story, the cat is male. A bachelor writes in to the paper, condemning the family for deserting its pet – and perhaps the paper is suggesting a certain affiliation between cat and bachelor, since both display aberrant sexuality. In all other respects, the narrative follows the pattern of those featuring female cats: the family regrets its action too late; though the cat found temporary shelter with a spinster, it is already dead.[44] In tales of feline suicide the cat is made to pay for her misdeeds – her liaisons and descents into vice – even though she has been betrayed by her family and left to fend for herself. The message is clear: she should remain true to her social station no matter what the cost. In the end, having transgressed sexually and otherwise, the cat must die anyway. The punishment is dire and the warning to women prescient.

These negative opinions of felines posed real challenges for cat fanciers who were fond of their pets. In seeking respectability for their hobby, middle-class fanciers founded the National Cat Club in 1887. The object of the NCC was "to do all in its power to protect and advance the interest of the Cat" by encouraging the breeding of "pure cats" of each distinct breed and defining the true types of such breeds.[45] The organization did its utmost to liberate the cat from its connections to femininity and perfidy. In this vein, the first *National Cat Club Stud Book and Register*, published in 1890, attempted to celebrate male participation in the cat fancy:

> It is only necessary to peruse the names of the present officials of the Club, to find men of most varied professions and sympathies, who have been drawn together by their common affection for and appreciation of the Cat. In all clubs and societies there are those who are especially attracted by the hope of pecuniary benefit, but the N.C.C., while offering solid advantages to the Cat Fancier, also cordially invites the co-operation of those who like many of the present members and warmest supporters, merely have the welfare of Poor Puss at heart without any idea of personal advantage.

Such assertions did little, however, to dismiss the notion that women and cats had a particular affinity. Cat fancying continued to be regarded as a female preoccupation, and the NCC was reputed to be dominated by women, who became, as we will see, objects of ridicule. Even after the foundation of the National Cat Club and its first show in 1887, cats continued to be regarded as relatively insignificant show animals, exhibited at most competitions alongside rabbits, cavies, and fancy mice. These were considered to be a lower order of fancy animals.[46] The NCC's efforts to rescue the status of cats met with limited success.

Cats had long been considered feminine creatures, and were believed to exemplify the emotive, independent, sly and promiscuous tendencies of women. For most of the Victorian era, the cat was scorned as a pet and used to theorize women's nature as inherently feeble and self-destructive. As such, it was used to educate women on their own fallibility and proper comportment. When the cat finally became a fancy animal of status, it remained associated with women and continued to be used to enshrine the social order.

Man's Best Friend

If cats were likened to women and looked to for examples of feminine behaviour, dogs were viewed as models of masculinity. Dogs were widely regarded as men's pets. It was widely believed that men enjoyed a special connection with dogs, and had done so since a mythic so-called primitive man had domesticated his first canine and transformed him into a special helpmeet. The dog was continually celebrated as man's best friend, and also as his loyal servant. In the words of the *Illustrated London News*, "from time immemorial [men] have found in the docile and affectionate dog an agreeable companion and a faithful and useful servant."[47] Dogs were believed to exemplify a chivalric heroism, guilelessness, and loyalty, traits which had long been associated with an idealized masculinity. They also possessed a special affinity with their owners, so much so that the two were thought to share characteristics. Moreover, as representatives of their masculine owners, dogs were considered to be guardians of women. Victorians viewed the relations between women and dogs as analogous to relations between men and women.

Depictions of dogs as masculine creatures were meant to inform conduct both inside and outside the home. These representations were highly didactic and portrayed codes of masculinity which celebrated loyalty, self-sacrifice, and chivalry. Interestingly, this stands in contradistinction to Victorian perceptions of middle-class men as sexually aggressive, immoral, and selfish, contaminated by the public sphere. It has been argued that there was a shift in codes of masculinity in the second half of the nineteenth century from an emphasis on moral earnestness to aggression and athleticism at the close of the era. With regard to men and dogs, it seems that some older ideas remained in play.[48]

Dogs were viewed as men's pets in part because they seemed to epitomize masculine characteristics. Victorians, it seems, never tired of considering the masculine qualities of the dog and associating it with ideals of Victorian manliness. An astonishing number of artistic representations extolled the virtues of the canine and granted it certain masculine attributes, associating the dog with selfless heroism and enduring faithfulness to his master. Early in the century these ideas were promoted in popular melodramas which featured dogs as stage actors cast in the leading role. These plays dramatized a plot in which the dog exposes intrigue and either saves his master or dies in the attempt, while an "evil" Indian or slave, the cause of misfortune, meets an untimely death. One particularly successful play, "The Forests of Bondy," reputedly "founded on fact," started with the murder of the dog's master. The dog then led the police to his master's body. A "dumb boy" was wrongfully accused of the murder and dragged off to prison. Just before his execution, the dog identified the true murderer: "Seizes the Murderer by the Throat! Tearing Him Down To The Earth!!!" This scene was followed by the "Triumph of innocence, and Grand Tableaux!" The play was so popular that one version, featuring a dog named Bruin, ran one hundred nights at the Theatre Royal, Covent Garden in 1837. Bruin, owned by a Mr Wood, achieved considerable fame and also appeared in three other plays titled "Military Execution or, the Dog of the Regiment," "Red Indian or, the Shipwrecked Sailor and his Dog," and "The Slave's Revolt; or, the Negro and the Dog." Sometimes canine actors played other animals, such as leopards, tigers, or lions, though they still demonstrated canine bravery. For example, a play staged at the Royal Surrey Theatre in 1836 titled "Leopards of Jumna" dramatized the "Fidelity & Sagacity of the Leopards!"[49] All of these productions helped reinforce notions of the dog as a gallant companion to man.

As the century progressed, canine heroism continued to be celebrated in painting, sculpture, and narrative representation. Large dogs, such as St Bernards, Newfoundlands, retrievers, and collies, were believed to be particularly intelligent and protective of humans. They were credited with saving the lives of drowning boys by swimming out into the river or sea.[50] These feats were depicted in sentimental paintings showing dogs holding fast to children in danger of toppling into torrential waters.[51] Sometimes dogs were pictured saving other dogs. For example, an image of a Newfoundland looking down at a spaniel struggling in icy water was accompanied by the following description:

> A little spaniel has incautiously slipped into a hole among the broken ice on the margin of a river or lake, and any bi-ped who has been similarly unfortunate … will know how frightfully difficult it is to draw oneself out of such a position. But a fine Newfoundland, with that wonderful instinct impelling him to save life which is so characteristic of this breed, as of the brave St. Bernard and some others rushes, in good time, to the rescue, like a true member of the Royal Humane Society …[52]

As the quotation indicates, certain dogs were reputed to be braver than others. The legend of St Bernard, the saviour of lost travellers in the Alps, for example, was widely publicized and informed heroic perceptions of this breed.[53] The Newfoundland was similarly associated with great courage, and many representations depicted it accomplishing feats of bravery. At the Great Exhibition in 1851, for example, a sculpture of a Newfoundland trampling a serpent became extremely popular. The statue had originally been commissioned in 1831 by Lord Dudley (1781–1833) as a private portrait of his favourite dog, Bashaw. The piece was intended as a personal monument commemorating Lord Dudley's wealth, power, and dignity. In the Great Exhibition, the meaning of the sculpture was changed so that it became a symbol of canine heroism and given the title "The Faithful Friend of Man Trampling Underfoot His Most Insidious Enemy." The sculpture of Bashaw became a symbol of canine bravery.[54]

The dog was depicted as a faithful companion, helpful in moments of strife and loneliness, even when his master was a miscreant or outcast and hardly deemed worthy of such fidelity. One print, for example, titled "His Only Friend" showed a musician, feet held in stocks, petting a dog. The narrative accompanying the illustration explained that the musician was a vagrant and criminal, and therefore undeserving of the dog's loyalty, "but still [he is] consoled by the affectionate caresses of his faithful dog." Another image with the equally sentimental title

"Keeping Himself Warm" showed a fiddler and pug dancing to music on a snowy evening. The narrative accompanying the picture suggests that it too is an allegory of canine devotion, and that the dog is ever loyal despite the drunken ways of the musician. Still another illustration showed a bachelor sharing a meal with a dog. The title, "Old Chums," conveyed the sense of fondness each felt for the other.[55] These pictures expressed the same sentiment: when a man has no other company, the dog is a devoted friend.[56]

The special relationship between men and dogs was believed to be so strong that certain breeds of dog were considered analogous to different classes of men. As one article stated esoterically, "Throughout brute creation the dog, by general consent, is the nearest approach to man – not only in intelligence, but also in variety of type and diversity of character."[57] Representations showing the similarities between men and dogs often ascribed masculine characteristics to dogs in order to emphasize class differences. For example, in 1829 Edwin Landseer, the acclaimed painter and sculptor of animal portraits, rendered two paintings titled *Low Life* and *High Life* of two anthropomorphized dogs. These paintings caused a sensation and remained so popular that they were reproduced in the supplemental section of the *Illustrated London News* in 1874. *Low Life* showed a dog that was terrifyingly human. It sat framed in a doorway next to objects representing the occupations of its absent owner – a pot, pipe, empty bottle, sporting boots, tie, butcher's block, and knife. *High Life* depicted a greyhound, sitting in a lavish room containing carpets, curtains, a desk with a lamp, books, gloves, and a pillowed chair. As the *Illustrated London News* suggested, viewers were to interpret the paintings as "analogies between the canine races and the different orders of men." The greyhound was to be understood as a dog of the purest breed, "thin, sinewy, agile, fond of field sports," evincing a "thoughtful and melancholy air"; while the "other dog [was] a vulgar cross of two plebian breeds," not active, graceful, or beautiful, though good in a fight. Given his fierce countenance, the mongrel seemed "perfectly content with the 'Low Life' he leads and represents." The Baron's noble hound, in contrast, was deemed "a fitting representative of 'High Life.'"[58]

The two paintings demonstrate the ways dogs were equated with men of different social standing. Pets, as we have already seen, were viewed as direct representatives of their owners, living symbols of social status, wealth, or poverty; Victorians believed they could identify the respectability of pet keepers through the appearance and conduct of

2.5. "Dog Sellers and Buyers in the East-End." From Frances Simpson,
"Cat and Dog London," 256

their pets. Men were considered to be masters of these animals, and the
dogs they kept, in turn, reflected their social identities (figure 2.5).

In this way dogs were objects of conspicuous consumption, especially for men. As one manual advised,

> It is a fact which can hardly be disputed that nobody now who is anybody
> can afford to be followed about by a mongrel dog. Since the institution of
> dog shows in this country, knowledge concerning the points of the differ-
> ent breeds has been gradually disseminated among the people, and al-
> though but a small percentage take the trouble to study these, still when
> any one takes it into his head to make a purchase of a dog, *he* will usually
> take little trouble to find out that *he* has the correct thing offered to *him*.
> [Italics mine][59]

Ownership of a high-bred dog indicated masculine character. These
ideas were also proclaimed in art. Thus, the greyhound in Landseer's
paintings epitomized English nobility and was a symbol of national
pride, while the mongrel signified a loutish, drunk, licentious, and

slightly cruel masculinity. The *Illustrated London News* praised the greyhound as representative of "our country due to their handsome figures and the sports connected with them."[60] Pet-keeping manuals additionally likened noble dogs, such as collies, greyhounds, St Bernards, Newfoundlands, and Great Danes, to English gentlemen.[61] At the other end of the spectrum, the mongrel dog – also an implicitly masculine figure – was generally viewed as a social threat and made analogous to the urban poor.

The association between dogs and plebian masculinity was not always negative, however, as demonstrated by the symbolic significance of the bulldog. Bulldogs had originally been fighting animals and were bred for this purpose. In 1835 the first cruelty laws regulating bull baiting came into effect and dog fights were censured. Bulldog keeping was revived later in the century when the bulldog took pride of place as a symbol of English masculinity. The bulldog was considered not only the "most courageous *dog*, but the *most courageous animal in the world*."[62] As a result, when fanciers were given directions on how to improve the physical features of this animal they were also implicitly advised to view their pets as analogous to British men. By breeding the bulldog, fanciers imagined they were creating soldiers to fight for empire. The following comments on the appearance of bulldogs are particularly telling if read as a prescription for the national character:

> It cannot be too frequently impressed that a Bulldog should look like a Bulldog … He is not a true Bulldog if he has a soft and benign expression of countenance; he is not a true Bulldog if he betrays any weakness of character. Physically and mentally he must be strong, as the Bulldog Club standard puts it; he must convey an impression of determination, strength, and activity …[63]

The fierceness of these animals was a source of national pride and the fact that they were ugly made them all the more endearing, as one pet-keeping manual made clear:

> From being the "Butcher's dog," and employed to bait bulls or assist in their slaughtering, he has developed into a fashionable craze, whose chief claim to consideration is his ugliness. The cult of the bull-dog is one of the most curious manias of fancy; "it is like the cult of the toad, I once heard a lady say with a shudder, as she regarded a bench of the breed at a dog show."[64]

By the end of the century the bulldog was a symbol of Britain's bullish island spirit – as well as a fashionable pet.[65]

The link between dogs, masculinity, and nationhood was hardly new in the nineteenth century, though it was more positive than it had been in times past. As Ian MacInnis demonstrates, in the early modern period the mastiff stood for English masculinity and was connected to ideas of the nation by epitomizing characteristics of strength, bravery, and tenacity; but being rough, stupid, and lazy, it could also represent a rougher masculine character. The spaniel was also associated with masculinity, representing a cultured and intelligent, if foreign and effete, manliness.[66] Curs evoked contrasting associations and were regularly culled because they were considered by medical men to be carriers of plague. Since these dogs were also associated with greed, idleness, and lust, killing them was understood as a symbolic cleansing of society.[67] In the nineteenth century, stray dogs were still blamed for the transmission of disease, especially during outbreaks of rabies. Strays were unlicensed animals, and licences were costly, so only a portion of the population possessed these registration tickets. Since licences were carried by owners (animals carried no sign of licensing), it was often the appearance of the owner that was believed to indicate the respectability and health of the dog. Middle-class dog keepers viewed their own canine companions, possibly muzzled and licensed, as legitimate participants in public and urban life, and not as potential carriers of disease. As Harriet Ritvo argues, middle-class dog owners were especially eager "to attribute rabies to mongrels and curs, foxhounds and lapdogs, and foreign dogs of all sorts – [that is] alien animals belonging to alien and ill-regulated people."[68] Dogs were believed to signal the status of their owners, and a vicious and disruptive dog was perceived as a social threat.

Art featuring dogs proclaimed the ambitions of pet keepers; it also informed viewers of the attributes which made dogs such potent symbols of masculinity.[69] When a woman was depicted alongside a dog, her relationship to the animal was shown to be entirely different. While the bond between men and dogs was one of mastership and alliance, women were pictured being guarded by the animal or struggling to dominate it. In images of women and dogs, the dog represented a masculine presence, and the rapport between women and dogs was likened to relations between women and men. The pictures consequently took on a didactic quality as readers were instructed simultaneously on proper gender relations and ways they might relate to their dogs.

When women were shown alongside high-bred dogs, in the *Illustrated London News*, for example, it was understood that the dog was a masculine presence. The woman was portrayed as defenceless without the dog; he protected her from physical harm and preserved her virtue. Some of these pictures were considered particularly romantic, and they presented a scene of epic adventure in which the heroine sets out alone in a forest glade under the watchful gaze of the dog. At other times the woman is pictured on the streets surrounded by men who might threaten her. The dog serves as her escort, protecting her safety and innocence (figure 2.6).[70] These images cast the dog as a male companion, acting in the place of brother, husband, or father, as the woman's public guardian. The dog defends the woman from harm and also prevents her from acting too impulsively as she embarks on adventure. The dog in these pictures is depicted as both chivalrous defender and agent of discipline.

These images and their accompanying narratives were intended to amuse and instruct readers of the newspaper. This was essentially light reading which had an underlying didactic quality. Readers were supposed to relate to these paintings and learn appropriate modes of conduct. For example, one of the few images showing children and a female dog – her gender made explicit by the presence of her puppies – was followed by a commentary suggesting what should be understood from this picture:

> the little girls, who take so naturally to playing at motherhood, or to the mimicry of nursing cares, with their inanimate dolls, instinctively recognize the exhibition of maternal affection in this watchful parent of a canine infant brood. They press forward, eager to look, but scarcely daring to touch, while the boy surveys the young dogs with an air of critical inspection, which is equally characteristic of future manly tastes.[71]

According to the narrative, the image showed the children responding to the dogs in a way that was appropriate to their gender. The girl instinctively understood the maternal affection displayed by the dog, while the boy took on the posturing of a future husband or father. In these images men were dominant, while women were maternal and passive. These pictures were prescriptions for proper behaviour that applied to relations between the sexes, within families, and with pet dogs (figure 2.7).

2.6. "A Frosty Morning," *Illustrated London News*, 2 March 1889

2.7. "A Nice Family," *Illustrated London News*, 3 December 1887

Images of female dogs could also be used to buttress pervasive ideas about race as they might be enacted in family relations. In a discussion of a painting by Stanley Berkley (1855–1909), the *Illustrated London News* urged its readers to once again "recognize in some degree, the traits of humanity in the character of dogs." The "humour" in Berkley's painting, according to the narrative accompanying the illustration, derived from the treatment of a black-faced puppy by its mother. The bitch apparently is "half-regretting that she has given birth to such a monstrously exceptional variety in her offspring; and the young ones apparently dispose to renounce their kindred of race." The newspaper very gently castigates this prejudice, stating, "It is sad, indeed, to consider that our unreasoning companions in the household, who might have thought their whole species born free and equal in a state of nature, may be infected with such illiberal views by imitating the conduct of men and women."[72] This article suggests that representations of dogs were used not only to reinforce the gender and social order, but also to support claims for the superior status of whiteness.

In images of dogs and young women, the girl rehearses her role as a future wife, teasing the dog and playing the coquette. For example, one illustration showing a dog begging a girl for a biscuit was accompanied by a narrative reflecting on the girl's future. The girl, apparently,

> promises a fine development of womanhood some ten years hence, when she may have lovers, one or several to be teased by playing with their feelings in a more direct and diplomatic way. But the time has not yet come, for which, perhaps, in the unconscious exercise of a social prerogative of her sex, this girl is most innocently practicing and trying her hand.[73]

The dog in the image is viewed as a masculine presence and the object of her attentions. In images which also featured a male child, the dog is aligned with the boy to show disapproval of the girl and her secret plotting for a husband (figure 2.8).[74] The notion that women were innately secretive and deceitful while men were affectionate and frank was put forward again and again in these images. Boys were shown acting out "manly performances" of mastership and ownership alongside and in alliance with their canine friends, while girls practised choosing a husband through trickery (figure 2.9).[75] These images were so popular that they were featured on postcards depicting many of the same themes: a boy mastering a dog and pretending to teach it to read,[76] a collie watching over and protecting a baby,[77] and a dog sitting alert at his master's feet, both awaiting the arrival of a new baby to the family.[78]

The only images in which women dominate their dogs figure lapdogs. As we saw in the opening of the chapter, the keeping of lapdogs by ladies was considered humorous, even outside the relatively narrow world of the dog fancy, and often ridiculed in language replete with sexual innuendo. The *Illustrated London News*, for example, described a Miss Monckton as "the typical old maid … who indeed is most frequently met with in society." She is "fidgety, crotchety and painfully disagreeable," probably because "she had no companions but her dogs, whom she kissed and scolded by turns."[79] Spinsters were believed to displace affection they would have spent on their children onto their dogs. The same opinion was perpetuated about domineering matrons whose children had long since grown. One, a Lady Tatel, was disdained for bringing up her grandsons "much as she educated her lapdogs – by letting them have their own ways, so long as they were agreeable, and

2.8. "The Secret," *Illustrated London News*, 6 December 1884

2.9. "Love Me, Love My Dog," *Illustrated London News*, 14 November 1885

cuffing them when they snarled."[80] These stereotypes were even found in pet-keeping manuals, showing the extent to which the pet-keeping enterprise repeated and reinforced widespread perceptions of women and dogs.[81] One, for example, found the pug dog particularly intolerable because it suffered from "obesity, somnolence and snappishness – generally in connection with proprietorship by an elderly maiden lady, which has done much to damn him."[82] These ideas remained current well into the twentieth century. In the popular children's novel *Mary Poppins* (first published in 1934), for example, the dog Andrew is emasculated by his domineering owner in much the same way. His desire for escape and the adventures that ensue are recounted in an amusing chapter titled "Miss Lark's Andrew."[83]

When young women were pictured with lapdogs – often small pugs – the animals were analogous to male lovers. Thus one pet-keeping manual stated coyly, "Ladies have more time and patience than men to attend to [these] pets, and probably more love to bestow on them, and the consequence is, a crowd of pet dogs has gathered round her skirts, so to speak."[84] (Here the sexual meaning of the verb "to pet" seems to find its nineteenth-century origin.) The illustrated press also perpetuated this stereotype, showing well-dressed women surrounded by adoring dogs (figure 2.10).[85] Lapdogs were considered fashionable accessories of wealthy young women and this too was the subject of satire. In 1903 *Vanity Fair* published a narrative in which a young aristocrat observes a girl in Kensington Gardens pretending to be a shop assistant. Her wealth is revealed by the three Pomeranian pups, "probably worth £20 apiece," that accompany her on her walk. The dogs attack the aristocrat's boots and this facilitates a conversation. When the woman's class identity is revealed, the two arrange to meet again. The keeping of lapdogs in this story occasions romance.[86]

As these stories suggest, relations between women and dogs had bearing on relations between women and men. Dogs were viewed as exemplifying traits long associated with idealized masculinity. The relationship between men and dogs was believed to be one of singular kinship in which the dog took on certain characteristics of its owner, be he a gentleman, cad, or lowly butcher. Consequently, when women asserted themselves as owners and breeders of dogs, this provoked gender trouble. The problem of the lady and lapdog was eventually deemed so acute that it became part of the anti-suffragist rhetoric, used to ridicule women's aspiration for enfranchisement. Female fanciers seemed unnatural in the order of things – unwomanly creatures with emasculated dogs.

2.10. "Lucky Dog," *Illustrated London News*, Christmas 1878

Female Fancies

When it came to participation in the animal fancies, women faced significant barriers. Specialist pet keeping was considered to be a masculine and scientific pursuit and the fancier in almost every advice manual – except those written by women – was gendered male.[87] Fancying was considered a male preserve because men were believed to be the rightful interpreters and manipulators of nature. From the 1850s and 1860s, when the natural sciences started to become professionalized, the right of men to speak in nature's name became a matter of common sense. Women who asserted themselves alongside men as masters of nature, in any capacity, challenged the prevailing ethic and called their femininity into question. Their actions were scrutinized by the mainstream press and used to warn all women of the reception they were likely to receive should they interfere in masculine spheres.

The pet-keeping enterprise was so intimately connected with scientific ideas about the proper gender roles of men and women that when Charles Darwin outlined his Theory of Sexual Selection in *The Descent of Man* (1871) he linked the process by which men chose wives to the activities of male fanciers:

> Each breeder has impressed … the character of his own mind – his own taste and judgment – on his animals. What reason, then, can be assigned why similar results should not follow from the long-continued selection of the most admired women by those men of each tribe, who were able to rear the greatest number of children?[88]

In outlining his theory of sexual selection, Darwin was attempting to explain the evolution of man and the ascendancy of Victorian society. He defined sexual selection as the struggle between individuals of the same sex to select a mate. Darwin argued that strength, aggression, and intellect were innate masculine characteristics, while women were inherently passive and their abilities were limited to childbearing. He speculated that, in more advanced societies, men actively choose mates according to their perceptions of female beauty and had a greater influence on the mental and physiological traits of their descendants. (The theory suggested that white male dominance was biologically determined.) In Darwin's view, similar processes directed men in the selection of wives and pets.[89] Sexual selection and fancying were portrayed as similar male prerogatives.

Newspapers devoted to fancy matters also perpetuated the view that most fanciers were men. Consider the following definition of a fancier:

> A fancier is one who has born love for dumb creation: this love once ignited will burn forever, hence the old saying, "Once a fancier, always a fancier" … We have known persons that have become possessed of a pet quite by accident that has been good enough to show, and the mere chance of that pet getting a card has led them into the highest ranks of the fancy. The man who is satisfied to plod along persistently, breeding the stock he shows, and by the condition you find them in has, in our opinion, the strongest claim to be called a fancier … Whether the position of a fancier be grand or humble, he is always welcome among his fellow-fanciers; as in no other walk in life are distinctions more easily forgotten than in the fancy, and no stronger introduction can be given by the fancier to another than is understood by the expression "He is a fancier."[90]

The quotation makes clear that pet fancying was a male recreation. The male fancier felt a sense of patriarchal responsibility towards nature, bred his animals with a great deal of patience, and regarded fellow fanciers in a comradely manner. This view was consistent with the idea that interpreting and controlling nature were exclusively male prerogatives. Moreover, as Harriet Ritvo points out, middle-class women were supposed to be ignorant of sex, the very opposite of the breeder.[91] Men of all social ranks were welcome in the institutions of the fancies, but female involvement did not provoke the same congeniality, and when female participation was acknowledged it was done reluctantly.

Though fancying was widely thought of as a masculine hobby, women did participate as breeders of animals, members of clubs, and exhibitors at shows. Their activities became more prominent in the last quarter of the nineteenth century, at which time their efforts were discussed in the various newspapers devoted to fancy matters. Many of the female fanciers who received attention were ladies of leisure, some of whom had a substantial coterie of servants to care for their animals. For example, an early edition of the *Fur Fanciers' Journal* reported on the cat-fancying activities of a Miss Florence Moore of Beckham, who had a large cattery made of brick and a "little manager, a sharp, intelligent looking boy of eleven summers, who, our hostess informed us, was a real treasure, inasmuch as she could depend on him to do for the pussies as she would do for them herself; it struck us that the fancy could do with a few more boys of this stamp." Moore had considerable financial resources at her disposal; this would probably not have been typical for most female fanciers, though their participation in the fancies depended somewhat on wealth.[92] The encouragement of husbands could also be beneficial. For example, in 1905 *Canary and Cage Bird Life* applauded Mrs McLennan for taking up hybrid breeding, while making clear that she was acting under the supervision of her husband. The paper expressed hope that "Mr. McLennan will render [his wife] all possible aid, even though his heart is so wrapped up in Belgians and Scotch Fancies." The paper went on to remind readers that canary breeding was "a most pleasing hobby for a lady to devote her spare moments to, as well as being a pleasant recreation from the ordinary cares of the home."[93] Though the presence of women in the fancies could be viewed as a positive development, their participation in these activities was often limited.

In the late nineteenth century, women became increasingly prominent in the dog and cat fancies. Their involvement in clubs and on the show circuit attracted considerable interest even outside the world of pet keeping, but this attention was rarely flattering. In general, female fanciers were viewed as a nuisance and they had a reputation for public displays of hysterics when their pets were critiqued harshly. One judge, a Mr W.L. Rae, claimed to be haunted by an encounter with a devoted cat lover who became incensed when her pet did not win a prize. She approached him, demanding "Where is the man what judged them cats?" He escaped her rage, but remarked, "there she stood, close up to the door, and with a look of determination that I shall never forget, whilst in her arms was the commonest Cat of all that common crowd."[94] Though Rae's judgment was inflected with class prejudice (note the grammar of the lady in the quotation), this was a fairly typical evaluation of how women behaved in the show ring, and it was repeated often.[95] Thus, as late as 1943 a novel described the antics of one lady exhibitor at a wartime rabbit show as follows:

> "Well what about this rabbit?" A sharp-faced, thrusting woman held out a rabbit which had been one of the first turned off the bench. "He's bigger than any of the others. Perhaps you'd tell me what's wrong with him?"
>
> "What's wrong with him? Well, look at him, madam. Gross. Like a pig, madam. Fat and muscle aren't the same thing, as any butcher will tell you." He handed her back the rabbit wrinkling his nose. "Gross," he repeated. The woman bore her rabbit away in a huff and Mr. Armitage [the judge] smiled round on his appreciative audience.[96]

These portrayals of female fanciers implied that women lacked the expertise – scientific and otherwise – of male fanciers and demonstrated excessive emotionality over the judgment of their pets.

Participation in the cat and dog fancies opened women to attack, and they were ridiculed because it seemed somehow improper for a woman to be successful in this public and masculine pursuit. This belief inspired satirical illustrations in the middle-class press showing the conduct of women on the show circuit. In these images female fanciers were categorized by type, shown as fashionable ladies, hysterical exhibitors, sour spinsters, and domineering matrons. They were often likened to their pets so that the two appeared to share characteristics. Thus, in a typical illustration the fashionable woman was accompanied by a prized animal with whom she presumably shared some affinity, the hysteric was shown pathetically consoling her losing pet, the bitter spinster was featured alone, and a contingent of yapping dogs represented the domineering matron.[97] By implication, female fanciers were being mocked as too vain, emotional, manly and/or motherly, and entirely unsuited for the rational world of the animal fancies. These caricatures were intended to apply to all women who would be similarly castigated should they assert themselves in masculine spheres.

Some male participants were also caricatured, but these tended to be more positive images. A typical illustration showed a gentleman in the company of his hound, and while the two were clearly being compared, neither dog nor man was an object of ridicule.[98] As we have seen, the association of men and dogs was often very positive, and the ownership of a canine of pedigree enhanced the social reputation its owner. When men and women were sketched together in illustrations of bird shows, they were comically compared to the creatures on display as "love birds," for example.[99] The humour of these illustrations was innocuous, and reflected the fact that the women in these images were appropriately accompanied by men. In contrast, alone on the show circuit, female cat and dog fanciers were objects of intense mockery. Male fanciers did not receive the same negative attention, nor did women who attended shows with male companions.

For their part, women were aware of and concerned by the negative attention they received while participating in the animal fancies. An article appearing in the *Ladies' Kennel Journal* in 1901 made the following comments, partly in jest, describing the ways such involvement might damage the social reputation of a lady:

A short time ago I was suggesting poultry keeping as an interesting hobby
for a lady who could not compose her peace of mind on the subject of pets.
Dogs she considered too masculine, and cats too feminine, and fowls, she
declared, were so utterly common that no respectable woman who valued
her reputation would suffer the crow of a cock or the cackle of a hen within her hearing … No; far rather would she join the ranks of the dog fanciers and have people alluding to her as a recruit to the ranks of the new
woman, or become a patron of the humble domestic cat and hear the same
people cherishing doubts as to her prospects of marriage …[100]

The author of the article implied that to be a woman and a dog fancier
was to take an overtly feminist stance, while joining the cat fancy
doomed a woman to spinsterhood. These statements were tongue-in-
cheek; the point of the article was to encourage women to join the poultry fancy by describing it as an eminently reputable recreation, the
hobby of duchesses and queens. Still, women who took up fancying as
a hobby were likely to become objects of ridicule. This was because
through pet keeping they asserted themselves as active participants in
public life and masters of nature alongside men. Their actions would
be used to reprimand all women seeking access to the vote.

The Ladies' Kennel Association

The organization that posed the most direct challenge to male dominance of the animal fancies in the last decade of the nineteenth century
was the Ladies' Kennel Association. The LKA was a group of female
dog owners who campaigned for the recognition of female dog fanciers. This was an implicitly feminist organization and understood as
such by those within and outside the animal fancies. The activities of
the LKA were seen as threatening and used to denounce all feminist
claims for emancipation.

Presenting itself as "a league unique in the history of women and
dogdom," the LKA was founded in October 1894 at the Kennel Club
Show in Brighton with a mandate to "form a Club in the interests of
women as exhibitors of dogs."[101] The idea was to organize a league "of
women for whom no social questions exist, but who, as a Kennel Club,
expect from each other, and will insist upon, becoming conduct in the
Club rooms and at Shows, the strictest integrity in all Sales, Exchanges
and other business, and cordial co-operation in upholding the reputation of the Ladies' Kennel Association."[102] This protestation of social

equality was mostly hubris. In fact, the LKA was an exclusive organization obsessed with social pretensions, manners, and good breeding, much like the Kennel Club itself. The LKA forged links with other associations, but only those with patrons of comparable wealth, such as the National Cat Club and the Ladies' Anti-Muzzling League.[103] Membership was expensive, as much as one guinea for an annual subscription, and each issue of its journal cost one shilling. This was an elite association, and women of the lower orders were actively excluded from its ranks.

The LKA was founded in order to remedy the problems that lady exhibitors encountered on the show circuit, where their dogs were sometimes "relegated to a place amongst the poultry and pigeons."[104] Members of the LKA believed they had been treated unfairly by Kennel Club organizers, in particular, who had not taken the participation of women fanciers seriously. Their primary purpose was therefore to "provide Premierships and Challenge and Special Prizes for Ladies' Exhibits at leading Shows." They also felt that their comforts had not been looked after by male organizers and they were particularly angered by the provision of inadequate refreshments and the lack of separate entrances and exits for women, as was deemed proper.[105] The provision of these comforts was not a frivolous matter, but essential for allowing women to leave their homes for extended periods of time, as Erika Rappaport argues with regard to the amenities, such as ladies' washrooms and tearooms, offered by late Victorian and Edwardian ladies' clubs and department stores.[106] The rules and regulations of the LKA therefore made resolving these issues top priority.

As an organization devoted to women's participation in a masculine pursuit, the LKA was an implicitly feminist institution, though no mention was made in the *Ladies' Kennel Journal* of other contemporaneous feminist movements. Nevertheless, the members of the LKA were active politicians – albeit for a non-political cause – and very public figures, writing for newspapers and competing in shows. They were also, as we shall see, explicitly linked to the pursuit of women's suffrage in the public imagination. The mechanisms of the LKA, its aims and public presentation, were similar to those of the suffragists, suggesting the extent to which the Victorian feminists had inspired women to seek equality in every aspect of public life, even in the seemingly less significant sphere of leisure.[107] The LKA attempted to assert women's right to participate in the dog fancy, and this was a radical goal. The organization sought to portray women as masters of nature alongside men by casting them as breeders and manipulators of dogs. This was an inherent attempt to change popular perceptions of women as natural creatures in need of male protection and stewardship. The aims of the LKA implied a more assertive position for women through the keeping of dogs. Since dogs were associated with masculinity and believed to have a special bond with men, proclaiming women as successful breeders of canines was a fairly novel idea. By skilfully rearing animals, the women of the LKA were declaring their ability to dominate nature. Just like male dog fanciers, the women of the LKA sought acclaim by exhibiting their dogs as objects of their success.

Equality with men was the primary objective of the LKA, but much like the suffragists, their feminism was grounded in beliefs of female distinction.[108] Though the LKA tirelessly asserted women's right to participate in the dog fancy, they insisted, like the suffragists, that women possessed innate moral characteristics that made them different from and even superior to men. They argued that as inherently ethical beings women would bring a moral dimension to the dog world that was lacking in the male-dominated Kennel Club. Their "Rules and Regulations" made this clear by including the object to "do away with faking and trimming of dogs; and generally, to improve the conditions under which dogs are shown, and by example and influence to raise the tone of Dog Shows and Dog-Showing."[109] With this mandate, the LKA was articulating a version of the view put forward by Victorian suffragists that women, as innately nurturing and compassionate beings, were morally superior to men and thus able to improve the tenor of public life. (For those opposed to female emancipation, these same characteristics made women suited only to the domestic sphere.) As we have seen, women had a reputation for volatility and viciousness in the show ring and were accused of extreme misconduct. Shows were plagued by frequent disputes and rampant fraud, and women were accused of causing these problems. The LKA attempted to counter this perception by demonstrating the moral authority and thorough respectability of its members.

As a result, its shows ran much like the pageants and marches of the suffragist movement.[110] They were lavish affairs in which wealthy women, decked out in the latest fashions, paraded around in an orderly and regal manner accompanied by their dogs. The thorough respectability of these events was always emphasized by the *Ladies' Kennel Journal*, which showed concern for preserving the "social lines" of these occasions. Women of lower status were actively excluded from the ranks of the LKA. By 1898, the LKA's dog shows occurred twice a year at the Botanic Gardens, Regent's Park, and were highly exclusive events. The ladies were careful to demonstrate model conduct, and their shows ran very smoothly. This attention to detail was hardly accidental, as a photograph of the Summer Show makes obvious. The ladies are carefully posed, showing off their fashionable outfits and their dogs. The newspaper wrote of the event: "The L.K.A. Show of dogs and cats at the Botanic was universally pronounced to be one of the most brilliant afternoon functions of the season. On the Thursday, the weather was simply perfect, and the garden party effect of the occasion was enhanced by the great charm of the ladies' dresses."[111] The women themselves were an integral part of the spectacle, and their exemplary conduct was important for the prestige of the organization.

As Sarah Cheang argues, events sponsored by the Ladies' Kennel Association were demonstrations of the women's claim to racial as well as class superiority. Chaeng documents the involvement of members of the LKA in Pekingese dog breeding and argues that these activities perpetuated a form of colonial nostalgia, allowing upper-class ladies to assert themselves as colonial masters in the metropole. The breeding of Pekingese dogs in Britain involved the construction of an elaborate mythology that connected the genealogy of these pets to the Chinese Imperial Court; the dogs became living referents to British perceptions of Chinese mandarins. In 1905 the LKA invited a Chinese ambassador to judge the authenticity of the Pekingese dogs on show, and the photograph of the event suggests the extent to which the LKA was embroiled in the complex politics of imperial, gender, and class relations.[112] The LKA promoted women's rights – at least in the animal fancies – by reinforcing claims to cultural, racial, and class superiority.[113]

In claiming to advance the cause of female fanciers, the *Ladies' Kennel Journal* devoted many pages to bragging about the achievements of the LKA. In its opinion,

No one, turning over the pages of the periodicals of the day, can fail to be struck by the extraordinary and rapidly increasing popularity of ladies' dogs as a subject for letterpress and illustrations. This change, of course, is entirely due to the Ladies' Kennel Association. Three years and a half ago, before THE JOURNAL started, the only dogs (except in occasional cases of Royalty or celebrities) which were written about and pictured were all men's dogs.[114]

To bring about this change, the LKA had made a substantial effort to encourage women breeders of dogs, and the *Ladies' Kennel Journal* had reported their successes with great pride. The dogs of women fanciers were increasingly recognized as objects of their achievement, and the *Ladies' Kennel Journal* therefore celebrated prize-winning female fanciers with great fanfare. For example, in July 1896, the paper included an announcement by a Miss Reston stating, "My own dear little Pointer, Jessie, has beaten fifteen men's dogs in a class, and little Dolly (given away by me) beat the crack dogs in the Field trials at Ipswich and Shrewsbury."[115] Similarly, in 1897 a Mrs Armstrong won with her collies thirty-three first prizes at eighteen shows. This, the paper remarked, "is certainly a splendid achievement, as it is admitted by everybody who knows anything about the subject that Collies are a most difficult breed for women to win with."[116] Still, these successes in a masculine sport were somewhat exceptional, and writers for the newspaper were well aware that they were fighting an uphill battle. It therefore made the following exhortation to its readers after reporting on a show at Birkenhead: "OLD ENGLISH SHEEP DOGS had no entry from women, a fact to be deplored, as lately this breed has given evidence of more popularity among lady exhibitors, and not to see them competing here was a disappointment."[117] The organization endeavoured tirelessly to fulfil their mandate and encourage women to participate in the male-dominated fancy.

To persuade women to breed large dogs, the newspaper also reported extensively on the pets of Queen Victoria, describing her as an exemplary breeder and gushingly suggesting that she might serve as a model for aspiring female fanciers:

> Here [Windsor Castle Kennels] the lap-dog is conspicuous by its absence, nor among the records of the Queen's Kennels, kept with admirable method from the first, are there any references to "Toys."
>
> Every one, of course, has heard the story – whether true or not, it is a very popular one among her subjects – of how our Queen only nineteen, hurried off in her robes of state, for she had just presided at Council, to console Dash, her King Charles, who was loudly lamenting her absence in an adjoining room. And is not Chico, a tiny Cuban dog, on record in the Register, and others of diminutive size, Looty to wit and Goliah?
>
> But these are only the exceptions, and except Pugs, which Her Majesty appears to have always appreciated, the chronicles of the Royal Kennels

tell us mainly of Collies, Spitzes, Skyes, Dach Dogs, Fox Terriers, with here and there a St. Bernard, a Greyhound, a Deerhound, or a Boarhound.[118]

In the view of the paper, the Queen was an example to be emulated, though she had just one fault: "but little ambition to breed dogs for Show … [which was] much to be regretted."[119] For her part, the Queen supported the aims of the LKA and eventually became a patron of the organization, even subscribing to its newspaper.[120] In turn the paper lavished praise on her dogs and depicted her as the ultimate dog-loving woman.

Despite these attempts to encourage women to take up the breeding of large dogs, the LKA achieved only partial success. The pages of the *Ladies' Kennel Journal* itself suggest that its most celebrated members remained attached to their toy animals. When the most celebrated members of the association had their photographs featured in the newspaper's glossy pages, the majority appeared alongside lapdogs, which they obviously viewed as ornamental objects, much like their lavish dresses and decorative fans. Ironically, the wealthiest members of the organization were photographed without their pets, suggesting perhaps that duchesses were not as fond of canines as the journal wanted its readership to believe. Some devoted fanciers were photographed with large dogs, but these were the exception and quite possibly women of slightly lower standing.

The work of the LKA was also hampered by considerable tension that existed between itself and the Kennel Club. During the early years of the LKA, the two organizations fought over almost every conceivable matter.[121] The most contentious issue was the attempt to gain stud book recognition for dogs that won prizes at shows held under the supervision of the LKA. For this to occur, judging had to be conducted according to the Kennel Club rules and the Kennel Club itself had to recognize the legitimacy of the show; it refused to grant this status to the LKA. In response, members of the LKA wrote in to the *Ladies' Kennel Journal* protesting the censure of the Kennel Club in the strongest terms – stopping short of accusing it of blatant sexism:

Furthermore, the Kennel Club could not see its way to granting Stud Book recognition to the L.K.A. Show, because, "a dog winning there, would have beaten only dogs owned by the one sex!" One would conclude, therefore, that a woman's judgment in canine matters is not accepted by the Kennel

Club, in spite of its recognition of awards by lady judges at the Kennel Club
Shows, and the frequent placing of women's exhibits at shows, both at
home and on the continent, over those of men, by recognized club judges,
some of whom are themselves Members of the Kennel Club.[122]

This censure was not an unusual action for the Kennel Club, which was
a fairly tyrannical organization. There were instances when clubs of
fanciers attempted to gain exemption from its rules, as occurred in 1895
with the Poodle Club. The Kennel Club responded harshly, issuing an
ultimatum and threatening to withdraw support. The Poodle Club
caved "unreservedly" before this might, withdrawing its demands.[123]

The belief that chauvinism motivated the Kennel Club's exclusion of
the LKA was not far off the mark. From the beginning, the reaction of
male fanciers to the LKA was mixed. In general the LKA was greeted
with a fair amount of derision. One writer to the *Fancier's Chronicle*, for
example, remarked, "this association seems to me started for the sole
object of giving prizes and specials to dogs mostly not worth their entry
fees," thus perpetuating the opinion that women were not capable of
breeding fancy dogs. This view was stated more directly by another
writer, who expressed the opinion that the "successful speculation of
the Ladies' Club cannot be seriously supposed to advance the cause of
scientific breeding."[124] In a twist of logic, another report on one of the
LKA's earliest shows supported the Kennel Club's decision not to include LKA winners in its stud book on the grounds that the LKA excluded men's dogs from competition: "Not one of the classes at this
show was open to everybody – a whole sex was excluded from competition. So for the purpose of stud-book recognition the fixture was informal, and future generations of exhibitors will be able to find no trace of
the exhibitions in the official records of the period."[125] This was a battle
of the sexes, and a small example of a much larger phenomenon taking
place in late Victorian society as a whole. The dog fancy was a relatively
insignificant forum where arguments for and against women's participation in public life were being aired. Yet from the dog fancy to national
politics and questions of enfranchisement was but a small step.

Once again, the connection between the efforts of the Ladies' Kennel
Association and the various groups advocating women's rights had
not been lost on contemporaries outside the dog fancy. In 1913, at the
height of the suffragette campaign, led by the increasingly militant
Women's Suffrage and Political Union (WSPU) founded by Mrs
Emmeline Pankhurst, an article appeared in the *Saturday Review* linking

the indulgent treatment of lapdogs witnessed at the Ladies' Kennel Show to women's struggle for the vote; its tone was meant to amuse, but its humour was distinctly nasty. The article rehearsed the main gender stereotypes discussed throughout this chapter, putting forward the claim that civilization was somehow endangered by female dog fanciers who, through their pet keeping, sought to transform men into pampered Pomeranians. The "average male," the article claimed, "loving dogs of most types, harbours a secret dislike for the Toy," whereas women love these diminutives; it "is woman who demands these dwarfs, woman who chiefly breeds them, and woman who makes most money out of the 'fancy.'" The "feminine craze for the pampering of pets" was described as "the maternal instinct gone astray" and "rather an exaggeration of the qualities of their sex, the maternal passion uncontrolled by any sense of proportion." In the absence of children, the "instinct of motherhood" would be focused on the coddled and infantilized lapdog, a creature implicitly gendered male and in danger of emasculation. This wasting of maternal instinct posed a national threat that might destroy a woman's reproductive capacities and endanger the health of future British progeny. The tendency of female lapdog enthusiasts to dote on their pets then became grounds to deny all women the vote:

> … one wonders what would happen to man if woman really became the dominant sex. Would she not try to mold him much as she had molded the Toy dog to her fancy? Men lag behind women in civilization, said Mrs. Pankhurst on her farewell to New York. What standard of civilization does the feminist desire man to reach? Something, one suspects, closely resembling the placid stupidity and dependence of a Pomeranian or a Pekinese.[126]

Female participation in the dog fancy and feminist demands for equality had been explicitly connected. In interfering in the dog fancy, women threatened the gender order and male supremacy in that system. (Leading feminists in fact owned Pekingese dogs: Christabel Pankhurst, Emmeline's daughter, kept one while in exile in Paris in 1913–14, as did the feminist and anti-vivisectionist Frances Power Cobbe.)[127]

In the first decade of the twentieth century, images linking cats and women also featured prominently in campaigns to discredit women's aspirations for the franchise. In particular, penny postcards sent to suffragettes show the ways cat iconography was used to disparage feminist demands. The images on the postcards feature vicious cats. For those familiar with the cat iconography that had been so prominent in representations of middle-class femininity over the course of the nineteenth century, the meaning of these images could not have been more evident: this was a spectacle of womanhood gone awry. One postcard, like the article in the *Saturday Review* quoted above, suggests that the plight of men will be dire, should women get the vote – only on this postcard, men are likened to tom cats. The postcard shows an angry cat holding a card stating, "Vote for Shes [*sic*] / THE 'SUFFRAGETTE.' / DOWN WITH THE TOM CATS."[128] Another postcard, dated October 1908, and sent to Christabel Pankhurst, showed a nasty-looking kitten, and the caption screeches, "I want my vote!" Though the postcard presents an anti-suffragist image, the sender inverted and poked fun at the message, writing to Christabel, "With wishes for greatest success" (figure 2.11).[129] A similar anti-suffragist postcard shows a photograph of a cat wearing an elegant hat, shawl, and button. The button displays the slogan "Votes for Women," and the caption on the bottom of postcard reads, "An Advokate [*sic*] for Women's Rights."[130] Another postcard likened the cause of women's suffrage to childish pursuits by showing a large white cat holding a hammer in its claws, wearing a suffragette's sash and sitting on a stool surrounded by children's toys, including a golliwog, bear, and two dolls. The cat is presumably lecturing the toys. The bottom of the postcard supplies the caption: "'FIFI' [presumably the name of the cat] THE MILITANT." In this case, the cat is bloated and ugly, puffed up with own ineffectual self-importance – ineffectual because only mute toys listen to its demands.[131]

Feminist artists responded to these anti-suffragist pictures by circulating other images that subverted longstanding negative associations of cats and femininity. This imagery was designed specifically to counter conventional representations of middle-class femininity. For the suffragists, dedicated to constitutional means of affecting change, such imagery took the place of militancy, while for the suffragettes these images accompanied and supported their violent actions.[132] One postcard, published at the Suffragette Shop, 31 Bedford Street, shows a drawing of a smiling black cat against a green background. The two captions read, "YOUR LUCK'S IN!" and "WHERE'S THAT VOTE YOU PROMISED ME?" The postcard maintains the association between cats and women, but disrupts the idea that black cats are unlucky.[133]

Perhaps the most powerful inversion of cat imagery, and best-known suffragette image, was the "Cat and Mouse" poster, likely created by

2.11. Anti-suffrage picture postcard sent to Christabel Pankhurst,
15 October 1908. © Museum of London

Alfred Pearse (1856–1933) for the WSPU in May 1914.[134] This image was produced in response to the Prisoner's Temporary Discharge (for ill health) Act passed in April 1913, popularly known as the "Cat and Mouse" Act (figure 2.12). Hunger strikes had been a suffragette tactic since 1909, but the militancy of the suffragette campaign increased after January 1913 when a Reform Bill proposing to grant the franchise to a limited number of women was withdrawn. The Cat and Mouse Act empowered the government to temporarily release hunger-striking suffragettes from incarceration and intern them again after they had received nourishment outside of prison. The suffragettes' attitude towards the Act is evident in the poster, which shows a listless woman trapped in the jaws of a cat. The caption makes the meaning of the poster explicit, exhorting "Electors" to "Vote Against Him [the Liberal Cat]! Keep the Liberal Out!" The "Liberal Cat" shown in the image represents the all-male Liberal government capturing the female mouse. The image inverted longstanding associations between women and cats; this cat is no longer an icon of womanhood, but a masculine animal exercising power over its female prey. Part of the reason for the lasting power and fame of the image may be the ways it overturns long-established associations between women and cats.

Conclusion

Pet keeping had bolstered the gender order by producing ideologies that defined differences between men and women. Cats had long been associated with a negative view of women as unreliable, independent, and sexually voracious. Dogs were considered genteel animals, paragons of masculinity, associated with chivalric heroism, guilelessness, and loyalty. Women and cats were viewed as analogous creatures, as were men and dogs. Ideas about masculinity and femininity had informed the management of these pets, and cats and dogs, in turn, were used to dictate how men and women should behave. As representatives of nature in the household, daily interactions with these pets helped construct understandings of what it meant to be a man and a woman.

When it came to matters relating to gender, pet keeping produced anxieties which were thrown into high relief by fanciers. In attempting to overcome the spurious reputation of the cat, fanciers mounted a quest for respectability and founded a club to advance the status of their pets. The success of the National Cat Club was significant insofar

2.12. Poster, "The Cat and Mouse Act Passed by the Liberal Government," made by the Women's Social and Political Union (1914). © Museum of London

as it improved the profile of the cat. The shows of the NCC also managed to replicate Victorian social hierarchies by exhibiting working men's pets under separate categories and failing to overthrow the negative association between cats and women. Female cat fanciers, as we have seen, remained objects of ridicule and satire. The dog fancy was a very different milieu. As a masculine preserve it was eminently respectable, and its institutional significance was hardly questioned. However, when upper-class women attempted to assert themselves as breeders of canines, they faced fierce resistance. In pursuing this hobby, female dog fanciers meddled with longstanding ideas about the special relationship between men and their dogs. They challenged ideas about the proper roles of men and women in relation to each other, to their pets and also in public life. Women's participation in the dog fancy was considered significant beyond the relatively narrow confines of the pet-keeping enterprise. The activities of female fanciers were directly correlated to women's struggle for the franchise and considered destructive to the gender order. At the same time, images associating women with cats circulated on penny postcards in the early twentieth century to discredit women's claims to the franchise. The activities of female fanciers, suffragists, and suffragettes forced a reconsideration of ideologies that posited men as masters of nature and defined men and women as being as different as cats and dogs.

Chapter Three

In the Zoo: Civilizing Animals and Displaying People

Although there were several zoological institutions in Britain by the mid-nineteenth century, the London Zoological Gardens enjoyed a reputation that surpassed all others. The London Zoo had become a fashionable site for recreation, and an institution that enjoyed increasing prominence in the burgeoning industry of Victorian entertainment. In an era that offered a variety of commercialized leisure activities, including music halls, theatres, circuses, seaside resorts, aquariums, pleasure gardens, and museums, the London Zoological Gardens was frequently celebrated as an especially popular site of amusement, especially on a Sunday, when the elite went to mix, mingle, and scrutinize each other.[1] *The Leisure Hour*, for example, proclaimed that in the Zoo "persons of all classes and of all opinions meet together, to see and be seen, to criticize and be criticized." For this purpose the paths of the garden were "occupied on each side by battalions of ladies, all in their smartest and best uniform."[2] The Zoo was a site for pleasure seeking and flirtation, as well as encounters with exotic animals, whose arrival in the Gardens fed a seemingly boundless demand for novelty. Visitors considered each other to be just as interesting as the animals on display, and ways of perceiving animals became ways of perceiving people, so much so that the lines between visitors and exhibits, humans and animals, were often blurred. So ubiquitous were witty comparisons of visitors and zoo-dwelling animals that in 1872 Gustave Doré and Blanchard Jerrold opened the eighth chapter of their book on London with the following description of the upper classes in the Zoo:

"Opera very full last night," – or "Didn't get home till two": or "Lady Ermine looks well after the crush" – are the greetings upon the grass on Sunday afternoons in the season, after Whitsuntide, in the Zoological Gardens.

> No wonder that the quiet lounges in the Gardens were so popular, be-
> fore they reached the honours of the burlesque, and the vulgar wits of the
> music halls. It is the very place for quiet easy talk in the open air – with the
> animals to point the conversation. The sentimental linger by the gazelles:
> the hoyden makes merry with the parrots: the humourists gather in the
> monkey house: the muscular-minded Amazon watches old Leo [the lion]
> rasping a shin-bone with his rough tongue.[3]

Doré and Jerrold depict the London Zoological Gardens as a stylish location for the elite to socialize, gossip, and flirt, regarding each other
with the same critical appraisal as others might inspect the animals. In
this description animals appear mainly as background amusement –
except to those habitués who share striking characteristics with the objects of their gaze. Doré and Jerrold capture the essence of an amusing
afternoon in the London Zoo where both animals and humans were
objects on display.

This chapter argues that that the Zoo was a site for collecting and
comparing humans and animals, and a complex way of displaying, describing, and ordering human beings and their experiences. By emphasizing the presence of people in the London Zoological Gardens, I am
interested in exploring the idea that visitors and keepers were on display alongside animals, and that the Zoo, like the cat and dog fancies
described in the previous chapter, was a space for the interrogation and
enforcement of etiquette as well as social hierarchies. As visitors entered the Gardens, they compared themselves to the animals on display
and tested socially acceptable behaviours; they also examined the work
of keepers, looking for demonstrations of imperial triumph, working-
class industry, and human mastery over beasts. Though previous scholars have examined the London Zoological Gardens as an exhibition of
Empire,[4] the Zoo has not previously been acknowledged as a site which
put people on display, perhaps because the people on show were visitors and working-class keepers. These constituencies were supposed to
be present in the Zoo; many were white Britons; they were not caged,
and it was mostly their behaviour and sometimes their dress that attracted attention and provoked comparisons with animals.

Like pet keeping, the London Zoo was a commercial enterprise. Many
of its central activities, especially collecting, exhibiting, and entertaining, were also consumer processes. Animals in the Zoo were living
commodities and incorporated into urban life as living exhibits and
objects of prestige. Since many of these creatures were foreign to the

British Isles, the Zoo became the site where they could be encountered. Brought to the outskirts of the metropolis in Regent's Park (which became a more central location as the city expanded), the Zoo became a domestic and public terrain where animals were managed and increasingly domesticated; these relations to animals received a great deal of public attention.

As a national and imperial forum, the London Zoo was a public site for Britons to explore their relationships to animals and to each other in very direct and often tactile ways.[5] The Zoo was celebrated as a space which reformed animals so that they no longer indulged their beastly proclivities, and visitors could test these claims by touching, feeding, poking, and teasing the fiercest animals as if they were tamed pets. So evocative were these interactions that they were celebrated outside the Zoo, recounted in newspaper reports, guidebooks, children's books, novels, and music, often with imperial connotations. These sources illustrate ways that the Zoo structured relationships between humans and animals, and also between groups of people. The experiences described in this and the next chapter gave rise to our relationships with zoo-dwelling animals and certain enduring cultural and consumer constructs – not in a teleological way but in ways that were so multifaceted, contradictory, and disruptive that they produced unintended and long-term consequences.

The first part of the chapter discusses the original aims of the Zoological Society of London, its scientific and utilitarian objectives, and its biblical underpinnings, as well as the broad significance of its collection practices. I then discuss how the challenges of keeping animals alive and on display undermined the classificatory intentions of the Zoological Society. Over the course of the nineteenth century, as the collection expanded, the Zoological Society built larger and cleaner enclosures and reorganized its collection so that visitors were often quite paradoxically presented with a disorderly spectacle. The architectural challenges of displaying living creatures sometimes made the taxonomic arrangements in the Zoological Gardens haphazard, and new architectural arrangements disrupted visitor expectations. Instead of encountering the same exhibit on each visit, the arrangement of the Gardens often changed. I then show how attempts at classification and exhibition inspired unintended actions and effects, as visitors reached through the bars of cages to pet, poke, feed, and tease even dangerous beasts. In so doing they exercised ambiguous forms of care and mastery, while testing claims that the Zoo domesticated and civilized all species. Finally, I suggest that the Zoo was widely acknowledged as a forum for comparing humans and animals in both appearance and behaviour. Keepers working throughout the gardens were meant to demonstrate British working-class industry, but sometimes foreign attendants were employed to enhance didactic effects. I show that the Zoo was ultimately a space for self-presentation. As visitors watched keepers and each other, hierarchical separations between humans and animals, as well as between people, became unstable; this made the cultural influence of the Zoo all the more potent because people as well as animals were on display.

Collecting Animals

The Zoological Society of London was the brain-child of Sir Stamford Raffles (1781–1826), who founded the Society in 1824. As Harriet Ritvo argues, Raffles's vision was explicitly imperial and very much in keeping with his career as a colonial administrator as well as his passion for natural history. Raffles felt strongly that London needed a living collection of animals that would rival the Jardin des Plantes in Paris and demonstrate Britain's beneficence and scientific acumen.[6] He was connected to Sir Humphry Davy and others in the British scientific community and able to drum up enthusiasm and support for his idea. At the time there were a number of menageries in London and throughout the country, as well as travelling menageries and circuses. These offered the public novel and amusing spectacles of exotic animals caged and on display.[7] The London Zoological Society, in contrast, would be devoted to the advancement of knowledge and not mere entertainment.

The development of the Regent's Park Zoo as a civic institution took many years. Initially the Zoological Society was intended as a research establishment, and admission to the collection of living animals was restricted to Fellows of the Zoological Society and those to whom the Fellows gave tickets.[8] Fellows comprised gentry, aristocracy, and the scientific elite. Until the paying public was granted access to the Gardens in 1847, the Zoological Society was privately funded. In 1847, it instituted a graduated policy of admission and so maintained social segregation in access to the Gardens. The charge for entrance was one shilling from Tuesdays to Saturdays and half-price on Mondays; the Gardens were open on Sundays only to Fellows and to those whom the Fellows gave tickets. The Zoological Society's motive in broadening its constituency was financial, so that it could continue to fund its scientific endeavours. From the beginning, the principal aims of the institution were inherently scientific, and they coincided, sometimes uneasily, with agricultural pursuits and recreational enjoyments. Zoological Fellows pursued their aims by drawing on colonial networks and slowly learning to manage the zoological enterprise.

When the original charter for the London Zoological Society was first issued on 1 February 1825, it made clear that the Society's ambitions were of vast scope, though not necessarily practical. The charter outlined a mandate of three components. The first entailed the introduction of "new varieties, breeds and races of animals" for domestication in the United Kingdom. This implied not only the importation of exotic species but also the creation of new species of animals. The second component called for the establishment of a "prepared zoological collection" – that is, a collection of taxidermic specimens so as to "afford a correct view of the animal kingdom at large, in as complete a series as may be practicable" for the purposes of scientific research. The third advocated for the improvement of breeding methods to increase "those races of animals which are most useful to man."[9] This tripartite vision was intended to satisfy two constituencies of Zoological Fellows. The naturalists were interested in advancing science and wanted to stock exotic species of taxonomic interest. The landowners were interested in the utility of these creatures and wanted to acclimatize animals that might be bred to augment the English diet.[10]

From these aims, it is evident that the Society intended to collect, if possible, every animal on the planet, dead or alive, and import it into London.[11] The ambitions of the endeavour were seized upon by the *Literary Gazette* in April 1826 after one of the first general meetings of the fledgling Zoological Society. In a scathing article titled "Zoological or Noah's Ark Society," the newspaper reported on the meeting, describing how Raffles "read an address recommending the formation of a society the object of which should be to import new birds, beasts and fishes into this country from foreign parts." Expressing great scepticism about this project, it opined, "But there is neither wisdom nor folly new under the sun," and proceeded to detail how the Romans and even certain British royals had held similar ambitions.[12] The religious allusion in the title referred to the biblical story of Noah's Ark, which is an ancient allegory about the dominion of man and practices of collecting.

The collection practices of the Zoo encompassed a variety of ambitious activities enacted by the Zoological Fellows, who aspired to scientifically discover new "races" of animals that they could import, tame, and subordinate to the utilitarian purposes of mankind. They envisioned acclimatization and breeding experiments to create new animal hybrids that would provide for the culinary and industrial needs of the British people. The Society appraised its own abilities in terms of a sincere belief in its capacity to improve upon and surpass nature, and in its power to render service to Britain. Born of confidence in British industrial and imperial achievements, this vast vision was deemed possible.

Though over time the original objectives of the Society were restrained by practical and financial limitations, for most of the nineteenth century it remained committed to breeding and acclimatization in order to domesticate and increase the utility of its animal captives. There had long been a popular fascination with animal hybrids, particularly with those exhibited in travelling menageries, circuses, and freak shows. Given the English obsession with manipulating the breeding of livestock and pets, it should come as no surprise that the London Zoological Society wanted to attempt similar feats, albeit on a grander and more scientific scale. Moreover, through the nineteenth century, many naturalists (and later biologists) inquiring into the generation of species conducted experiments crossing both plants and animals.[13] The breeding of exotic animals particularly appealed to the aristocratic financiers of the Zoological Society, many of whom were also interested in high stock breeding.[14] Thus, for the purposes of careful experimentation, to understand properly "all matters relating to breeding and points of animal physiology connected therewith," the Society established a farm at Kingston Hill, in addition to the collection of living animals in Regent's Park.[15] Breeding experiments on the farm were intended to rectify the ad hoc manner of previous crosses and to create hybrids as well as naturalized breeds "likely to supply the objects of food, clothing, medicine, or draft."[16] Crossings between goats and sheep, Dorset ewes and Wallachian rams, and zebras and asses, to name a few, were attempted, but, by 1833, the establishment was deemed financially unviable and the farm was sold.[17] Despite the disappointment of the farm, the Society continued to pin hopes on the utility of individual species housed in the London Zoological Gardens.

To this end, both the eland and the hippopotamus were considered new meats for human consumption. Interest in the culinary merit of the hippopotamus was expressed mainly in guidebooks, which reported that its flesh "is delicate and succulent; the layer of fat next to the skin makes excellent bacon."[18] The eland, a large African antelope, more successfully caught the gastronomic imagination of the Society when it first procured a herd in 1851. Elands had been introduced to England by Lord Derby in 1842 to be used for breeding and crossing with domestic cattle.[19] The Zoological Society's Annual Reports boasted of the progress the Society made from efforts to breed the eland, stating, for example, that by June 1858 sixteen calves had been born in the Gardens. This merited the comment that "the success with which this animal has been managed is one of the most effective points in the History of the Zoological Society."[20] Many, particularly in aristocratic circles, hoped that the eland would be consumed regularly as meat, and some kept elands in private menageries in an effort to breed them for food. In 1859, a letter to *The Times* described a dinner held to taste the beast. The letter concluded "that a new and superior kind of animal food had been added to the restricted choice from the mammalian class at present available in Europe."[21] These optimistic sentiments were echoed in the *Saturday Review* in 1861, which quoted Sir Cornwallis Harris, a self-proclaimed "experienced sportsman," who claimed that both in "grain and colour, [the eland] resembles beef, but is by far better tasted and more delicate."[22] The search for new meats was one that Fellows of the Zoological Society found particularly inspiring, and in this they were not alone. (Many Fellows were also members of the short-lived London Acclimatization Society.) As late as 1867, for example, the *Pall Mall Gazette* reported on Lord Hill's attempts to breed elands in his park at Hawstone. In that year, according to the paper, the London Zoological Society sold its surplus stock at the price of £150 per pair, a cost "for the table [that] will probably be somewhat high."[23] By eating these meats, some Fellows of the Zoological Society demonstrated their refined taste, enjoying exotic flavours as signifiers of upper-class distinction. The ability to offer for dinner the same exotic beasts that had been secured through colonial networks became a symbolic expression of control over the natural world – and by extension, British imperial territories.

Confidence derived from Britain's imperial success was similarly evident in other aspects of the Zoological Society's endeavours, particularly in its collection practices.[24] Over the course of the nineteenth century, the Zoo became a quintessential collection – an amassing of (animal) objects that were removed from contexts of origin and organized into sets.[25] In the Zoo, animal captives were assigned new meanings and unique qualities, and the zoological collection became an index of national prestige.[26] The Zoological Society sincerely engaged a mandate to acquire, identify, and classify all natural phenomena, and as early 1833 the Annual Report of the Zoological Council asserted:

> With every succeeding year the probability of acquiring animals not previ-
> ously possessed will evidently become less; but those which are obtained
> will generally be invested with additional interest and importance on ac-
> count of their comparative rarity … there are [also] many [animals] which
> … appear to have been undescribed until the period of their arrival in the
> Society's collection.[27]

Animals considered rare and as yet "undiscovered" (by Europeans)
were the most prized acquisitions since their possession contributed to
the goal of amassing a comprehensive taxonomic arrangement of the
animals of the planet.[28] By 1835, the Zoological Society had procured
over one thousand living animals, many through donation.[29] The arrival of each new animal was reported with excitement in various
newspapers. These events were considered matters of great importance
and therefore national news in part because they fuelled a seemingly
endless demand for novelty on the part of the Victorian public. Through
the processes of collection, ordinary animals (quite common in the
places from which they came) were transformed into objects of particular significance and attention in the Zoological Gardens. They were
now representatives of their species and referents to the British power
to collect animals indigenous to far-flung territories. In a very direct
sense, the animal collection became a celebrated measure of Victorian
imperial prestige.

Given the increasing notoriety of the London Zoo, it therefore seemed
only logical to the Society's Fellows that their objectives should be "met
with peculiar sympathy among residents in the colonies, among Men
of Science in the most distant regions, and among the most powerful
princes."[30] While some of the animals in the collection were purchased
from animal dealers, the Zoological Society could also express desire
for particular specimens and then expect local and colonial contacts to
incur considerable difficulty and expense to deliver the animals.[31] In
1830 the Report of the Council gave instructions on the rearing of animals destined for the Society's collections and suggested the best
methods of transport to London.[32] This section concluded with a list,
six pages long, detailing the locations of correspondents who could
procure animals.[33] The Society was therefore willing and able to ma-
nipulate long-distance networks, rendered increasingly accessible by
steamship and railway since the 1830s and 1840s as well as through
colonial diplomacy, to obtain acquisitions.[34] For example, in 1858 when
Dr Livingstone offered to procure large animals of the Zambezi region

for the Society's collection, the Society acted to ensure his success. At its request the King of Portugal gave "orders that the Governor-General of Mozambique should transmit directions to the Governor of Tete, and the other authorities of Zambezi, to afford all the aid and assistance in their power for the acquisition and transport of such animals as Dr. Livingstone may desire to procure."[35] (This was a form of animal diplomacy – securing ties of patronage through exchanges of beasts.)[36] Such seemingly benign appeals hid the colonial labour and violence involved in the procurement of animals for the Zoo. No mention is made of the large numbers of attendants who accompanied white hunters on their expeditions and may have captured the animals and secured them for transport.[37]

Yet, the ability to secure patronage from all over the world was not merely hubris on the part of the Zoological Society. Eminent persons wanted to be associated with the project. The early Annual Reports recognized and expressed gratitude for donations made by the British Royal Household, His Highness the Viceroy of Egypt, Abbas Pasha, various colonial administrators, and members of the British aristocracy.[38] Less illustrious individuals were equally eager to donate to the Society. By 1870 the list of patrons in the Annual Reports was eleven pages long and encompassed even upper-middle-class individuals, who were also collecting and donating.[39] In 1885 the donations included more mundane animals. Their banality was emphasized, for example, in their being listed as a "common pole cat," an "ordinary frog," and "seven common vipers."[40] These contributions to the Society's collection ensured that a broad constituency had a stake in the zoological endeavour.

The success of the Zoological Society was widely acclaimed in the popular press, where the practice of collecting was endowed with the noble purpose of rescuing animals. The Zoo was praised for fulfilling an imperial and civilizing mission vis-à-vis its animal captives. The so-called civilizing mission was a justification for colonial expansion, whereby Europeans considered it a moral imperative to bring their technology, religion, and education to those they deemed less enlightened.[41] *The Leisure Hour*, for example, argued that it showed "a high state of civilization when a great and overcrowded city devotes part of its energies and space to the preservation and kindly treatment of animals, which the savage looks upon as things made solely on purpose to be hunted and destroyed."[42] This statement is most remarkable for its lack of apparent irony, since the British proclivity for hunting game as "sport" was widely praised and considered integral to the national character. Nevertheless, animals "imported into this peaceful and common home" were supposedly protected from the "savages" who, according to this logic, hunted them needlessly (only for food).[43] In other articles the animals were considered analogous to Britain's colonial subjects, and deserving of similar treatment. In 1880, for example, the *Daily News* reported, "The Queen's rule is as extensive over the races of beasts as of men. Every sort of wild creature in every zone, from the Arctic regions to the tropics, and from the tropics to the Antarctic, inhabits her Empire. A visit to the Zoological Gardens illustrates the variety of the fauna which we may count in a certain sense as our fellow subjects."[44] Inside the Zoo, the beasts of the planet were transformed into imperial subjects.

The Challenge of Exhibiting Animals

As the zoological collection expanded, the upkeep of animals in overcrowded conditions became an increasingly serious concern for the London Zoological Society. The challenge was to keep the animals alive and on display for as long as possible. Many of the creatures that arrived in the Zoological Gardens soon perished in the harsh conditions they encountered, and there were disputes over how best to house these creatures and keep them alive. High rates of mortality among Zoo animals were believed "to be owing to the want of ventilation in the dens."[45] Fellows of the Zoological Society were divided on whether the animals should be kept inside heated enclosures or in open-air spaces.[46] This concern reflected the Victorian belief that disease was transmitted through bad air.[47] Despite the high death rate, it was considered important to continue acquiring exotic specimens, since this would "gratify the curiosity of the Fellows and the Public."[48] As had been the case with the pet-keeping enterprise, the well-being of animals was less of a priority than satisfying the interests of their owners. Nevertheless, the "sanitary condition of the menageries" remained a pressing issue, and slowly the Zoological Society built larger and cleaner enclosures and reorganized the collection.[49]

This constant upheaval meant that the Zoo remained a fairly chaotic place, as animals were moved between cages and enclosures were renovated and rebuilt. The Annual Report for 1885 discussed this process, alluding to the separation of the "Carnivorous Animals from the Rodents and other Frugivorous Animals." To accomplish this task, the former reptile house was fitted up with cages suitable for the exhibition of smaller cats and allied Carnivora, and it was proposed to build a new house for the wild species of the genus Canis to relieve the congestion of the mammal house.[50] Over the years a single enclosure could be used to house very different animals. For example, a reptile house built in 1882 was later converted to a bird house, and a refreshments building later became the parrot house.[51] Exhibit areas were based on classifications of animals, with houses dedicated to the display of primates, reptiles, carnivores, and so on, but these could be reorganized.[52] The temporary nature of some installations meant that the organization of the gardens was impermanent and visualization of taxonomies could be difficult. These expediencies may have made it difficult to organize the animals in a clearly educational way.

In addition, the requirements of animal display posed serious architectural problems for the Zoological Society. Paddocks, huts, and cages had to permit the best possible view of the animals, while also protecting the public from danger. Balancing these imperatives took decades and was a long learning process. For example, the eastern wing of the giraffe house was given to the newly acquired hippo in 1850 because this enclosure was believed to fulfil "the primary object of preserving the Animal in health." In addition, to "obviate, as far as possible, the inconveniences to which Visitors were subjected during the summer of 1850 from the inadequate dimensions of the portion of the house devoted to spectators, the Council have constructed a TANK in the open air, 33 feet square and of suitable depth, commanded by platforms, from which they calculate that about 1000 Persons will be able to see the Hippopotamus at the same time."[53] While renovating other enclosures, mitigating danger was a serious consideration. To this end, a "very strong and convenient iron fence" around the paddock opposite the zebra house was constructed in 1867 to better contain these animals and safeguard the public.[54] These improvements suggest that the Zoo was regularly renovated and reorganized throughout the nineteenth century.

To promote appropriate interpretations of the Gardens, the Zoological Society made careful attempts to promote understandings of its collection as ordered and domesticated. Unlike the Berlin and Amsterdam zoos, which called attention to the exotic origins of their animals through architectural design by housing elephants, for example, in buildings resembling temples, the architecture of the London Zoo alluded to domesticity. In London the animals were installed in huts, cages, and paddocks called "houses." These enclosures functioned as a conceit of human habitation, visually conveying the impression that animals had been taken from the chaos of the wilderness and quite literally domesticated in buildings similar to those made for people. The London Zoo's first architect, Decimus Burton (1800–1881), appointed to his position in 1830, designed rustic enclosures consistent with ornamental garden architecture that blended gothic and classical styles. Burton's buildings were scattered throughout the highly landscaped grounds so that the site resembled earlier menageries in private gardens.[55] Contemporaries complimented Burton's designs for their similarity to his other buildings, particularly those in the wealthy suburb surrounding Regent's Park. The author of one guidebook, for example, felt that "the dens and houses in these gardens are not a whit less picturesque than the villas and mansions which we have elsewhere noticed from Mr. Burton's designs."[56] Subsequent architects remained consistent with Burton's vision, continuing to build in his classical style.[57]

Enclosures built later in the century conveyed similar impressions. Over time, Burton's highly decorative buildings gave way to more complex structures, which retained some of the same architectural style. The monkey house, for example, built in 1864 by Anthony Salvin (1799–1881), had an iron and glass roof that resembled a garden building. The elephant and rhinoceros house, built by the same architect in 1869, also approximated Burton's style. This was a brick structure with large windows, rounded archways, and a gothic roof.[58] Animals were often exhibited in the yards outside these enclosures. The interiors also offered visitors various views of the beasts. For example, the first reptile house, built in 1849, permitted visitors to inspect creatures housed along the walls behind glass. Light for viewing was provided by skylights along the vaulted ceiling.[59] Visiting the animal cages was thus akin to entering houses, looking into rooms, and peering through windows. These buildings elided distinctions between "natural" and "artificial," "outside" and "inside," "nature" and "artefact," as well as between "animal" and "human." By displaying exotic animals in enclosures that looked similar to human habitations, the Zoo simultaneously promoted and linked domestic and imperial ideologies. In these dwellings the animals might appear benign and interaction with them could appear routine as visitors wandered between cages to peer at and pet their inhabitants.

The freedom to enter the enclosures remains one of the most celebrated conceits of Zoo architecture. Humans were the only species completely free to roam in the Gardens, while most animals were confined to pens. A visit to the Zoo was therefore a confirmation of the human ability to order, capture, and confine the animal inhabitants of the planet. This message, suggested by the architecture, was reinforced by official guidebooks, published by the Zoological Society in the 1830s and updated at semi-regular intervals until the 1930s.[60] Visitors to the Zoo could purchase these books to learn about the animals on display, to remember their time spent in the Gardens, or to give away as presents.[61] Guidebooks provided narrative coherence and organization to what might otherwise have been understood as a chaotic amassing of animals; they instructed readers on how they should interpret a visit to the Zoo and suggested an itinerary through the grounds that could last between three or four hours.[62] At every enclosure, guidebooks advised visitors to ponder facts concerning the strength, size, character, provenance, and potential utility of each beast. This information was copious and ponderous. For example, a guidebook published in 1860 listed the scientific nomenclature of all twenty types of birds housed in the "Water-Fowl Enclosures."[63] By reading this information as they walked along the prescribed path, visitors could actively order the collection on display. This route was mapped in the front page of the each guidebook and indicated by a dotted line.

The maps provided a bird's-eye view of the area and implied that the best understanding of the collection was attained by following the suggested itinerary, but the route was random. If maps from 1828, 1860, 1894, and 1912 are viewed together, one can see how over time the Zoo became crowded with increasing numbers of animals and their enclosures; the itinerary becomes increasingly winding, folding in on itself in a crisscrossing manner. The plan to be followed, with its priorities of what to see first and last, where to pause for rest and refreshment, and what to notice along the way, demonstrates only the imperative to adhere to the route. The significance of these maps is their very existence and the linear order that they impose. Comprehension of displays was achieved by moving from one cage, aviary, or tank to another, and by stopping at various locations, reading information, and considering the exhibited animals.[64] At each enclosure, sounds, smells, and sights invited palpable contemplation of the animals on display, inspiring visitors to poke and feed the beasts.

Interacting with Animals

As part of the suggested itinerary, guidebooks recommended feeding even the most dangerous inhabitants of the Zoo. Food could be brought from home or purchased on site from a stall, near the bear pits, "where a person attends for the sale of cakes and fruits, which the visitor may feel disposed to give to the different animals."[65] Bears were the most popular animals to feed. Visitors would place a bun or other item at the end of a long stick and dangle it in the bear pit. Part of the amusement was watching the bears clamber up a pole in the centre of their enclosure in an attempt to reach the food. The ability to come close to these creatures was touted as one of the more exciting opportunities offered to visitors by the Zoological Gardens (figure 3.1). Even guidebooks aimed at children encouraged approaching and feeding these beasts.[66] An elaborate pop-up book, first published in the late nineteenth century, exaggerated this encounter, showing children reaching through the bars of the cage to hand apples directly to the bears![67] Here fantasies of what could be experienced at the Zoo are imagined and celebrated at home during the privacy of reading. Similarly, a postcard from 1905 showing a bear up a pole in the "old bear pit" suggests the enduring popularity of this amusement.[68] Via these media, visitors were encouraged to interact with the Zoo's most dangerous animals as if they were pets. These encounters presumably gave visitors opportunities to contemplate the animals at close range and exercise ambiguous forms of care and mastership through teasing (providing and denying food), much as they did with their own pets.

Many animals, in fact, died from the consumption of harmful objects given to them by visitors.[69] Even the Fellows of the Zoological Society took pleasure in these activities. For example, in 1836, it was revealed that the chairman of the Society enjoyed giving cigars and snuff to the monkeys.[70] In 1852, *The Times* reported that "two well dressed young men" were charged with drunkenness and administering gin to a badger in the gardens.[71] Sincere efforts to prevent the feeding of injurious objects to zoo animals began in the twentieth century. In 1915 the official guidebook strongly urged visitors not to tease or irritate the animals. Feeding was still allowed, but visitors were told "that the giving of tobacco in any form is noxious to the animals, and that persons detected in this, or in offering any other noxious substances will be prosecuted."[72] These regulations marked an important shift in Zoo policy, since feeding the animals had long held a particular significance, connected to imperial discourse and the so-called civilizing mission. In the 1830s, for example, great optimism was expressed about the improvement of a carnivorous parrot with a taste for New Zealand sheep. The parrot and its habits were juxtaposed with assumptions about the

3.1. "At the Bear Pit." From Kearton, "The Zoological Gardens," 345

supposed cannibalistic proclivities of the Maori. Whereas Britons deemed aboriginal New Zealanders unregenerate, there was hope for the parrot: it might be induced to eat seeds like the other varieties of its species after it "has been educated a bit in England."[73] Similar sentiments were expressed in regard to the feeding of a troublesome python.[74] In the 1880s, the diet of the snake became an issue for some humanitarian activists. The sight of a python eating live rabbits, guinea pigs, and pigeons (common pets) was considered a demoralizing exhibition. One proposed solution was to educate the python to abandon its carnivorous habits.[75] The Zoological Gardens in Regent's Park, it was argued, brought order and civility to the chaos of nature. Increasingly the imperial rhetoric of the civilizing mission was linked to the Zoo's domestication of its animals.

These insinuations were particularly strong when it came to discussions and exhibitions of apes, which were frequently compared to humans in blatantly racist terms.[76] For example, Sally, a chimpanzee, brought to the Zoo in 1883, soon became a celebrity because she was considered primitive and "capable of being taught many things." When she died in 1891, the *Illustrated London News* wrote a lengthy obituary describing the processes of her tutelage. In the Zoo, Sally had acquired the trappings of civility, learning to count and, most importantly, to eat human foods. Apparently, she had been quite "savage" as a young creature, adroitly catching birds and violently consuming them by biting off their heads. After a time, she abandoned these tendencies and "became more civilized, when cooked mutton and beef-tea were substituted for this part of her dietary." Despite these changes, Sally never forgot, or overcame, her origins, "and evinced an extraordinary amount of interest in coloured people, whom she would receive with a loud cry." The obituary concludes with the reminder that the "chimpanzee may be regarded as the animal which approaches most nearly to man." The implication could not be more evident: human-like apes (and the paper includes in this category orang-utans, gibbons, and gorillas, alongside chimpanzees) "constitute the nearest of our poor relations" – humans who were perceived as racially inferior.[77] At the same time, these observations could be combined with other prejudices, including class antagonisms. One reporter at the turn of the century, for example, described a "witty" conversation he overheard whilst looking at an orang-utan in which a young boy exclaimed, "Oh, ma, isn't he [the ape] like a working man?"[78]

The treatment of Sally was not exceptional. She was not the first or only zoo-dwelling ape to undergo "education," nor was the London Zoo the only institution to attempt such feats. Other chimpanzees and even some orang-utans in zoos across Britain and elsewhere were taught to wear clothes, as well as eat and drink with utensils.[79] Many visitors enjoyed watching these animals drink tea, including Queen Victoria. Mrs Owen, wife of the morphologist Richard Owen, captured the Queen's delight in this amusement as follows:

> We saw Jenny have her cup of tea again. It was spooned and sipped in the most ladylike way, and Hunt, the keeper, put a very smart cap on her head, which made it all the more laughable. Hunt told me that a few days ago the Queen and Prince Albert were highly amused with Jenny's tricks, but that he did not like to put the cap on the orang, as he was afraid it might be thought vulgar![80]

(The Royal Family, in fact, visited the Gardens as least once a year in the 1850s.)[81]

Similar fantasies of civilization were conveyed in popular descriptions of other exotic beasts possessed by the Zoological Society. Very often these creatures were likened to pets, and their dispositions were said to reform under British tutelage as they became increasingly domesticated. As early as 1832, for example, the *Mirror* complimented the Zoological Society by admiring how "the habits and structure of some of these animals [in the Zoo] adapted to the wants of man ... Consider but for a moment that the cat which crouches at our fireside is of the same tribe as the 'lordly lion,' whose roar is as terrific as an earthquake ... that the faithful dog 'who knows us personally, watches for us, and warns us of danger,' is but a descendant of the wolf, who prowls through the wintry waste with almost untamable ferocity."[82] In 1876 Gordon Stables, a popular writer of adventure stories for boys as well as tales about cats and dogs, mused, "may not the time come, in the distant future, when a large variety of feline animals shall become fashionable – when domesticated tigers, tame lions, or pet ocelots shall be the rage?" He then forecast that ladies would lead wild cats out on the lawns: "A lady beside a lion on the lawn would, I think, make a prettier picture than one by the side of a peacock."[83] Pet-keeping narratives of zoo animals circulated as late as 1927. In that year another author, P.N. Hart-Scott, related the story of a lioness which had been the property of the Duke of Orleans. She was commonly regarded as "bad-tempered and uncertain," but when the Duke came to visit her, she "sprang at the bars, her eyes ablaze, her huge body arched like a cat's." Though she seemed angry, the presence of her master provoked kindly feelings in the feline. She even permitted the Duke to tickle her nose, rub her neck, and play with her "like a puppy."[84] These stories confirmed beliefs in the power of the Zoological Gardens to tame beasts of the wilderness.

The Zoo profited from impressions of the domestication of its animals, especially those that were deemed favourites of the public and explicitly likened to pets. In 1850, for example, viewing the newly procured hippopotamus became the latest fashion, and visits to the Gardens soared. *Punch* reported that "hippomania" inspired well-dressed individuals to wear breast-pins in the shape of the hippo, which were sold in a shop in the Strand, and a Hippo Polka dance celebrated the animal.[85] The hippo trend was helped along by reports of the animal's docile nature. Newspapers described it "following like a dog, close to his [keeper's] heels."[86] *Punch* went one step further, portraying a hippo decked out in ribbons being happily led about by a lady.[87] Sometimes these fantasies were realized, and the public had opportunities to handle even dangerous animals as if they were tamed. For example, the riding of elephants, occasionally with very little supervision by their keepers, was considered a favourite activity. Similarly, as late as 1938, children could embrace an adult chimpanzee in the Children's Zoo. Though handled like a pet, this creature was strong enough to do serious harm.[88]

The success with which the Zoo convinced visitors of the docility of its captives produced some unexpected results, since animals did not always respond kindly to how they were treated by visitors. Newspaper reports were filled with accounts of accidents involving reckless visitors to the Zoo. In 1861, one woman lost several joints of her hand as she passed too close to the wolf cage.[89] Stories of incautious women losing hats and purses while feeding the animals were frequently described as humorous incidents.[90] There was often a gendered component to these accounts – and this had an effect on attempts to regulate the conduct of female visitors to the Zoo. In the 1830s, for example, a notice reading "LADIES ARE RESPECTFULLY REQUESTED NOT TO TOUCH ANY OF THE ANIMALS WITH THEIR PARASOLS, CONSIDERABLE INJURY HAVING ARISEN FROM THIS PRACTICE" was posted in the Gardens.[91] Tales of men interacting with the animals were given a different emphasis suggesting foolish bravado. A sensationalized case in 1867, first related by a letter to the editor of *The Times*, described a young man who lost his hat while "amusing himself with the bears." He descended into the pit to recover the hat and was saved by the keeper. According to the letter, he was "hugged" by the bear, but got away unhurt. Tellingly, when "asked by the keeper how he came to do such a thing he quietly replied that 'he did not know their nature.'"[92] He had assumed they were not dangerous. The incident was dramatized again in two illustrations over the next several days. By that time, the facts of the case had been altered and the episode was recast as human mastery over nature. The *Illustrated Police News* portrayed the showdown between man and bear as an equal fight; the *Penny Illustrated News* went further, showing the man beating the bear.[93] In these accounts the reckless stupidity of the visitor was transformed into heroic action whereby man combats and overcomes beast. Several months later the *Illustrated Police News* wisely took a different approach when it published a story of a "foolhardy" man who teased the bears and was rescued by their keepers. This occurrence, according to the paper, "ought to act as a warning to people who have a penchant for teasing the dangerous animals in the gardens."[94]

Such admonishments ignored popular perceptions of the Zoological Gardens as a site where humans had triumphed over beasts and rendered them tame. These ideas were repeatedly given currency. On several occasions, newspapers offered harrowing descriptions of the transfer of animals between cages. These articles featured exaggerated stories, describing, for example, the rage of a tiger transferred to a new cage.[95] The ability to relocate dangerous animals seemed to prove the Zoo's mastery of these creatures, and visitors presumably found the opportunity to view wild animals outside their enclosures immensely appealing. In January 1876, *The Times* reported on the popular desire to witness the transfer of lions and tigers to the new lion house: "It seems to have been imagined by some people that the lions and tigers would be led out by the keepers with chains round their necks like house dogs, and transferred simultaneously into their new abode in a kind of procession."[96] For several weeks, in anticipation of the event, there was an increase in the number of visitors to the Gardens.[97] This was particularly remarkable because the same rumours had circulated ten years previously; nevertheless people seemed to remain tantalized by the prospect of viewing animals, including the most ferocious carnivores, walking together in harmony under the guidance of their keepers.[98] One can speculate that biblical understandings of the Zoo influenced the popular desires to witness such incidents. Indeed the Zoo encouraged these biblical associations and sometimes portrayed itself as an idyllic Eden. For example, images on some admittance cards showed animals living together in harmony and not separated by enclosures.[99] Certainly, these episodes reveal a fascination with the Zoo's most dangerous animals, and a naïve belief in the rhetoric celebrating the extent to which they had been rendered docile by the civilizing influences of the Zoo.

At the same time as they published these stories, newspapers criticized the actions of the London Zoological Society and the folly of visitors who tested this rhetoric. In 1850, for example, *Punch* published a cartoon of a young visitor prodding a lion with an umbrella while the keeper stands idly by. The image made fun of the irresponsible visitors who irritated the animals and the ineffective attempts of the Zoo keepers to prevent such incidents.[100] Similarly, in 1861 the *Observer* concluded a report on a woman injured by a wolf with the comment that it "is unpardonable that the society not provide for the safety of those who visit the gardens." Responding to the charge of mismanagement, the Zoological Society asserted that there was no risk of injury in the gardens "unless the fingers be thrust through the wires into the dens."[101] In 1879, while reporting on the killing of a keeper by an elephant, the *Daily Telegraph* laid blame for the incident with the Zoological Society. In the Zoo, according to the article, even "otherwise humane and kindly-disposed persons, are too often possessed with a feverish anxiety ... to rouse [the animals] into activity with stick, umbrella, or parasol ... for the sight of an animal in a cage seems accompanied in some minds by an irresistible impulse to prod at him and to dig him in the ribs."[102] In this particular instance, the elephant had been provoked to violence by a nagging visitor, but the problem was the way visitors were encouraged to use and understand the Zoo:

> The gardens are open and exposed; and the visitors are confiding almost to a fault. In fact, so much trust do they place in the organisation of the institution that in nine cases out of ten they needlessly and obstinately expose themselves to danger which common sense would surely prevent. Taught by experience that the soothing influence of the Regent's Park, where lions crouch in obedience to the keeper's whip, where dogs keep company with the fiercest tiger, where seals indulge in gymnastic and oscillatory exhibitions, and where the most venomous snakes contentedly roll themselves up in a blanket, has a certain taming effect upon the wild

beasts therein contained, the happy public has chosen this dangerous playground as a field for the miscellaneous purposes of education, amusement and flirtation.[103]

The quotation implies that the Zoo had so successfully convinced the public that it had "a certain taming effect upon the wild beasts therein contained" that visitors behaved incautiously. Yet, despite such warnings, the popularity of the London Zoo did not wane, in part because animals were but a small component of the entertainment on offer. Those seeking education, amusement, and flirtation entered the Gardens to see and be seen – but they were not, necessarily, looking at the animals; for people, too were on display in the Zoo.

Humans in the Zoo

The London Zoo was widely acknowledged as a forum for comparing humans and animals in both appearance and behaviour. The Zoo was a location to socialize, and visitors took the opportunity to watch and critique each other in the same ways that they viewed the beasts. Starting in the 1880s, for example, the *Illustrated London News* began a series called "Odd Sketches at the Zoological Society Gardens" in which the distinction between visitor and exhibit becomes increasingly fuzzy, and both exemplify certain beastly behaviours. These illustrations figure stereotyped individuals, who evince similar habits in "costume, temper and moral disposition" to the animal inhabitants of the Zoo.[104] In the words of the newspaper, "Our sketches are designed, in the spirit of grotesque or comic art, to represent a few of the queerest and most obvious instances of a fanciful resemblance … between well-known inhabitants of the dens and cages and the accidental bystanders or spectators."[105] The illustrations accompanying this and similar narratives made the juxtaposition obvious, placing people next to cages. In one such illustration (figure 3.2), we see a "Yankee" with his beard cut in the "American fashion" standing next to a goat; and in another image, a woman, "Mrs. Tabitha Teacham," obviously owlish in her dress and deportment, standing next to an owl.[106] Such images, poking fun at people and classifying them into "types," were the stock in trade of the illustrated press in the second half of the nineteenth century and part of the popular discourse on physiognomy and also on Darwinism.[107] Physiognomy gained popularity in the nineteenth century, and involved seeing facial features as indicators of inner qualities, including personality, intelligence, and moral capacity. As the century progressed, the judging of physical presentation became increasingly complex as facial characteristics were scrutinized alongside stature, modes of dress, and styles of hair. Victorians believed themselves to be particularly adept at interpreting pictures for evidence of character and also reading the crowds they encountered in the modern city, on the streets and in places of education and entertainment, such as exhibitions, museums, tea gardens – and zoos.[108] Illustrations of people in the Zoo presumably reflected and had influence on how visitors were seen and also enforced rigid social hierarchies by making plain the visual characteristics that made deviance supposedly identifiable. Any anomaly or marked difference would be amplified in these illustrations to support a way of viewing others that was patriarchal, imperial, and classist. This was essentially an exercise in definition – all, especially those perceived as misfits, would be put in their place.[109] As they viewed the illustrations, newspaper readers were instructed to consider the "likenesses between the different species of animals there placed on view, and the variety of characteristic human figures met with inside or outside the precincts allotted to the zoological collection."[110] In addition, the illustrations may have called to mind Charles Darwin's evolutionary theories, which received wide publicity in the late nineteenth century. Since viewers of these images were urged to contemplate the precise demarcations of the human-animal boundary, they may also have considered evolutionary theory and the question of their own descent. In visualizations, which likened people to zoo-dwelling animals, the Zoo was used to identify, categorize, and discipline all sorts of people.

Earlier in the century, comparisons between humans and animals in the Zoo were deployed in ways that were simultaneously humorous and chastising to enforce modest behaviour and proper gender roles, just as representations of cats and dogs were intended to teach sexual propriety. These descriptions suggest that the Zoo was a venue for the pleasures of socializing and flirtation. In this regard, the Zoo operated in a similar fashion to other sites of Victorian leisure whose reputations were less savoury because some of their entertainments were explicitly sexual. For example, the Westminster Royal Aquarium, a pleasure palace near Charing Cross that hosted a variety of entertainments, including freak acts, variety shows, theatrical events, and exhibits of marine animals, was a known haunt of prostitutes and a site which concerned Victorian moralists.[111] In contrast to the variety shows of the Aquarium, the Zoo was intended to offer more refined forms of educational

A COUNTERFEIT PRESENTMENT.

THE GOATEE BEARD.

THE MEDITATIVE MARABOU.

MINERVA AND HER OWL.

3.2. "Odd Zoological Sketches," *Illustrated London News*, 20 November 1880

entertainment. Nevertheless, discussions about flirtation in the London Zoological Gardens may have been informed by concerns about sexual conduct at other venues. The Zoo wished to maintain (at least the pretence of) social respectability. In the Zoo, vice would be highly circumscribed and its potential only hinted at.

To this end, in 1866 *Punch* published an image of a young woman requesting permission to go to the Zoo (figure 3.3). She receives consent by assuring her mother that she intends to mingle, rather than inspect the animals:

> "Mamma, dear, Mrs. Robinson has written to ask if I will go with her to the 'Zoo' next Sunday. I *should* so like to!"
> "*What*, my dear! On *Sunday!* Never!"
> "Why, but we go to the Kensington Gardens!"
> "I disapprove of looking at Beasts on Sunday!"
> "But the People look at each other, Mamma; not at the Beasts."
> "If you are *sure* of that, my dear, you may accept Mrs. Robinson's invitation."

The beasts in this scenario are men and women seeking opportunities for flirtation and courtship in ways that are construed as improperly bold and overtly sexual. In another cartoon, *Punch* made the humour more explicit. A woman, dressed in her finery, approaches a man sitting on a chair. The cartoon, titled "Beasts at the Zoo," makes fun of the woman's brazen conduct, but the man does not escape unscathed. Both man and woman are described as beastly: the woman for making advances and the man for spurning them.[112] Those who visited the Zoo for flirtation were clearly being observed, and this could be both amusing and censuring.

Signs posted within the Gardens drew attention to other opportunities for contrasting visitors and caged animals, and their equally "beastly" behaviours. These placards, like the cartoons and illustrations discussed above, were intended to enforce orderly conduct, but they emphasized the instability of hierarchical separations between humans and animals (as well as between people). For example, a photographic postcard of the monkey house, circa 1905, shows three warnings directed at visitors posted directly on the exterior of a cage. The largest and most prominent states, "BEWARE OF PICKPOCKETS," while the two smaller signs declare, "NOTICE. VISITORS especially those WHO WEAR GLASSES are cautioned … TOO NEAR [the rest if the sign is

3.3. "All the Difference," *Punch*, 7 July 1866

obscured in the photograph]" and "THE KEEPERS have strict orders to prevent Visitors IRRITATING THE MONKEYS."[113] Such notices suggest that comparisons between humans and animals could be fraught with anxieties. Visitors are instructed to be simultaneously mindful of monkeys and of each other in much the same ways, since both could engage in thieving. Suspicion is directed towards the animals and towards pickpockets – a certain lower class of criminals who might be hiding amidst more respectable pleasure seekers. At the same time, the notices empower working-class keepers to discipline visitors, even those who might be their social superiors.

Keepers were ubiquitous in the London Zoological Gardens and their presence became integral to associations between the Zoo and Britain's expanding empire. Keepers interacted with visitors and conveyed information about their animal charges.[114] The number of keepers in the employ of the Zoological Society varied over time and depended on the financial health of the institution. In 1835 the Society employed fifteen keepers (including a head keeper, two assistant head keepers, one steward, and ten under-keepers) to look after all animals.[115] At the turn of the twentieth century, one publication estimated that the Zoological Gardens employed one thousand people – but did not specify the number of keepers.[116] Keepers occupied an ambiguous place in the organizational structure of the Zoo somewhere between the fellows of the Zoological Society, visitors, and animal wards. Most keepers were white working-class male employees of the London Zoological Society. They were akin to servants, living on the grounds (in a sense, like the animals) and carrying out work in the Gardens. As a constant presence in the Zoo, they were most familiar with the habits of the beasts in their charge, though for the most part their expertise was not acknowledged, and all acclaim went to Fellows of the Zoological Society. The Zoo was completely reliant on their labour. Keepers cared for the collection, supervised visitors, and facilitated certain amusements, such as riding elephants, camels, and zebras. Their work was highly visible: it brought them into close proximity with the animals and provided the visiting public with a spectacle of British and masculine working-class authority over beasts.

The presence of the keeper, in fact, became iconic. Old photographs from the second half of the nineteenth century show these attendants posing with their animal charges.[117] Similar photographs were featured in the second volume of a book, titled *Living London: Its Work and Its Play, Its Humour and Its Pathos, Its Sights and Its Scenes*, on all "forms and phases of London life" at the turn of the twentieth century.[118] The chapter on the Zoological Gardens drew attention to the work of the keepers, showing them alongside their animals and inviting comparison between keeper and beast. In each photo, we see all sorts of creatures submitting to the ministrations of their keepers. As they work, keepers feed, lead, and restrain the animals, as well as clean their enclosures.[119] These images are arresting depictions of working-class industriousness showing the exertion of human authority over animals through careful management. Each picture provides an impression of orderliness, showing how working-class (white) keepers tame, discipline, and civilize even vicious beasts. The most striking image is of a keeper, the sleeves of his shirt rolled up, leaning over and muzzling an alligator with what looks like a fairly thin rope (figure 3.4). In these images, the keepers' uniforms of caps, suits, and practical shoes convey impressions of orderly authority, institutional affiliation, and working-class respectability.[120]

At times, the presence of foreign keepers dressed in exotic clothing could be equally important. For example, in the 1830s, when the Zoological Society acquired an Indian elephant that became a great attraction, one visitor wrote to the assistant secretary suggesting that the keeper should be dressed "in something of an Asiatic costume" made of cloth or calico. The letter stated, "The elephant thus attended and placed in (what will by-and-bye be) your North Garden, will fancy himself at home, and visitors suppose themselves transported into Asia."[121] This letter is remarkable for the fantasy it expresses: the presence of the animal has become a vehicle to imagine the Zoo as imperial space, but understanding of this conceit depends on the presence of a keeper in colonial drag. In this instance, the keeper is displayed as exotic in order to make the exhibition of the animal appropriately comprehensible.

Perhaps to indulge such fantasies, certain significant animals were cared for by a coterie of European keepers cross-dressing in Arab costumes and accompanied by foreign attendants in their native clothing. This began within a decade of the Zoo's opening and continued periodically throughout the nineteenth century. One instance of this occurred in 1836 when the Zoological Society succeeded in purchasing several giraffes. According to a report in the *Morning Herald*, when the animals were conveyed to the Zoological Gardens they were accompanied by M. Thibault, the agent hired by the Zoological Society to procure the animals. Thibault, "who was attired in an Arab dress," arrived with the giraffes in the company of Nubian and Maltese attendants.[122]

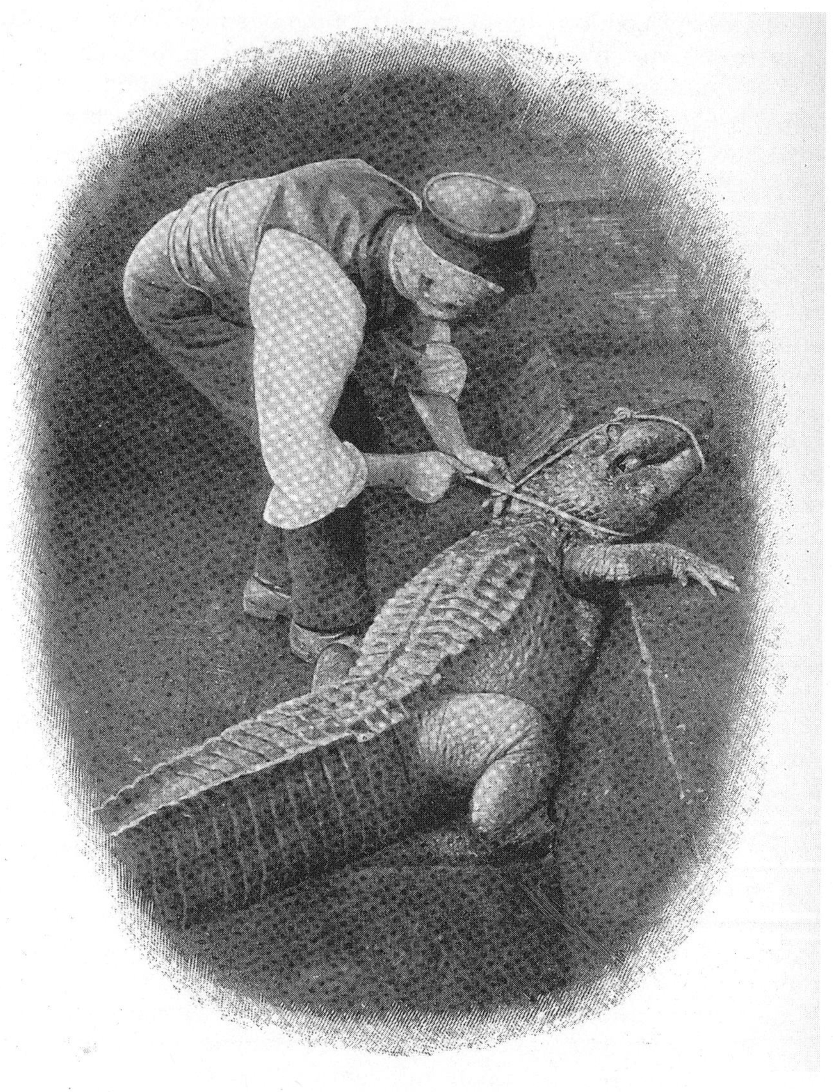

3.4. "Muzzling a Vicious Alligator." From Kearton,
"The Zoological Gardens," 348

In illustrations of the animals, Thibault is clothed in Arab regalia, and his presence is clearly indicated so that he is not confused with the other non-European keepers.[123] Foreign attendants lent an aura of exoticism to the exhibition of certain animals, as occurred with the hippopotamus, acquired in 1850. In illustrations, the hippo is accompanied by his Arab keeper in native costume.[124] This keeper, Mr Hamet Saafi Cannana, was considered the hippo's favourite attendant. Much was made of Cannana's ability to tame the beast, which was portrayed as so docile it would submit to him. According to *The Times*, he could interpret its language and provide the best care. In such descriptions it is implied that Cannana is primitive and so close to nature that he can commune with animals.[125] Later in the century, as we will see in the next chapter, even more attention would be paid to foreign attendants, and the press would describe in ethnographic detail their mannerisms, dress, food, and ritual objects. These reports encouraged comparison between humans and animals and established a hierarchy whereby visitors to the Gardens were positioned outside (and above) animals and keepers. If the Zoo was about collecting, comparing, and categorizing humans and animals, this involved describing and defining hierarchical gradations of the British imperial self.

A Man in the Zoo, 1924

Through the early twentieth century, the Zoo remained very much a nineteenth-century institution, perpetuating nineteenth-century ideologies and human-animal relationships. This is perhaps best exemplified by the ideas put forth in a novella from the early twentieth century, *A Man in the Zoo* (1924) by David Garnett. As the plot unfolds it brings together all the themes of this chapter, linking the practices of collection, organization, exhibition, domestication, and domesticity with the Zoo as a site for exhibition, amusement, and flirtation. The story deconstructs and reaffirms the imperial relationships of power that were enacted in the Zoo. Boundaries between visitors and spectacle are breached, and hierarchies of gender, race, class, human, and animal are momentarily destabilized, only to be strengthened and confirmed. The religious connotations of the Zoo are evoked, and it is described both as the Tower of Babel and as Noah's Ark.[126] Most important, the novel describes a scenario in which a man is put on display in the Zoo.

The novel begins when a courting couple, Josephine Lackett and John Cromartie, argue about their relationship while visiting the London

Zoo – like others, they have come to the Gardens as part of their courtship. Josephine is of aristocratic lineage, while John is of middle-class
background. Josephine is reluctant to marry John out of consideration
for her family, insisting that she is "not going to live with you [John], or
do anything they would mind if they find out." (Though not stated
outright, the sexual implications of this conversation are clear – just as
they were in the *Punch* cartoons where beastliness was a euphemism
for flirtation.) When they fight during a visit to the Zoo, Josephine employs the language of Social Darwinism and accuses John of being a
"silly savage" as well as "atavism at its worst." She suggests that he
"ought to be shut up and exhibited here in the Zoo."[127] Thus stripped of
his whiteness and its associated privileges, John acts on her outburst,
writing to the Zoological Society and requesting exhibition as "an ordinary member of the human race" (read: white, middle class, and well
mannered). John's witty letter rehearses many of the conceits discussed
throughout this chapter, particularly the ways in which the Zoo amass-
es and organizes its collection and encourages comparison between
men and beasts. He writes,

> … the more I have thought over this omission, the more extraordinary
> has it appeared to me … It may seem unimportant at first sight, since the
> collection is formed for man to look at, and study. I admit that human be-
> ings are to be seen frequently enough walking about in the Gardens, but
> I believe that there are convincing reasons why the Society should have a
> specimen of the human race on exhibition.
>
> Firstly, it would complete the collection, and secondly, it would impress
> upon the mind of the visitor a comparison which he is not always quick
> to make for himself. If placed in a cage between the Orang-outang and the
> Chimpanzee, an ordinary member of the human race would arrest the at-
> tention of everyone who entered the Large Ape-house.[128]

With relatively little ado, the Zoological Society accepts John's proposal
(seeing in it the prospect of a great attraction that would increase gate-
money) and installs him in the ape house.[129]

In most respects John becomes a regular inhabitant of the London
Zoological Gardens, and he agrees to "be subject to the usual discipline,
as though he were one of the ordinary creatures."[130] He is given a cage
between the orang and the chimp, and assigned a keeper. He is maintained in comfortable conditions. His cage is properly decorated in a
manner that exemplifies his social station, with carpet, table, upright

chair, armchair, lamp, library, and writing materials.[131] (He becomes an ethnographic exhibit, displayed amidst material culture representing his station.) A sign announcing his classification as "Homo sapiens" and "presented to the Society by John Cromartie, Esq." (that is – himself) is affixed to the outside of the enclosure. Soon John becomes a great sensation, attracting a large crowd, which comes to ogle and gape at "The Man" in the Zoo.[132] John's installation in the ape house becomes the cause of a public debate about "the propriety of exhibiting a man," and the ways this destroys hierarchies that position humans over animals, men over women, wealthy over poor, and Britons over their imagined racial inferiors. The debate rages in Parliament as well as "in every train, in every drawing-room, and in the columns of every newspaper in England. Jokes on the subject were made at public dinners, and at music-halls, and Mr. Cromartie was referred to continually in *Punch*, sometimes in a facetious manner."[133] John himself cares nothing for these controversies. As a creature in the Zoo, he has become thoroughly integrated with his fellow inmates. Most of the beasts treat him with the same "cynical indifference" as they treat each other. John wonders at this and is at a loss to explain the shared attitude of "such heterogeneous a collection of creatures."[134] As John pines for Josephine, pacing his cage and weeping, the reader is let in on the mystery. Like the other animals in the Zoo, removed from context and collected, John has been weakened, emasculated, and entirely stripped of his power – he is now no more than "The Man."

Towards the end of the story, the Zoological Society decides to "establish a 'Man-house' which should contain specimens of all the different races of mankind, with a Bushman, South Sea Islanders, etc., in native costume, but such a collection could of course only be formed gradually and as occasion offered."[135] John is moved to a new enclosure and caged next to a black man by the name of Joseph Tennison. In characterizing Tennison, Garnett employs several racial stereotypes: Tennison is clownish, irritating, and sexually aggressive.[136] This is most evident when Josephine comes to visit John and Tennison makes several lewd remarks about her presence.[137] Tennison is also likened to an animal in his relations with the keeper. The keeper has no trouble disciplining Tennison, while he treats John, his social superior, with the utmost respect.[138]

Because this is supposedly a light-hearted tale, all conflicts are soon resolved. Josephine regrets her pride, consents to marry John, and decides to join him in his enclosure, thereby agreeing to exchange her gilded cage for one of a lesser metal. The Zoological Society, however, cannot countenance this arrangement, and releases John from his obligation to the institution. As the curator explains (again with euphemisms), "It is impossible for various reasons, for us to keep married couples." Immediately John and Josephine leave the Zoo, slipping "through the turnstile into Regent's Park. There, still hand in hand, they passed unnoticed into the crowd ... chiefly composed of couples like themselves."[139] On this note, normalcy is restored: Josephine is repentant, John triumphs, and the Zoological Society is left with a "Man House" for the housing of racial inferiors. This last point is incidental to the novel, barely remarked by its protagonists, and perhaps for this reason all the more crucial and insidious. Tennison is left inside the Zoo. His predicament, apparently, merits no further comment because of its supposed normalcy.

Indeed in 1924, the year *A Man in the Zoo* was published, twenty-seven million people, most of them local, flocked to the Empire Exhibition at Wembley, where they could encounter colonial peoples on display, some in "native villages" and "native workshops."[140] For its part, Garnett's novel imaginatively actualized what had long been implicit – that the Zoo was a site for comparison of human and animal behaviour, and a complex way of displaying, describing, and ordering human beings and their experiences. Also in 1924, the notion of a "zoo" was (officially) applied to people, according to the *Oxford English Dictionary*. The word "zoo" entered English vocabulary as a colloquial term in 1847, the same year that the London Zoological Gardens was opened to the public. The definition positions the London Zoological Gardens as the prototype for all other zoos: a "zoo," according to the *OED*, refers very specifically to the "Zoological Gardens in Regent's Park, London; [and is] also extended to similar collections of animals elsewhere." In 1924, the second definition became common, and by this time "zoo" also referred to a "(diverse) collection, esp. of people; the place where they are assembled. (Freq. mildly contemptuous.)"[141] *Webster's Dictionary* also dates the origin of "zoo" to 1847, but does not privilege the London Zoological Gardens. *Webster's* offers two definitions for the term: "a garden or park where wild animals are kept for exhibition," and "a place, situation or group marked by crowding, confusion or unrestrained behaviour." The second definition is principally a (North) American use of the term – and not mentioned by the *OED*. It is worth noting that when the *OED* applies the term "zoo" to humans, it maintains the idea of a collection with the associated implications of order and orderliness. In contrast, the North American use of the term implies disorder. When North Americans describe a situation, gathering (of people), or place as "a zoo," they are suggesting that it is chaotic.[142]

According to the *OED*, the application of the word "zoo" to people originated in *The White Monkey*, a novel by John Galsworthy, also published in 1924 and later famous as part of the Forsyte Saga. In Galsworthy's novel, the term "zoo" is used when Wilfred Desert says the following to Fleur Mont, with whom he is in love, though she is married to his best friend:

> "You won't keep me in your Zoo, my dear. I shan't hang around and feed on crumbs. You know what I feel – it means a smash of some sort."
> "It hasn't been my fault, has it?"
> "Yes; you've collected me, as you collect everybody that comes near you."[143]

Here the notion of a "zoo," though applied to people, maintains the connotation of a collection and all the selective acquisition and ordering that this implies. The quotation also suggests flirtation and impropriety. The London Zoological Gardens and all it stood for is evoked in this scene and attached to this definition of "zoo."

Conclusion

In the hundred years since its foundation, the Zoological Society of London had engaged in collection practices that were imperial and biblical in zeal. Strategies of exhibition, reinforced by architectural design and guidebooks, conveyed the impression that the Zoo had domesticated and civilized zoo-dwelling animals. The reform of certain beasts was deemed proof of the British ability to rescue and civilize creatures with the most animalistic proclivities. Some visitors, believing this rhetoric, tested the claims of the Zoological Society by reaching through the bars of cages to pet, tease, prod, and feed dangerous animals, even bringing food from home for this purpose. The ability to interact with zoo-dwelling animals encouraged visitors to compare themselves to the creatures on display and designate certain individuals as more beastly than others.

The Zoo was a site where the consumer practices of collection, organization, exhibition, and domestication were used to deconstruct and reaffirm relationships of power in ways that were educational and amusing, sometimes so much so that they were barely noticed by visitors who entered the Zoo to socialize and to flirt. The Zoo breached boundaries between visitors and animals, and destabilized, then strengthened, hierarchies of gender, race, class, human, and animal. By likening certain visitors to zoo animals, Britons drew attention to perceived aberrance of appearance and behaviour. There was no privacy in the Zoo, and anyone could potentially fall prey to censuring humour and allegations of beastliness. This was a means of regulating the social order by reducing everyone to a type and encouraging self-reflection. Even keepers, employed by the Zoo, were the objects of intense scrutiny, providing a spectacle of working-class industry that demonstrated mastery over animals. The presence of European keepers in colonial drag, or foreign keepers in their native costumes, was believed to authenticate exhibitions of animals. When they became spectacles of colonial otherness, keepers were conflated with the beasts, and both beasts and men were on display. In the Zoo, the line between humans and animals was often blurred as Britons explored their relationships to animals and to each other, verifying and testing ideas about the white human self; in the process, as we shall see in the next chapter, they questioned white superiority and even exposed it as a consumerist sham. The Zoo, in many ways, was a nether-space, a site for imaginative colonial encounter that was entirely self-reflexive, encouraging Britons to contemplate what it meant to be white and what it meant to be British. In a sense, Britons were on display in the Zoo.

Chapter Four

The White Elephant in London: On Trickery, Racism, and Advertising

The publicity promoting the exhibition of the white elephant Toung Taloung began portentously in the winter of 1883 with an assertion of authenticity. A small notice, appearing in *The Times*, announced the purchase of an elephant by Phineas Taylor Barnum, the famous American circus proprietor and self-professed humbug, for the enormous sum of £40,000. The elephant had already left Rangoon and was en route for New York, but would stay for a time in the London Zoological Gardens. "This," the paper proclaimed, "is the first and only genuine white elephant ever imported."[1]

The arrival of the Toung Taloung was eagerly anticipated on both sides of the Atlantic. To the British, white elephants were objects of curiosity and mystery, a view perpetuated by nineteenth-century adventurers who described the religious significance of these beasts in memoirs recounting voyages to Siam and Burma. For European observers, the way these animals were treated indicated widespread decadence and ignorance in these territories. At the same time, the worship of whiteness, particularly when it manifested across the body of an elephant, seemed to confirm the European sense of enlightenment and superiority. The body of the animal would become a symbol of British imperial ambition and an emblem of the British imperial self.

Toung Taloung was scheduled for a brief stay in the London Zoological Gardens before joining the retinue of the Barnum, Bailey, and Hutchison Circus in New York. When the elephant docked in Liverpool, reporters clamoured to glimpse the beast, eager to publish descriptions of its features. The disappointment was immediate. In *The Times*, cries of fraud were barely suppressed. The terms of the controversy over the authenticity of the animal were immediately set:

> At first glance, the beast … looked very much like any other elephant, ex-
> cept that it had been lying in dust. He is 15 years old. A more careful ex-
> amination, however, showed it to be of lighter complexion, though it
> seems to be a stretch of language to call it "white." It has a mottled appear-
> ance, but it may be that when the animal has had a good scrubbing he will
> approach much nearer than he does at present to what a "white elephant"
> ought to be. The head and neck are of a much whiter hue than the other
> parts of the body, and it is this circumstance that gives the animal its *right*
> to be described as a "white elephant." [Italics mine][2]

In the article, whiteness was construed as an attribute that could be assigned or denied; it was a demonstrable indicator of status evidenced
by skin tone and hygiene, and it commanded respect. When first in-
spected, Barnum's elephant seemed to merit the description so marginally that it had to be qualified by quotation marks. For the moment,
final judgment was reserved. A good scrubbing, the article implied,
might improve matters – cleanliness, after all, was next to godliness –
and to be white and of high rank, at the very least, was to be clean in
appearance. At stake here, and in the ensuing debate over the authentication of the elephant, were definitions of race – what it meant to be
identified as white (or white enough) and what it meant to be identified
as non-white. With all this discussion of cleanliness, it is no surprise,
perhaps, that eventually Toung Taloung's image would be used as a
soap advertisement.

This chapter explores how the exhibition of Barnum's white elephant,
housed in the London Zoological Garden between January and March
1884, became a forum to discuss nineteenth-century theories of race
that entered nineteenth-century consumerist discourse in particular
ways. The Zoo, I show, became a site to explore anxieties and work
through frustrations about racial discourse and imperial authority. In
the space of the Gardens, divisions between humans and animals were
often blurred as Britons considered their relations to animals and to
each other, and, in this charged context, the exhibition of an elephant
became highly significant. By exhibiting the elephant, Barnum staged a
trick enacting the English definition of a white elephant, playing on
British perceptions of "Eastern" decadence and Burmese corruption. To
nineteenth-century Britons, white elephants were potent but misunder-
stood symbols. Popular travelogues had generated certain expectations of these animals: they were alleged to be holy to the kings of Siam
and Burma, and worshipped because of their white colouration. The

elephant's white pigmentation was expected to provide visible proof of white superiority. And it did – for some. Others were disappointed. They found its skin lacklustre, splotchy, and insufficiently white. Many could not distinguish this elephant from others of its species. As the authenticity of the animal was questioned, Barnum's trick provoked anxiety about the maintenance of racial purity and white privilege. The ensuing controversy became an opportunity to discuss the precarious status of whiteness, and the subject of an important Pears' Soap advertising campaign, where the meaning of the white elephant reached its apotheosis.

The discussion that follows explains how the exhibition of Toung Taloung occasioned a debate on racial ideologies. In recent years historians have highlighted the great significance of popular and consumer culture as ideological apparatuses of empire, disseminating notions of scientific racism. The presence of empire, far from being a distant and abstract idea, was pervasive in lived practices "at home" in the metropole.[3] So-called "objective" knowledge on race produced by the emerging disciplines of anthropology, eugenics, and biology was made accessible to and consumed by a non-academic public in museum exhibitions, music halls, zoos, and circuses, and in advertisements that were plastered on billboards, featured in newspapers, and stamped on household items. These cultural productions implicated ordinary citizens in imperial ideologies, presenting ideas of racial difference as fundamental and inescapable truths.[4]

The scientific discourse on race in the late nineteenth century was based on two premises: first, that there were observable physical differences between whites and non-whites; and second, that these differences were innate and linked to intellectual, moral, and physical capacities. These supposed differences justified the construction of hierarchies placing the "races" in a relationship of inferiority or superiority.[5] At the same time, racial status was closely tied to notions of class and ethnicity, ideas that were brought to the fore on the Victorian show circuit where working-class English and Irish performers were often costumed and painted to pass as black Africans and ethnic Others. As we have already seen in the previous chapter, the London Zoo engaged in these entertainments, sometimes employing white keepers in colonial drag to care for and be seen alongside exotic animals. As Nadja Durbach shows, the exhibition of "fake" Others was quite pervasive, and these exhibitions reflected the complexity of racial categories, suggesting that blackness – and its corollary whiteness – could be assigned and performed.[6] The casting of actors who were poor in these roles was an extension of popular discourses which equated urban slums and slum dwellers with racial Others and degenerates, often using the imagery of the "Dark Continent."[7] The expansion of the franchise to include working men in 1867 and 1884 made these anxieties all the more potent for airing in popular entertainments. Audiences used to enjoying fake savage shows were no doubt also prepared to experience the exhibition of a marginally white elephant and debate the animal's racial status.

As a novelty, the elephant became a cipher through which to focus concerns about the status of whiteness. If whiteness, as Durbach suggests, was relational, requiring the presence of an Other for identification, then the animal body suited this purpose.[8] During the exhibition of Toung Taloung, whiteness became a moving target, sometimes assigned to the elephant and at other times disavowed. The elephant became the being against which Victorians of all classes could measure their status. Whiteness was contested and negotiated as people viewed the elephant, sought entertainment, perused pages of advertisements, and purchased seemingly innocuous bars of soap. The ambiguous status of the elephant and claims about the whitening power of soap became powerfully linked.

Barnum's shows, in particular, were famous for promoting and exploiting racial differences. As Benjamin Reiss, Bluford Adams, and James Cook have shown, entertainments sponsored by Barnum were embroiled in the racial politics of post–Civil War America and they pandered to sentiments of white solidarity among audiences.[9] Moreover, in Barnum's American Museum, he offered audiences views of Leopard Children, Albino Families, and Negroes turning white. These exhibitions addressed the needs and anxieties of different audiences with regard to debates on the origins of skin colour and the possibilities of racial transformation.[10] The episode of the white elephant was no exception – but the way in which it tapped into racial ideologies was more subtle because it was an *animal* that was on display. Mobilized in the service of colonial ideologies to verify certain imperialist attitudes, the elephant's body became anthropomorphized. The spectacle of the elephant inspired a "scientific" discussion of skin pigmentation and the nature of human racial difference.

The following analysis will discuss how the elephant became the subject of these fantasies. First, I will provide context for the controversy that occurred in London in 1884, focusing on Anglo-Burmese and Anglo-Siamese relations. I will then discuss the significance of white elephants in Buddhist cosmology and how European observers misinterpreted the importance of these creatures. Their stories, published in travelogues about voyages through Southeast Asia, suggest that Barnum's exhibition of Toung Taloung enacted the English definition of a "white elephant." Second, I will examine Barnum's exhibition of the elephant and the various debates about authenticity that it provoked. Here we will see how the episode became a forum to express anxieties about the maintenance of racial purity. Finally, I will show how consumer culture adopted the controversy over the elephant and used the image of Toung Taloung to advertise for Pears' Soap. As the elephant was sent on to America, the expression "white elephant" became more firmly entrenched in the English lexicon.

The Significance of White Elephants

British dissatisfaction with the political situation in Burma and genuine fascination with "white elephants" formed the context of the controversy over the authentication of Toung Taloung as a genuine white elephant. The timing of Barnum's exhibition coincided with a period of heightened tension in the ongoing conflict between the British and the heartland of the Burmese kingdom, an area the British called "Ava" or "Upper Burma." The Anglo-Burmese rivalry had accelerated over the course of the nineteenth century. In close proximity to Calcutta, one of the presidencies of the British East India Company, Burma was of strategic importance to the British. By the 1880s, British businessmen were intent on exploiting Burmese resources, especially teak, minerals, and gems. The Burmese mountains also offered the possibility of large-scale trade to China, and the opening of new routes to China through Burma became a major objective.[11] Britain had slowly annexed Burmese territories over the course of three wars, occurring in 1824–6, 1852–3, and 1885. From the mid-1870s, the British had been discussing the possibility of further intervention in Upper Burma and increasingly regarded this as their right. In the 1880s, media depictions of Burma became progressively more hostile, creating perceptions of King Thibaw, the Burmese monarch, as an incompetent and unfriendly ruler who did not sufficiently support British commercial interests.[12] As the French consolidated their hold over Vietnam, Laos, and Cambodia and received increasing attention from Thibaw, British influence in Ava was considered all the more important. Mounting unrest in Thibaw's kingdom added to the excuse for annexation. In 1886, after the third Anglo-Burmese War, Britain abolished the Burmese monarchy and established direct rule.[13] As an object of British interest that was also symbolically linked to the Burmese monarchy, Barnum's elephant, Toung Taloung, became a living referent to this ongoing conflict and a trophy of Britain's imperial ambitions.

In Siam, better relations with European powers contributed to the evasion of direct colonial rule. Siam steadfastly resisted all colonial power, though its borders were demarcated by British and French surveyors.[14] The Siamese King Mongkut (Rama IV, reigning 1851–68) maintained cordial ties with both the English and the French, and used white elephants as symbols of these amicable relations. Having been sent to report on the Siamese court, Sir John Bowring, Queen Victoria's envoy, returned home with several valuable state and personal gifts, among them a talismanic offering of white elephant hairs. In his two-volume treatise, *The Kingdom and People of Siam*, Bowring described the gift as follows: "Amidst the most valued presents sent by his Majesty to the Queen Victoria, was a tuft of white elephant's hairs; and of the various marks of kindness I received from the King, I was bound to appreciate most highly a few hairs from the tail, which his Majesty presented to me."[15] This was not the only souvenir of the white elephant Bowring received from King Mongkut. After the death of his white elephant, the Thai monarch gifted the former envoy a portion of the pachyderm's skin preserved in alcohol.[16] Bowring subsequently bequeathed this present to the Museum of the Zoological Society of London, and possibly contributed to that organization's fascination with these creatures.

In scientific terms, albinism in elephants is not hereditary, and a pale-hued elephant born in the wild "is merely a fortuitous conjunction of events and of genes."[17] As part of Hindu and Buddhist cosmology, white elephants were ancient religious symbols in Siam and Burma, and closely tied to concepts of righteous kinship. As Rita Ringis explains, in the "Thai language, the term 'white elephant' is *changpheuak*, which literally means 'albino (or strange-coloured) elephant', the usual word for the colour 'white' being different entirely." A ruler possessing a white elephant would be recognized as an exalted and righteous monarch and "Lord of the White Elephant." Regarded as a celestial creature, the elephant was considered a symbol of legitimacy that could be "spontaneously" acquired in each reign. If an albino elephant was found bearing the physical characteristics considered auspicious, it was brought to the royal retinue. These elephants were not smooth and spotlessly white (as European observers desired), but usually had pink or cream eyes, nails, hair, and a tail tuft. Possession of a white elephant was perceived as a sign of sacred approval of the earthly state and its ruler, and occasioned ceremonial rejoicing. Conversely, the untimely death of a white elephant became a calamity.[18] These elephants were therefore not worshipped, as European observers would claim, but viewed as symbols of the divine.

Nineteenth-century Europeans were intrigued by these customs and recorded their observations of Buddhist ceremonies in tales recounting voyages through Southeast Asia. In these stories, writers offered personal accounts of travel and adventure. They cast themselves as investigators of rituals and riddled their descriptions of strange peoples, exotic customs, and tyrannical kings with orientalist representations. Through the use of what Mary Louise Pratt has called "numbing repetition," these narratives recounted similar incidents which created certain enduring perceptions of Siam and Burma.[19] Each narrative reveals a fetishistic fascination with white elephants, viewing them as objects of myth, desire, and repulsion.

One trope repeated in these stories is a visit to the stable of a white elephant kept by the retinue of a king. Bearing such titles as *The Mission to Siam and Hue* (1826),[20] *Narrative of a Residence at the Capital of the Kingdom of Siam* (1852),[21] and *The Land of the White Elephant: Sights and Scenes in South-East Asia* (1874),[22] these narratives use sensationalism to describe white elephants and the manner in which they were kept. European observers were particularly fascinated by the colour of these creatures and assessed each elephant's whiteness. George Finlayson, for example, recognized the animal he saw as an albino, differing minutely from its counterparts, and wrote that the "appellation white, as applied to the elephants, must be received with some degree of limitation."[23] His description of the manner of keeping such elephants seems not to have been exaggerated: "Fresh-cut grass was placed in abundance by their side; they stood on a small boarded platform, kept clean; a white cloth was spread before them, and while we were present they were fed with sliced sugar-cane, and bunches of plantains."[24] F.A. Neale, on the other hand, observes of "the brute" that "his skin was as smooth and spotless and white as the driven snow." He describes the flooring of the room housing this elephant as covered with mat-work "of pure chased gold." For Neale this treatment smacked of animal worship and was "more terribly emblematical of the oppressive yoke of tyranny than anything that I know of, at least in my own humble opinion."[25] Other travellers and dignitaries, including Anna Leonowens, who was hired by King Mongkut as a governess to teach his children English in 1862, and Sir Henry Yule, who reported on the British mission to Burma in 1855, echoed Neale's sentiments to varying degrees, repeating the suggestion that the animal was an object of worship and excess.[26] In most of these accounts the elephant was described as a living talisman of Siamese and Burmese superstition and decadence.

Given the repetition of these stories, it is reasonable to suppose that these narratives were used to formulate the definition of "white elephant" in the English language – which was quite at odds with the meanings Buddhists ascribed to the animal.[27] A "white elephant," according to the English definition, is a rare albino elephant venerated in Asia; it is also, in the figurative sense, a scheme considered to be without use or value. The term entered the English language in 1607; the first mention of worship, according to the *OED*, dates from 1841, and the beast was first associated with deceit in 1851, just decades before Barnum staged his spectacle. The exact definition in the dictionary reads as follows:

> **a.** A rare albino variety of elephant which is highly venerated in some Asian countries. **b.** *fig.* A burdensome or costly possession (from the story that the kings of Siam were accustomed to make a present of one of these animals to courtiers who had rendered themselves obnoxious, in order to ruin the recipient by the cost of its maintenance). Also, an object, scheme, etc., considered to be without use or value.[28]

If taken together, the literal and figurative definitions contradict and refute each other in a racist and malicious way, implying that the religious significance of the elephant is a scheme without use or value, and this is precisely how European travel writers perceived the treatment of white elephants in Siam and Burma. European observers felt that the rituals associated with these beasts were excessive. The term "white elephant" enshrined these assessments of Buddhist practices in the English language. Barnum's exhibition dramatized these meanings of the phrase.

Other stories exploiting the symbolic implications of white elephants proliferated alongside travellers' tales about these creatures as examples of excess and ignorance. Barnum was therefore not the first to exhibit an elephant that was reputedly worshipped in Asia. Narratives celebrating circus proprietors and white elephants were published widely in the years prior to Barnum's exhibition of Toung Taloung. The tales of white elephants and showmen all described the same scenario. For example, on 17 January 1880 the editorial section of the *Illustrated Sporting and Dramatic News* related a convoluted account of a hoax in which a painted elephant is pawned off as the genuine article. The humbuggery is then discovered by an "astute personage" who is angered by the deception:

> There was no mistake about its [the elephant's] whiteness, especially on Mondays, when the colour was renewed by the aid of a big brush and a pail of whitewash, but after a time the elephant grew less white, because it was found that the mixture got into the pores and interfered with the elephant's health. An astute personage … observed this with amazement, and one day when looking closely at the elephant discovered that the colour comes off … The astute personage was angry because he had been deceived, and he began to think big thinks, and find out a plan to cause anguish to the circus man who had deceived his trusting nature.

The "astute personage" then forges a letter from the King of Siam, attempting to expose the circus proprietor's trickery. The letter plays on the assumption that white elephants are religiously significant to the Siamese monarchy and people. The circus man falls for the trick, assuming the letter to be authentic, and finds himself in a quandary. He faces potential exposure and ruin, until he hits upon a stroke of brilliance. He understands that the offer actually authenticates his forgery. The King's letter transforms this ordinary beast into an authentic white elephant – that is, an elephant (supposedly) holy to the King of Siam and a worthless object for which vast sums have been offered. Even if the whitewashing of the elephant is disclosed (assuming it wasn't already known by everyone but the astute personage), only the distant King seems humbugged. The circus man is thus able to make peace with his audience:

> He [the circus man] went into the ring and addressed the people. He had received, he said, this tempting offer from a monarch whose only regret was that he could not come over and see the circus, of which he had heard so much, and … the offer of £20,000 was tempting. But, as tempting as it was, he could not find it in his heart to deprive "the nobility and gentry of

the Borough-road" of their favourite animal. For their sakes he had refused the kingly offer, and decided to retain the white elephant ...[29]

The story is a dramatization of the English definition of a white elephant, and such narratives generated expectations of the entertainment
that Barnum would provide during the exhibition of Toung Taloung.
Spectators supposed that Barnum's elephant would be uniformly
white, even if it was chalked, and they anticipated forged letters au-
thenticating the animal. While inspecting the beast, they also sought
evidence of "Eastern" decadence and hoped to witness scenes of animal worship.

The narrative related in the *Illustrated Sporting and Dramatic News* was
repeated almost verbatim by the Norwegian naturalist and explorer
Carl Bock, who told a similar tale in his travelogue *Temples and Elephants*, published in 1882. After describing in great detail a ceremony
held to honour the acquisition of a white elephant by the Siamese King
Chulalonkorn, Bock writes of a "performance of a rather different nature, and with very different motives," which took place in Bangkok
some days after the King's festivities. The performance was given by
"Wilson's English Circus" and had "been witnessed by the king, princes, and nobility." In the midst of the performance two clowns began
jesting about white elephants, claiming to be in possession of "the only
genuine white elephant in the world," which appeared "as white as
snow; not a dark spot could be seen anywhere." The elephant had been
chalked. The Siamese, according to Bock, "were annoyed that fun
should be made of their religious beliefs," and they cursed the circus
proprietor, forecasting that he "would be punished by Buddha, and
that the elephant would die. And their prophecy came true." For his
part, Bock agreed "that the performance was, to say the least, in very
bad taste."[30] The similarity between Bock's story and that published
by the *Illustrated Sporting and Dramatic News* is remarkable and suggests that tales of white elephant forgeries and circus proprietors had a
broad circulation.

Bock's travelogue would be referred to in the heated discussion of
the authenticity of Barnum's elephant, showing the influence of these
travelogues and jokes on the staging and interpretation of the exhibition of Toung Taloung in the London Zoological Gardens.[31] Some of
these letters may have been written by Barnum's agents. The first letter
to the editor of *The Times*, penned by "F.E.W.," argued that there "is
nothing sacred, according to Buddhist teaching, in a white elephant or

in any other elephant." Implicating Bock in the fray, the letter adds, "Mr. Bock ought to know [this], professing, as he does, to be a scientific traveler."[32] Three days later, a letter from Charles E. Fryer, editor of Bock's *Temples and Elephants*, attempted to counter charges made by F.E.W. against Bock.[33] Finally, a letter written by Nai Pleng made another reference to Bock. Pleng also contested Barnum's claims of the sacred nature of white elephants. He wrote to "protest against what the showman says about the 'sacred' white elephant, which is foolishly supposed to be worshiped by Buddhists of those countries in the Far East." He concluded his letter with the sudden statement, "Perhaps, Mr. Carl Bock never saw a Temple in his life, so he thinks the elephant's royal stable is the Temple."[34]

The circulation of these narratives and the style of Barnum's showmanship make interpretation of the 1884 exhibition of the white elephant a difficult task. Barnum's success, as James Cook has argued, derived from his skill to artfully deceive. Barnum made a career of exhibiting curiosities (Joice Heth, Automaton, Feejee Mermaid), celebrating their anomalous features and inviting their inspection. He was particularly adept at drumming up publicity for his shows.[35] Barnum used the press as a forum to question the authenticity of his own productions. During the course of an exhibition, Barnum would let it slip to newspaper editors and reporters that he was showing a fake. In their zeal to sell papers, outdo competitors, and even expose hoaxes, editors and reporters complied with and fell prey to Barnum's schemes. The effect on audiences was palpable. People felt compelled to examine his exhibits. The possibility that the spectacle might be real fuelled their curiosity; conversely, the scent of imposture was irresistible. His reputation as a prankster proved no deterrent. Spectators flocked to his shows, where they were willingly duped by the master showman and became active participants in fraud. As a "purveyor of public amusements," Barnum was a shrewd interpreter and manipulator of popular sentiment.[36] By offering contradictory interpretations of his own exhibits, Barnum invited debates over their meaning. His shows provided nineteenth-century audiences with representations whose significance they could actively negotiate.[37] This characteristic stratagem produced contradictory results during the display of the white elephant. The rub is that Barnum's elephant was authentic; it was a genuine white elephant in so far as its skin pigmentation was natural and had not been tampered with. Moreover, the elephant was reputed to have been acquired at great expense and was ultimately deemed worthless. This meant that despite his predilection for hoaxes, Barnum faced disgruntled London spectators with the real deal – a white elephant according to the English definition of the term.

The majority of those who commented on the elephant did so in letters to the editor of *The Times*, which became the main forum for the debate on the elephant's authenticity. These correspondents were an assortment of individuals, including university scholars, eminent scientists, medical men, Anglo-Indians, colonial administrators, Buddhists living in London, and curious onlookers; it is also entirely possible that some of them were Barnum's representatives writing under pseudonyms. The most vocal participants in the debate therefore possessed (or claimed to possess) scientific or colonial expertise, but working-class individuals were just as likely to partake in the drama. Records kept by the London Zoological Society show an increased number of visitors to the Zoo when the elephant was in residence. The number of "privileged" visitors approximated the number of lower-class visitors. These class divisions are known because the Zoological Society recorded visitor numbers in categories. Members of the London Zoological Society (or guests of members) paid an annual subscription rate. Their admission was recorded under listings of "Privileged Visitors." Paying visitors were divided into two classes, those who paid the shilling entrance fee and those who entered the Gardens for half a shilling. The half-shilling rate was implemented specifically for a working-class constituency.[38] Admissions spiked on days when well-publicized trickery was scheduled to occur. Between the months of January and March 1884, while the white elephant was in residence, over ninety thousand visitors came to the London Zoological Gardens.[39] Given that the exhibition of Toung Taloung was reported in almost every London-based newspaper covering news and/or leisure, this widespread interest in the elephant is not surprising.[40]

By 1884, Barnum had been in the entertainment business for fifty years and he was a master of trickery. At every turn one should suspect his manipulation and be wary of the spectators and their innocent protestations against fraud. British spectators had been attending Barnum's exhibitions for fifty years and it would be a mistake to assume them naïve.[41] Barnum's elephant would have been received by a public that was used to entertainments figuring "trophies" from Burma and the surrounding region. For example, during the first Anglo-Burmese war in 1825, a "Burmese Imperial State Carriage and Throne" was displayed at the Egyptian Hall. Similarly, in 1883, one year before the exhibition of the white elephant, "Kroa, the Missing Link," a seven-year-old girl from "Indochina whose body was covered in hair," was exhibited at the Royal Westminster Aquarium. Kroa was seen "as a prize, a souvenir of imperial conquest."[42] The excitement provoked by Barnum's elephant should be understood in the context of these other exhibitions that gripped the public imagination. Visitors to the London Zoological Gardens likely came to inspect and feed the white elephant because they wanted to be entertained and scandalized as they had been at other exhibitions and performances figuring exhibited bodies and objects from the region.

These expectations explain the contradictory reception of the elephant. When Barnum's elephant arrived in London, it generated immediate disappointment. Spectators found that it was insufficiently white (figure 4.1). Apart from the odd pink patch, Toung Taloung was virtually indistinguishable from other elephants. During the course of the elephant's exhibition, Barnum and his agents employed trick after trick to prove that this was a genuine specimen. But they seemed ill prepared for the extent to which evaluations of the elephant's authenticity would depend on assessments of its colour. In the controversy that ensued, the animal came under close scrutiny and was the subject of intense debate. During the fray, Britons evinced a willingness to believe in the mysticism of the creature, hoping that it would verify notions of white supremacy and confirm perceptions of their imperial selves.

The White Elephant in the Zoo

From the beginning, the exhibition of Toung Taloung was controversial in ways that were unanticipated, even by Barnum. Though never the most trustworthy commentator, Barnum later stated that his interest in white elephants derived from their reputation as sacred animals.[43] Along with his contemporaries, Barnum claimed to be intrigued by the possibility that whiteness was venerated in the East. He certainly saw potential profit in exploiting this belief. But whiteness could be a matter of degree. How white did the elephant need to be to satisfy Barnum and his viewing public? Upon first inspecting the elephant, Barnum is reputed to have stated, "Well, it's whiter than I expected to find it!"[44] Echoing the sentiments of the various European travellers who witnessed the ceremonial arrival and keeping of white elephants, Barnum claimed in his autobiography that he expected Toung Taloung to be of pure white pigmentation:

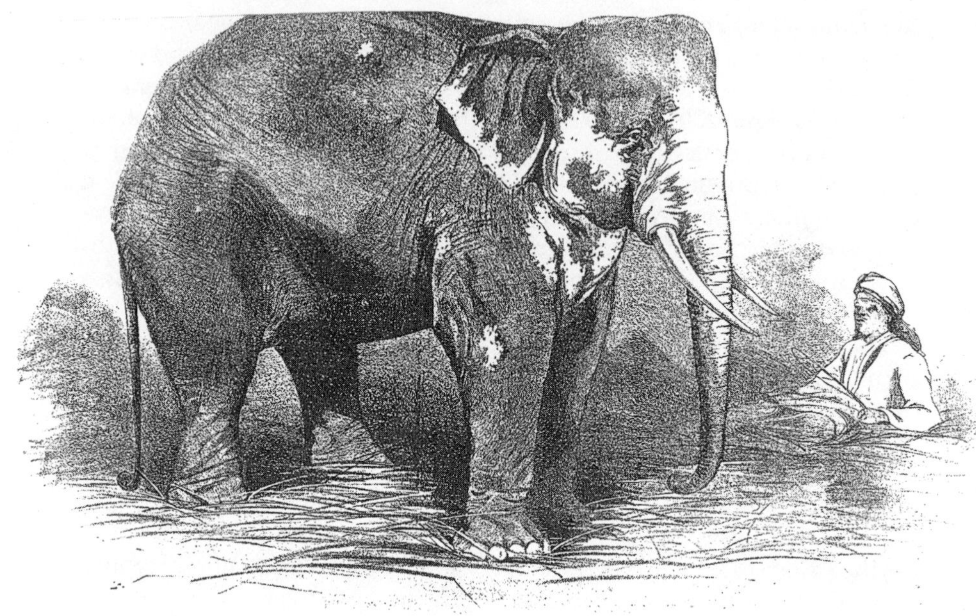

THE BURMESE WHITE ELEPHANT, "TOUNG TALOUNG."
Imported by Mr. BARNUM.

4.1. "The Burmese White Elephant," *Illustrated London News*, 26 January 1884

Until my agents first visited Bangkok, the capital of Siam, and there saw the king's "Sacred White Elephant," I had supposed that they were literally white, instead of technically so. Those who had not seen these animals, nor read descriptions of them, had the same idea as myself, when, therefore, my Sacred Elephant arrived in London, a large portion of the public having expected to see a milk white elephant, were disappointed.[45]

As the quotation demonstrates, Barnum aligned himself *ipso facto* with the spectators who came to see the beast and pronounced it insufficiently white.

The majority of spectators who recorded observations of the elephant stated that initially they had supposed it to be white, but were disappointed by their inspection of the beast. As one observer put it in a letter to *The Times*, "When I was taken to see the white elephant I naturally expected to see an albino – that is to say, an animal entirely white or faint pink."[46] The dark colouration of Barnum's elephant was unexpected and caused much speculation and confusion. One correspondent wrote to the Zoological Society and inquired, "Is the specimen a bonafide White Elephant? I certainly agree with what descriptions we have. But is it a cross breed – a mongrel? Horace alludes, I think to White elephants, but as he uses the word 'albi' – I concluded they were white, and not like this … Are there any whiter than this one – or are they all like this"?[47]

During his stay in London, Toung Taloung was intensely scrutinized. According to *The Times*, the elephant was even viewed by various dignitaries, including MPs, ministers of the Crown, ex-ministers, members of the House of Lords, Indian officers, and the Prince of Wales.[48] A chorus of self-proclaimed experts announced their assessment of the animal's colouration and found it wanting. Many judged the animal from direct experience, claiming to have prior knowledge of the genuine article. One traveller, John Guy Laverick, pronounced Barnum's elephant fake based on his observations of white elephants in China. In a letter to the Zoological Society Laverick wrote, "I have seen them myself. They are not white in patches like Mr. Barnum's specimen, but are all one colour and certainly answer to the description of White Elephant much better."[49] Taking cues from the opinions offered by Laverick and other correspondents, *The Times* veered between enthusiastic endorsement of the elephant and derision of Barnum's humbuggery. Other newspapers quoted *The Times* in their reporting of the elephant's sojourn in London. The main issue in the coverage of the elephant's exhibition was the nature of whiteness.

The debate over the authenticity of the white elephant was linked to popular conceptions of racial difference, ideas of racial purity, and notions of racial hygiene. Three main points were considered in discussions of the beast: the pigmentation of the elephant's skin, the elephant's monetary value, and Buddhist religious practices. Belief in the elephant's monetary value and religious significance came to depend on opinion of the elephant's colouration. Though this debate was circuitous and layered, it was ultimately one-sided in that it was held in Britain (and later in the United States). Throughout the course of his exhibition, Toung Taloung was personified and made representative of Asia. As the president of the London Zoological Society argued at the height of the controversy, "the chief interest that remains in [the elephant is] … that those of us who have never been in the East, see for the first time an animal presenting a condition of colouration said to be common in its native land."[50] The elephant's colouration was a subject of intense interest because it was believed to have implications for the categorization of human populations into taxonomies of "race." As a natural phenomenon, the elephant was a potent symbol. Through the elephant, nature itself seemed to be validating cultural constructions of race.

From the moment the elephant arrived in England, it was examined as evidence of the position of whiteness in the "East." To make this comparison, the animal's skin colour and "gentle" comportment were immediately juxtaposed with that of his "native" attendant, Radee. In the press, Radee was referred to as a "half-caste boy" and "a half-breed of one of the hill tribes," by implication of lesser status than the animal.[51] The attendant's appearance was described in *The Times* in a derisive tone:

> his mahout, who, with his long black hair falling on his shoulders, his dark swarthy complexion, a silk handkerchief of tawny gold, worn as a turban, white linen jacket with lace edging, and a pinky silk garment loosely enwrapping his thighs and leaving the legs from the knees downwards bare, seemed to divide with Taung the curious regard of the visitors. He would not wear shoes, and stood bare-foot on the damp brick, an imprudence which should surely be checked.[52]

The illustrations covering the arrival of Toung Taloung in the *Illustrated London News* also compared the attendant and the beast, calling attention to Radee's outward conduct, including his dress, long hair, bare feet, and culinary habits (figures 4.2 and 4.3). The attendant was judged according to Victorian standards of hygiene and dress, to which his bare feet were an affront. The elephant was the subject of the same inquiring gaze, focusing on appearance (even dress!) and feeding habits. Toung Taloung was said to "behave with perfect equanimity on the first day of his appearance in public, and seems to be ready to make himself comfortable."[53] In contrast to the attendant, the elephant was initially perceived as a paragon of hygiene and purity – demonstrating the superior status of whiteness. Across the body of the elephant, colonial ideologies and racial doctrines were visually represented to the British public.

Initially, *The Times* promoted the possibility that the elephant was a genuinely white specimen, and continued to do so even as it questioned the animal's authenticity. Claims of the elephant's fastidious character and bodily hygiene were particularly important for this process – and laid the foundation for the appropriation of the controversy by advertisers to sell soap. Toung Taloung was increasingly assigned attributes that distinguished him from other elephants and "befitted his claims to distinction." His mild temper, in particular, was emphasized to illustrate his rank as "a high-caste elephant."[54] Elephants were generally likened to "slaves" consigned to manual labour in the colonies. In Britain, elephants could be actors, performing in theatres or circuses, or zoo pets, like Jumbo, giving rides to generations of children. Toung Taloung was described as elevated above other elephants, rarely condescending to eat common hay and oats.[55] When he was eventually permitted to snack on the food sold to the public for feeding the Zoo's animals, he apparently distinguished himself from these other elephants by consuming it "without any greedy response. Such, indeed is the animal's care over its delicate constitution."[56] *The Times* even suggested that he be treated like royalty and ritually anointed.[57] In imputing meticulous habits to the elephant and advocating for his exceptional care, the press drew on assumptions that connected racial superiority to bodily hygiene and validated claims of the beast's whiteness.[58] Despite the disappointment evident in early reports of the elephant's colouration, he was continually granted attributes that might befit a high-ranking personality. In this way, *The Times* colluded with Barnum, at the same time as it encouraged speculation about the authenticity of the animal.

Yet close examination of the illustrations raises certain questions – for us and, no doubt, for nineteenth-century audiences – about whiteness as a potentially artificial production. In the lower left corner of figure 4.2 we see the elephant being scrubbed in "The Great Wash." Cleaning supplies – a bucket, brush, and soap – are also depicted in the lower right corner of figure 4.3 as "Necessities of the White Elephant." These images provoke questions about the elephant's cleanliness and whiteness: is his cleanliness a product of his whiteness (and presumed civilization)? Or, is his whiteness a result of vigorous scrubbings, and thus a fraud? The illustrations also emphasize the contrast between white and black, and make the "white" splotches more clearly defined than they would have been in reality, thus perhaps perpetuating the expectation that the elephant should appear white when seen at the Zoo.

Not all newspapers were willing to entertain the possibility that Toung Taloung was in any way special, however. The *Illustrated London News* reported, for example, that Toung Taloung "is regarded as a great

4.2. "Arrival of the 'White Elephant' from Burmah," *Illustrated London News*, 26 January 1884

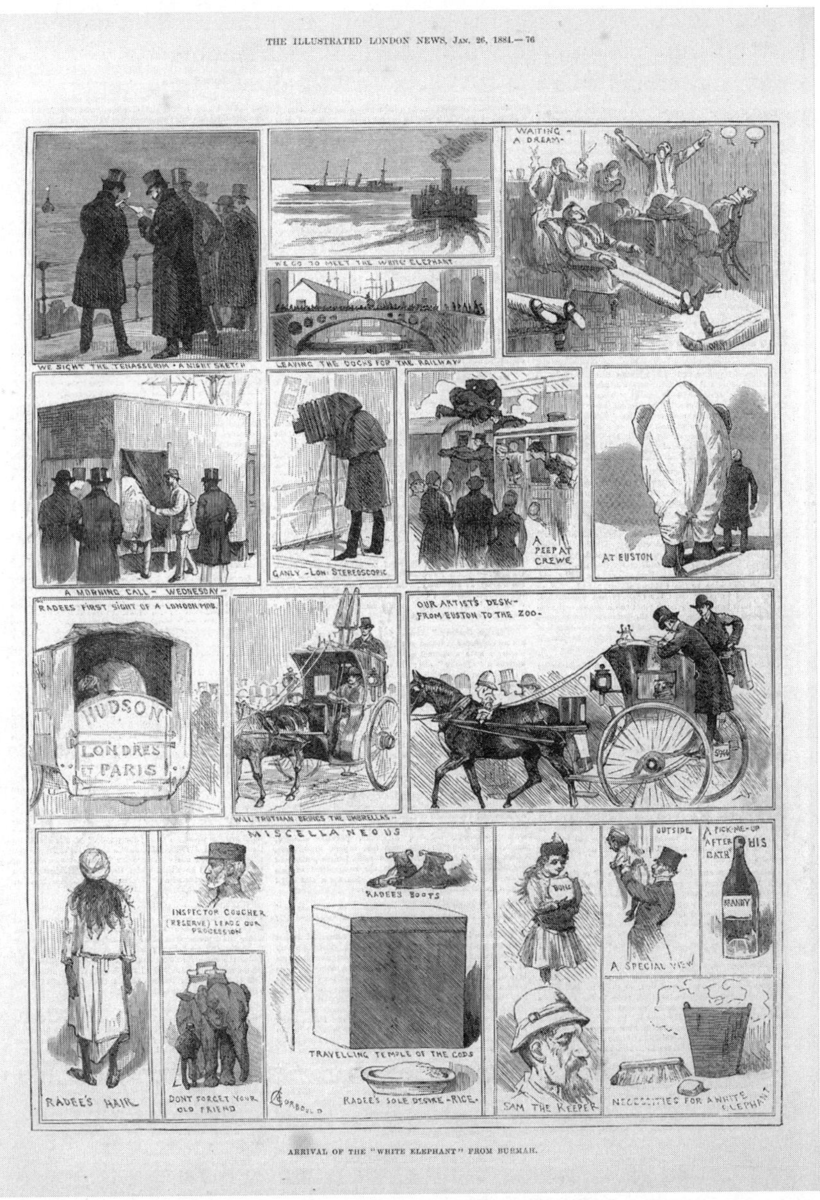

4.3. "Arrival of the 'White Elephant' from Burmah," *Illustrated London News*, 26 January 1884

curiosity in London, being the first example of this freak of nature that has been shown here; but we are told by Mr. Sanderson, the best authority, that many like it are to be seen in India."[59] Some reports even demonstrated a remarkable understanding of Barnum's style of showmanship. The *Illustrated Sporting and Dramatic News*, for example, claimed that the elephant "is in every respect an ordinary beast, except that he belongs to Mr. Barnum who understands the art of advertising."[60] The *Spectator* went to great lengths to decry the extravagant attention lavished on the beast by *The Times*:

> Mr. Barnum … has sent over a beast purchased in Burmah, which he declares to be of the "white" variety held there to be semi-sacred. The daily journals are helping him, and publishing minute accounts of the creature, and of the "gentle" way in which it walks up gangways, but we suspect he will be disappointed. The public fancies that the white elephant is white, and will hold that a slate-coloured brute with pink patches, not eight feet high, and not otherwise remarkable, is not the animal it is looking for … but Toung is neither big nor beautiful, nor anything else, except possibly "sacred" among a people who are less known in England than any race in Asia. Mr Barnum should give some sharp Yankee chemist a few thousand dollars to invent a new bleaching process, and then show his elephant in the colours which the populace expect.[61]

In addition to emphasizing the unremarkable pigmentation of the elephant, this report suggests that there was widespread disappointment with the fact that its colour was not artificial. Referring to the stories of trickery and chalked elephants, the *Spectator* suggested that a bleached specimen would have satisfied those who came to view the elephant in the Zoological Gardens. Even when the elephant was not fake, assessments of its colour were based on expectations generated by the travelogues and other narratives of trickery.

Given that the elephant's pigmentation was natural, speculation about its causes became a concern of the British scientific establishment, and a number of scientists attempted to understand the colouration in relation to their knowledge of skin diseases. The medical professionals who entered these discussions questioned whether the elephant suffered from a pathological condition, or whether the splotches were a sign of transformation from blackness to whiteness. Their understanding of skin diseases was imbued with racial ideologies. W.H. Flower, president of the London Zoological Society, and Balmanno Squire, surgeon to the British Hospital for Diseases of the Skin, became the main participants in the debate about the elephant's pigmentation. Flower and Squire attempted to diagnose the skin condition of the elephant, speculating that the whiteness was either congenital or a disease. Flower was the first to suggest that the animal was "not a pale variety of the ordinary elephant, as some have supposed the so-called 'White Elephant' to be, but one characterized by a local deficiency of the epidermic pigment." The elephant was not diseased, argued Flower, but it did manifest a birth "defect" approaching "albinism."[62] Squire, in contrast, was of the opinion that the elephant suffered from a malady called "leucoderma," during the course of which light patches spread over the skin. Claiming to have previously witnessed a few cases of this affliction, Squire suggested that the disease was more obvious among "the black races of man, who go about more or less completely unclothed." His assessment of the elephant compared it to a "well-marked example of the piebald negro."[63] Another letter similarly referenced the case of an "African Albino" in a medical discussion of the elephant's condition.[64] The *Illustrated London News* also made reference to the discussion playing out across the pages of *The Times*, concluding, "In rare instances, both among negro human beings and brute animals, there is a partial absence of the dark colour matter in the epidermis, and this sometimes presents the appearance of light-coloured patches. It may even affect the whole body."[65] In these discussions the elephant was likened to a person. Explaining away the whiteness of the elephant as a disease became a way to assure readers that whiteness on black bodies was abnormal and anomalous, rather than a marker of privilege. At the same time, discussions of disease raised the possibility of whiteness as contagion which could make mayhem of observable racial categories. Through these discussions, assessments of the elephant's condition were linked to medical discourses on race, which became a part of the public discussion about the elephant – and also, presumably, part of the commercial entertainment on offer as newspaper editorials opined on these possibilities.

In fact, the commercial potential of Toung Taloung outlasted interest in him as a scientific object. As a scientific curiosity, the elephant was not considered worthy of prolonged consideration. Thus, discussion of the elephant's exhibition was scant in the leading medical journals, and Toung Taloung was only mentioned in a brief article in the *British Medical Journal*, which discussed the elephant in a dismissive tone, stating that the "British public has been much disappointed with the

animal, which, during the past week, has been the talk of London." In
the journal's view, "a perfect 'white' elephant is a real albino and the
natural colouring-matter of the epidermis being absent, the colour of
the blood in the cutaneous vessel gives a pale pink tint to the hide."
Verifying Toung Taloung as a common elephant, "very frequently seen
in British India" and "not a fine specimen of his kind," the *BMJ* did not
compare the animal to humans or discuss human colouration and
skin diseases.[66]

Nevertheless, the non-medical press continued to speculate on the
scientific significance of the elephant. In an editorial, *The Times* immediately seized upon the medical discussion and its anthropomorphic implications, in an attempt to reassure readers and maintain the status of
whiteness. In a convoluted and confusing argument, the article stated
that Toung "should be called not a white, but a piebald elephant" that
likely suffers from a condition of the skin "not uncommon among negroes."[67] The significance of this discussion pertained to people, not to
animals. At stake were issues of racial identification and fears of racial
degeneracy. The elephant seemed to challenge taxonomies of racial
types. On the one hand, a disease which transformed black to white,
The Times argued, "may be ennobling." But what if the disease could be
cured and the transformation reversed? Taking on the racist humour so
characteristic of Barnum's showmanship, the editorial asserted, "Mr.
Barnum will never feel safe so long as Taloung sojourns in England,
that Mr. Squire might not at any moment practice his skin-curing blan-
dishments upon the fortunate victim of an ennobling malady, and turn
it as healthy a blue-black or brown plebian as its neighbours." The
newspaper then did an about-face and predicted the later use of the
elephant in soap advertisements, asserting that Toung Taloung "is [de-
finitively] not a white elephant. It is neither white all over nor in patches, and the best advertised patent soap would not whiten it sufficiently
to be accepted as white in the tempered sense of a London laundry."
Recognition of true whiteness, the newspaper asserted, was the prerogative of white Europeans, who would not be fooled by a skin condition:
"An elephant may be white to Burmese or Siamese eyes which is nothing of the sort in Regent's Park." The same article insisted that the "real
disenchantment is that of white elephants such as it there seems to be no
especial scarcity. Inability to reach a standard of pure whiteness might
be forgiven. Tuang's inexcusable guilt is that Asia apparently contains
plenty as good in the way of dirty whiteness as itself."[68] The elephant
seemed to challenge fixed categories of racial distinction and white

superiority. As such, it was not deemed white enough to be of monetary value or religious significance. The animal seemed to be a sham.

Claims of the elephant's financial worth and religious importance became increasingly dependent upon assessments of its colouration. The British public, it seems, could not accept that this ostensibly plain elephant was an object of religious merit and monetary value. They had expected the animal to be white and were disappointed by its colour. As the RSCPA's *Animal World* reported, "the same remark has rolled off the tongue of the visitors on their approaching him – 'What a shame to call him white! It's a swindle!'"[69] For their part, Barnum's representatives in London were prepared to entertain speculation about the elephant's value and religious significance, but they had trouble fending off denigrations of the elephant's colouration.

During the course of its exhibition in London, Barnum's representatives circulated rumours of the elephant's value by providing fraudulent testimonials. These documents ridiculed Buddhist religious practices and also smacked of trickery.[70] Indeed, an earlier report suggested that French missionaries had been involved in the procurement of the elephant in an effort "to break down the superstitious veneration of their proselytes for a representative of the last animal whose form was assumed by Guatama before he became Buddha."[71] To add to the confusion, *The Times* reported that "Mr. Barnum's representatives have offered a premium of £5000 for an insurance of £40,000 for one year on the life of his 'sacred white elephant' – no insurance company has been found to entertain his proposal."[72] These statements were presumably intended to continually publicize the animal's valuation and thus confirm its authenticity. This was a trick. In order for the animal to be authentic – that is, a real "white elephant" according to the English definition of the term – it had to be worthless, no matter the expense incurred at purchase.

Two self-proclaimed experts wrote to *The Times* to make this very point. By claiming that the elephant was of no financial value (or religious significance), they paradoxically confirmed the authenticity of the creature. Their opinions were based on disappointment with the elephant's colour. The first letter, signed by Robert Gordon, stated that the elephant was "a very ordinary one, such as can be purchased in Burma from £100–£140, and with no more white about him than several animals I have seen there."[73] A Mr Sanderson, superintendent of Government Elephant Catching Operations in Bengal, supported Gordon's view, asserting that "[n]either in the general colour of his body, in the flesh-coloured blotchings on his face, ears, and chest, nor in the smallest particular whatsoever, does he differ one whit from the hundreds of elephants of the commissariat … carrying the baggage of troops or dragging timber down the banks of rivers." Sanderson valued Barnum's elephant at £150–£200, and concluded by denying the existence of white elephants entirely: "We must not, however, be too hard on Mr. Barnum for not obtaining a white elephant, for the sufficient reason that such an animal does not exist." The elephants of the Burmese King, Sanderson argued, are quite ordinary except that they possess "certain 'lucky' marks."[74] These assertions validated the authenticity of Barnum's animal as a purchase for which vast sums had been paid, but which was actually worthless.

The amount of money Barnum paid for Toung Taloung remains uncertain.[75] The first announcement of the elephant's purchase in *The Times*, as we have seen, stated that the cost was £40,000. A *New York Times* article later reported that Barnum swore under oath that the elephant was worth $200,000.[76] In his autobiography of 1889, Barnum claimed he was willing to spend half a million "to procure a curiosity which centuries of unsuccessful endeavor had seemed to prove utterly unattainable."[77] The showman had apparently been trying for some time to purchase a white elephant from Southeast Asia, using the contacts of John A. Halderman, the United States minister to Siam, and later of his own agent, J.B. Gaylord, in Bangkok. Gaylord's first attempt to export a specimen failed when the elephant he acquired suddenly died. It had allegedly been poisoned by fanatical Buddhists angry that so sacred an animal had been sold for the profane purposes of circus exhibition. (There is reason to doubt the truth of this claim, since it is suspiciously similar to Bock's tale of vengeful Buddhists. The circulation of discourses, tropes, and narratives about white elephants was once again evident here.) Gaylord finally succeeded in obtaining Toung Taloung in 1883 – possibly from King Thibaw of Burma. According to A.H. Saxon, Thibaw, facing mounting encroachment by the British, was strapped for cash and agreed to the sale.[78] As we have seen, other stories of the elephant's provenance, circulated by Barnum's agents, alleged that it was acquired with the aid of French missionaries, or directly from devout Buddhists. These conflicting reports raise the possibility that Barnum actually purchased the elephant easily and inexpensively. Rumours that the animal was acquired with difficulty and at great expense may have been another ruse, but were also standard components of exhibitionary culture. To drum up excitement and attract spectators, showmen very often claimed in their promotional materials that they had acquired their exhibits after several attempts and with great difficulty.[79]

The other deception which became important for the elephant's authentication was a spectacle of Buddhist "priests" venerating the beast. This was arranged by Barnum and his agents and took place in the elephant's enclosure on 26 and 27 January 1884. These spectacles were calculated to shock British Christians, who viewed animal worship as the antithesis of proper religious conduct.[80] Before the arrival of the "priests," the nature of Buddhist religious practice was debated in letters to the editor of *The Times* and became part of the controversy associated with the elephant. Though a contested issue, this correspondence reveals a persistent unwillingness to understand the true significance of these animals, as well as the extent to which fantasies of Buddhists venerating whiteness appealed to those seeking verification of white supremacy. The possibility of animal worship excited the imagination and seemed to prove imperialist perceptions of Burmese savagery and excess. The first letter, signed only "Ayaybain," was the most sensational. Paraphrasing an anecdote published in a popular travelogue published in 1874, Ayaybain claimed that a white elephant had been honoured by "handsome well-developed young women of the respectable [Burmese] middle class, who, exposed to the waist, proudly acted as wet nurses."[81] (One can only imagine how Barnum's audience received this tale. In the Victorian imagination the submission of middle-class girls to a beast would be perceived as barbaric.) Linking this story to England's territorial ambitions in Burma, Ayaybain then confirmed British assessments of King Thibaw's weakness, stating, "And it is the more extraordinary that King Theebaw [*sic*] should allow the exportation of one possessing the critical marks." If the animal proved authentic, Ayaybain predicted, Thibaw's reign would be in danger.[82]

Other travellers and scholars protested the so-called religious spectacle. One authority on the matter, Thomas William Rhys Davids, an honorary professor of Pali and Buddhist literature at University College London, objected to the "disgraceful scene" of "Burmese priests" in the Zoo. Displaying remarkable acumen about representational politics, Rhys Davids wrote, "what should we think of men dressing themselves up in the dress of Catholic priest and going through a sham mass before a sham altar to attract the Burmese to a wild beast show in Burmah? And if it should be the descriptions [in the newspapers] that are at fault, and the men should be real Bhikkhus (which I should be

very surprised to learn), the matter would not be much bettered."[83] In a
follow-up letter one week later, Rhys Davids stated that he had "received the best possible evidence of the deep personal pain given to
Buddhists resident here [in London] by the mock ceremony against
which I felt it my duty to protest."[84] Rhys Davids, however, was a lone
voice of protest in the storm.

The arrival of the "priests" in the London Zoological Gardens was
reported by the press in a manner evincing the characteristic waffling
between a desire to collude with Barnum and an attempt to expose his
humbuggery. Not surprisingly, the "priests" were objects of media fascination from the moment they arrived in Liverpool. Their purpose was
to provide visible proof of white elephant worship in Asia. Yet, their
authenticity, according to *The Times*, was doubtful, and "the title priest
may be used in their case, probably, with some such modifications as
attached to the white elephant."[85] Nevertheless, newspapers presented
them as objects of extreme curiosity, reporting their lavish headgear,
tunics, stockings, and slippers (figure 4.4). Their religious performance
was described in a manner confirming prejudicial notions of "Eastern"
practices.[86] Newspapers were eager to decry their religiosity at the same
time as they relished reporting its details. Even if their ceremonies
seemed fraudulent, worshipping whiteness was described as the proper occupation of Eastern "priests."

At the same time, these demonstrations caused problems for the
London Zoological Society. One letter from Frederick Brine to Philip
Lutley Sclater, secretary of the Zoological Society, stated, "I don't think
the 'Sacred White Elephant' was ever in Siam. What a pity for the Z.S.
to be connected thro' Barnum's agent with such falsehood and deceit."[87] Nevertheless, some Fellows were certainly intrigued by the
spectacle. At least one wrote to the Society to inquire, "Are the two
natives priests?"[88] Other correspondents felt that the religious performances were not consistent with the scientific objectives of the Zoological Society. Their letters expressed concern for the reputation of the
organization, as well as xenophobic reactions to Barnum as an American upstart. A letter from Joseph Charlton Parr condemned the arrival of the priests, stating that such an event "might form an attraction
in an American Peep Show but for the Zoological Society to degrade
itself to such a level" was most shocking.[89] Another letter suggested
similarly that "the time has come for a prompt severance between the
Society and Mr. Barnum. The connection has never been a very desir-
able one and the Society is held responsible for every mendacious

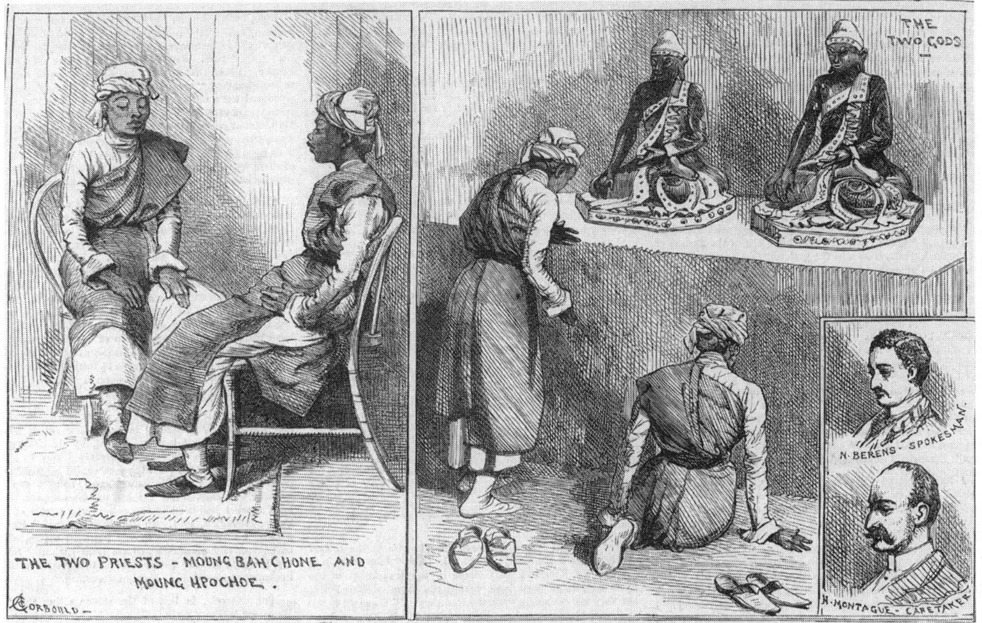

4.4. "Priests of the Burmese 'White Elephant' at the Zoological Gardens,"
Illustrated London News, 2 February 1884

statement concerning Mr. Barnum's Elephant made by his agent and we are gradually sinking from the position of one of the most reputable Societies in England to the lowest … gardens in New York."[90] The exhibition of Barnum's elephant made obvious the extent to which the Zoo was a commercial venture, alongside other venues of Victorian entertainment, and not solely devoted to science, public pedagogy, and moral erudition.

The trickery of Barnum's exhibition, in particular, threatened the credibility of the London Zoological Society. In a letter to the editor of *The Times*, a man identified only as an "Anglo-Indian" thoroughly reprimanded the organization for agreeing to house and display Toung Taloung, suggesting that there "is nothing even remarkable about this elephant. He has only a few more of the cream-coloured spots to be found on most elephants … It is humiliating to see the public taken in by such a gross piece of humbug, and the Zoological Society ought to

be thoroughly ashamed of themselves."[91] Another letter written directly to the Society by Sir Edwin Ray Lankester, a prominent zoologist,
tempered accusations he had made in the *Pall Mall Gazette* implicating
the Society in Barnum's tricks. Lankester wrote, "I say 'the press *seems*
to have entered into a conspiracy with Mr. Barnum and the Zoological
Society' to persuade people that Black is White. That of course is not a
serious hypothesis. No one imagines that the Society wishes to make
people believe that black is white."[92] The letter assures Sclater that the
imperialist integrity of the Zoological Society remained intact, though
apparently it was momentarily compromised by the exhibition of an
elephant deemed insufficiently white. Would an artificially whitened
specimen have satisfied these critics?

The Zoological Society may have agreed to house the animal because
Fellows were interested in observing its pigmentation and habits. This
is made evident by the archives of the Society, which record the arrival
of the creature as a male "'Sacred' Elephant Elephusindieus (From
Burmah)." Someone later modified the entry several times, crossing out
the word "Sacred" and replacing it with "Indian Elephant Pale Variety."
This too was changed to "Indian Elephant Mottled Variety."[93] These re-
classifications suggest, perhaps, that the elephant's colouration disappointed the Zoological Society and diminished the creature's scientific
worth. Though genuinely fascinated by the elephant, the Zoological
Society denied sanction of the so-called religious display. In this vein,
Flower, its president, wrote,

> When the Council of the Zoological Society gave permission for the ani-
> mal to be deposited in their gardens, it was with the belief that it would be
> one in which the Fellows of the society and visitors to the gardens might
> take a legitimate interest, but they are in no way responsible for the state-
> ments made about it by newspaper writers, or the adventitious excitement
> which they have created. It is perhaps hardly necessary for me to say that
> the so-called "religious rites" announced in a letter to *The Times* of to-day,
> as about to be performed in public in the presence of the elephant, will
> certainly not be permitted.[94]

Despite these meek protests, the sensational ceremonials did take place.
In a show of excess politeness that was, not surprisingly, ineffective,
Sclater wrote to Barnum's agent, stating, "I am sorry to have to trouble
you again about the Burmese Bonzes, but I hope you quite understand
that we can only permit their presence in the Gardens as ordinary

attendants upon the Elephant, and that no ceremonies of any sort or kind whatsoever are to be performed by them."[95] It is not clear why the Zoological Society was unable to stop this occurrence. Financial arrangements with Barnum were probably a decisive factor, though these are not on record.[96]

Indeed, the Zoological Society had similarly profited from a previous controversy associated with Barnum during the sale of Jumbo, another elephant, to the showman in 1882. In the months before Jumbo sailed to America, Londoners thronged to the Zoological Gardens for a chance to ride and feed their favourite beast. Admissions to the Gardens soared, and the Society reaped the proceeds.[97] In view of that incident, housing Toung Taloung was likely perceived as another lucrative opportunity for the Zoological Society.[98] Perhaps the revenue from increased admissions to the Gardens during the two months of the white elephant's residency also justified the negative publicity of the incident.[99] During its stay in the London Zoological Gardens, the elephant became a liability. Increasingly, it was felt that "Mr. Barnum's keeper ought not to have been allowed to exhibit the 'White Elephant' at the Zoo."[100]

Advertising Soap

Yet on the day Barnum's elephant was sent on to New York, the *Pall Mall Gazette* informed its readers that the "elephant has greatly improved during his stay in the Zoological Gardens, not only in flesh but in colour, being now a very light ash."[101] Somehow, the newspaper implied, the pigmentation of the beast had changed and Toung Taloung had become "whiter." The timing of this change coincided almost precisely with the decision of A & F Pears, manufacturers of Pears' soap, to use the elephant as a commercial mascot. Adopting various Barnumesque tricks, Pears' seized upon the references to soap made during the course of the elephant's sojourn in London. The animal became a consumer good linked with soap and concerns of racial hygiene. This association was important in the history of early pictorial advertising, which was in its nascence at this time. Perusing the pages of the illustrated press, a reader can easily note the sudden emergence of images in advertising, which became more common in the late 1870s and early 1880s as technologies made the production and reproduction of lithographic images more economical. Images in turn were important for the creation of brands, and soap was one of the first branded products, alongside cocoa, cigarettes, tea, patent medicines, and a handful of other product types.[102] Brand identities were not yet fixed, and products could be associated with very different ideas. A & F Pears played a particular role in this process by mounting very successful publicity campaigns which linked soap to a number of diverse concerns, including class difference, childhood innocence, and imperialism.

The managing director of A & F Pears, Thomas J. Barrett (1829–1896), was a pioneer of modern advertising and played a particular role in this process by associating Pears' soap with famous paintings and making reproductions of these images available to wide audiences. One famous example of this phenomenon began in 1886, two years after the exhibition of Barnum's elephant, when Barrett purchased the copyright to the painter John Everett Millais's "The Child's World" (1886), a celebrated portrait of childhood innocence in which a small boy sits blowing bubbles. Barrett changed the painting into an advertisement by inserting a bar of Pears' soap into the lower right corner so that it seems as if the bubbles, which so delight the child, are produced by the soap. A reproduction of the painting had already circulated in the Christmas supplement to the *Illustrated London News* in December 1886, but Pears' really popularized the image, circulating it after 1896 in the *Pears' Annual* and in different formats including postcards, showcards, and billboard posters.[103] By the 1880s, soap advertisements were also popularizing images of empire and peddling what Anne McClintock calls "commodity racism." These ads produced and reinforced colonial ideologies and sentiments.[104] Toung Taloung, as an object of European fantasy and a symbol of whiteness, seemed perfectly suited to this purpose. Advertisements figuring the elephant laid the groundwork for more famous and racist advertisements figuring people.

On 8 March 1884, a full-page advertisement for Pears' soap was published depicting a white elephant with similar markings to Toung Taloung being washed and scrubbed by an attendant resembling Radee (figure 4.5).[105] The attendant holds a bar of soap, which he has presumably used to whiten the elephant's forehead, trunk, and ears. Soap, the ad claims, has artificially whitened the elephant by washing away dirt or somehow applying whiteness. The ad capitalizes on the anxieties about racial purity articulated during Barnum's exhibition of Toung Taloung and reinstates, in visual form, the notion that the white colour of the elephant is a humorous trick. Whiteness, and the status associated with this colouration, have been conferred to the elephant by the soap.

4.5. "The Real Secret of the White Elephant – Pears' Soap,"
Illustrated London News, 8 March 1884

Viewers of the ad, presumably white Britons, are informed of the secret used to create the elephant's colouration. The caption for the advertisement states, "THE REAL SECRET OF THE WHITE ELEPHANT – PEARS' SOAP. Matchless for the Complexion." In this way the advertisement visually reinstates the narratives of white elephant forgeries that had circulated before Barnum's exhibition of Toung Taloung. In these stories, the circus proprietor exhibits an artificially whitened specimen, claiming that it is an object of worship in the "East." His white audience is aware of the hoax and complicit in the deception. Similarly, the Pears' ad discloses the secret that creates the object of veneration; it is the soap that conjures the elephant's white colour. Through the ad, white viewers were implicitly in on the trick – as presumably the Burmese who had allegedly worshipped white elephants were not.

Versions of the advertisement were published widely. One appears, for example, in a collection of clippings in the Museum of London Archives. In this ad, Pears' capitalizes further on the trickery associated with Barnum's elephant by including the following addendum:

Lord Mayor's Show.
This liberal offer was refused.
The Citizen states that the Lord Mayor and Sheriffs' Committee have received the following letter: –
"Sir, – We hear that several elephants will form part of the procession on the 10th proximo, and although you perhaps may consider the inquiry novel, we venture to think it worthy of consideration. It is to know whether your Committee is disposed to entertain an offer of £500 to paint all the elephants white, with 'Pears' Soap' in red letters on their sides. Your reply in the course of the day will much oblige. Faithfully yours.
A. and F. Pears.
38, Great Russell Street, Oct. 17. 1884."

By issuing this challenge, Pears' apparently intended to engage in similar strategies to the showman. The caption for this ad also read, "THE REAL SECRET OF THE WHITE ELEPHANT – PEARS' SOAP. Matchless for the Complexion." In this advertisement Pears' associates itself with whitewashing in the most literal sense.[106]

At the same time, in a clever reversal, these advertisements redirect the trickery associated with Barnum's exhibition towards white consumers (the implicit targets of the ads). This is made evident by the attendant's outstretched hand, which offers consumers a bar of soap to whiten and cleanse themselves. Through this gesture it is implied that human whiteness is an ephemeral condition that can be regenerated by the commodity. The ad promises white consumers the ability to pass as the whitest of whites, and maintain the social, moral, and racial benefits that the whiteness of being accords.

This advertisement, figuring the whitewashing of Barnum's elephant, was a direct precursor to another famous Pears' ad that rehearsed the same themes. Seven months later, in December 1884, Pears' released an advertisement depicting the whitening of a black child (figure 4.6). A white child, fully clothed and wearing an apron, offers a naked black child, sitting in the tub, a bar of Pears' soap. The next frame shows the "results" of the cleansing. The black child has emerged from the dirty water and is sitting on a stool. His entire body has been whitened – except for his head. The caption for the advertisement reads, "For improving & preserving the complexion." The ad claims without subtlety that the black child's complexion has been "improved" by the commodity, even if it has not been fully transformed.

This advertisement has been analysed extensively by Anne McClintock and Anandi Ramamurthy, who interpret its imagery in light of the Berlin Conference, held between November 1884 and February 1885, when representatives of the European powers gathered to partition Africa. McClintock argues that the advertisement "offers an allegory of imperial progress as spectacle," in which the soap magically regenerates the black body, washing away the stigma of racial and class degeneracy. The violence of colonial conquest and the civilizing mission, McClintock argues, are portrayed in the ad as the outcome of benign domestic processes – that is, washing.[107] Ramamurthy interprets the ad differently, suggesting that it should be understood in the context of trade competition. British soap manufacturers, she argues, wanting to secure West African supplies of the ingredients used to make soap (principally palm oil), had a vested interest in the negotiations taking place in Berlin. The image of the child happily being washed, she maintains, should be understood as a "celebratory statement from a company whose interests were tied to this trade" and also as a denial of the brutal partition of Africa carried out by European powers. The black child, she suggests, is shown to acquiesce in his own conquest: he has whitened himself. His body is therefore metonymically all African bodies submitting to British control. Britain, meanwhile, represented by the white child, shoulders the "white man's burden" in order

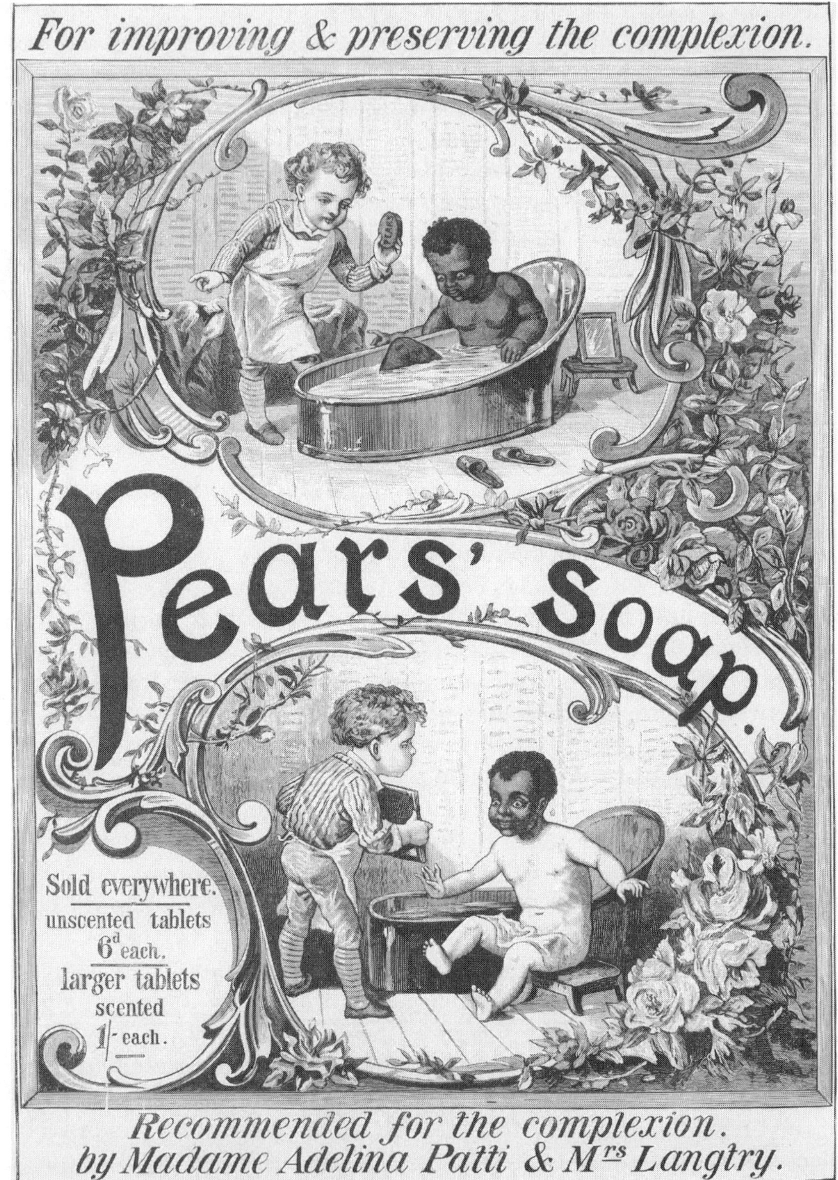

4.6. Pears' soap, *Illustrated London News*, 22 June 1885.
(This image was first published in the *Graphic* in December 1884.)

to tutor Africa in the ways of hygienic civilization.[108] Neither McClin-tock nor Ramamurthy acknowledges the extent to which the ad employs Barnumesque trickery to sell ideologies of racial hygiene to white Britons. As Joanna de Groot suggests about Ramamurthy's reading of the ads, "It is equally worth noting how these images of 'Africans' played a role in shaping British perceptions of their imperial selves."[109] From whitewashing an elephant to whitewashing a human child was but a small step. The advertisement depicting the children expressed the same racist humour as Barnum's exhibition of Toung Taloung and the ads featuring the elephant. This is made evident by the portrayal of the black child and the ways the advertisement both allays and incites fears of passing. Though his body is transformed, the child's head remains black, and this leads to two possible interpretations: either the child can never pass as white, or his face can be cleaned too. (The same suggestion is being made in advertisements figuring the elephant, since most of his body remains black, even after the washing.) Yet as he looks in the mirror, the child seems delighted at the change wrought by the washing. In this way the ad showed consumers, imbued with imperialist ideologies, what they presumably wanted and feared to see – a black child desiring to be white, but for the moment remaining essentially black. White consumers are positioned outside the advertisement, given the ability to distinguish the authentic white child from the fake. They are made complicit in the trick by holding the power to assign or withdraw the status of whiteness.

At the same time, whiteness is shown to be an arbitrary status, so that the trick rebounds on white consumers. The advertisement suggests that whiteness is not an innate or permanent condition, but a colour that must be artificially created and renewed by ministrations of soap. The caption, "Recommended for the complexion by Madame Adelina Patti & Mrs Langtry," refers not to the image of the black child being whitened or to the elephant, but to other ads featuring testimonials of famous Victorian actresses and their ivory complexions (figures 4.7 and 4.8). These ads, printed in black and white, emphasize the stark whiteness of the actresses' faces. Taken together, the imagery and wording instruct white consumers to use Pears' soap to cleanse themselves of dirt, which is figuratively linked to blackness, poverty, and lack of civilization. The ad capitalizes on fears of the precarious status of whiteness and offers Pears' soap as the solution to maintaining and creating white superiority. The soap can be used to make oneself even whiter; therefore whiteness is maintained as an arbitrary status that provokes anxiety.

4.7. Pears' soap advertisement, *Illustrated London News*, 15 March 1884

4.8. Pears' soap advertisement, *Illustrated London News*, 29 March 1884

Subsequent advertisements for Pears' soap perpetuated these anxieties, and in fascinating ways made reference to previous publicity campaigns – and, implicitly, the exhibition of Toung Taloung. For example, a famous advertisement of a woman scrubbing a young boy was featured in several newspapers and publicity campaigns, first appearing, perhaps, in the *Graphic* in 1887 (figure 4.9). The copy directly references previous ads, telling viewers that "PEARS' soap [is] recommended by Mrs. Lillie Langtry." Moreover, the image repeats several visual tropes that had been established in illustrations of Toung Taloung, so that once again viewers are presented with buckets of water and bars of soap – the same cleaning supplies that apparently served as "Necessities for a White Elephant" (figure 4.3). The intensity of the scrubbing, conveyed by the tense muscles of the woman and the puckered face of the child,

4.9. Pears' soap advertisement, *Graphic*, 5 March 1887

also mirrors the illustration of "The Great Wash" of the elephant (figure 4.2) in which we see the attendant, presumably Radee, using all his strength to scrub the creature. In these images dirt is not merely filth but also a cultural category symbolizing racial and class degeneracy. Here, once again, class is brought into discourses of race and hygiene. The hope is that degeneracy can be washed away. Whiteness is understood as something fragile that can be regenerated and reassigned to social inferiors (and equals) through cleanliness.[110] The image was powerful, and its symbolism should not be underestimated. In the 1890s a reproduction of the advertisement in canvas was placed on Yarmouth beach. This version had circular holes in place of the faces. As they enjoyed the seaside, Victorians could photograph themselves literally inside this advertisement, poking their heads through the holes and replacing the faces of the woman and child with their own. Similar portraits, with the "You Dirty Boy!" canvas, could also be taken in photographic studios.[111] In this way, the meanings of the ad were proliferated and imbibed in a variety of venues and even, presumably, taken home in photographic form to be displayed in albums and on mantels.

In this way, Barnum's exhibition of Toung Taloung became associated with definitions of whiteness and used to sell ideals of whiteness to Britons. The exhibition of the elephant had questioned the status of whiteness. Ironically, in order to be considered secure, the creature's whiteness had to be artificial. Responding to this sentiment, the Pears' advertisements exhorted consumers to create and maintain whiteness with soap – a colouration and status they already possessed. In the process, human whiteness was established as an artificial production, and a status of the most superficial kind.

American Coda

There is an American coda to this story and the ideas of racism it materialized, for it was in New York that the allusions to deception and bleaching became a terrifying reality. While Toung Taloung garnered media coverage in London, Adam Forepaugh, Barnum's chief rival and fellow circus proprietor, secretly procured an elephant of his own.[112] Forepaugh had his elephant painted in Liverpool and shipped to Philadelphia.[113] Claiming to possess the real "Light of Asia," an elephant of truly white colouration, Forepaugh managed to upstage the arrival of Barnum's elephant in New York by eight days.[114] The playbill advertising Forepaugh's elephant declared it "Too White for Barnum"

and pronounced "Barnum's 'Sacred White?' Elephant and all its Sur-
roundings a Rank Fraud."[115] Barnum, the famous trickster, was left
quite literally in possession of the genuine article, a white elephant of
mottled complexion that was of less interest than the forgery. Crowds
flocked to see Forepaugh's elephant, even after it was exposed as a
sham. Not to be outdone, Barnum bleached one of his own elephants
and advertised it as "A White Elephant Just like Forepaugh's Whitewashed One."[116] The rivalry between the two showmen ended when
Forepaugh's elephant died at the end of the season, poisoned by repeated administrations of toxic paint.

While the showmen engaged in these stunts, the discussion of racial
differentiation provoked by the exhibition of the elephants reached an
insidious pitch. The *New York Times*, never subtle in its commentary,
speculated on the human implications of the bleaching processes used
on the elephants. (This article might have been authored by Barnum.) It
is worth quoting at length:

> Mr. BARNUM'S plan of making an elephant white by artificial means in
> order to contrast it with the dark and genuine white elephant is an inge-
> nious one, but it is of less interest to elephants than it is to another class of
> our population. The inventor of the process of bleaching elephants claims
> that it can be applied without the slightest injury to colored people, and
> that it furnishes a complete answer to JOB's famous inquiry as to the pos-
> sibility of whitening an Ethiopian. The experiment now making with the
> elephant is watched by the entire population of Thompson-street with the
> utmost interest, and if it succeeds the colored man will be as rare among
> us as the sacred white elephant himself.
>
> The bleaching process, as now conducted, will not make the complex-
> ion of the colored man identical with that of the white man. The cleansed
> Ethiopian will be of a dazzling whiteness, rivaling that of the snow. The
> purest blonde of Madison-avenue will appear dark by the side of the
> beauties of Thompson-street, and what was once the white race will sud-
> denly become the colored race.
>
> It will be a curious sensation for white people to find themselves treated
> with contempt on account of their color by the bleached colored people. All
> the laws and regulations still existing which are aimed at the colored people
> will then apply to the Caucasian race. We shall have to pass a new Civil
> Rights bill to secure admission to hotels and sleeping cars, and we may
> even hear ourselves contemptuously described as "niggers," should the
> bleached colored people condescend to adopt white methods of expression.

To avoid such an embarrassing situation it is to be hoped that the bleacher of Mr. BARNUM'S elephant will find some way of accurately imitating the Caucasian complexion. In that case the ex-colored man will be distinguished from the original white man only by the quality of his hair. Probably a method of straightening Ethiopian hair and repressing the exuberance of Ethiopian lips will soon follow the grand discovery of bleaching Ethiopian skin, and in that case all distinction between the two races will at once disappear, and the negro question will vanish from our politics, never to reappear.[117]

The article makes it explicit that the exhibition of Toung Taloung was a forum to discuss theories of race. This article drew upon the conceits of the narratives of circus proprietors and sham white elephants that had circulated prior to Barnum's exhibition of Toung Taloung in London, and turned anxieties about the maintenance of racial purity and white privilege into a repulsive joke – this time perpetrated against African Americans. In post-Reconstruction America, in the context of the debate about the political future of the union which was bound up in race relations, the significance of bleaching an elephant was all the more resonant.[118] The Pear's Soap Company could not have penned it better, and indeed similar ads playing on fantasies and anxieties of racial transformation circulated in the United States.[119]

Conclusion

Curiously, the British press made almost no further mention of Toung Taloung, but allusions to white elephants appeared frequently and suggest the lasting cultural resonance of the episode – and enduring image of the white elephant.[120] In 1892 *Punch* published a satirical cartoon showing John Bull contemplating whether he should take over direct responsibility for Uganda from the British East Africa Company or permit the territory to fall into German hands. Uganda is depicted as an elephant which is uniformly and conspicuously white. His keeper, the "present proprietor," presumably a representative of the financially strapped Company, states, "See here, Governor! He's a likely looking animal, – I can't manage him. If you won't take him, I must let him go!!"[121] In this use of the term, white elephants remained symbols of Empire. The cartoon also evokes the English definition of a white elephant, suggesting that annexing Uganda as a protectorate (which occurred in 1894) represents a financial burden not worth its price.

The connection between white elephants and white superiority remained equally popular. One children's book, for example, featured a story about an ordinary elephant, Chunee, who envies the luxuries granted to his white elephant brother. The white child with whom Chunee converses explains the situation: "'I believe it was because your brother was *white*,' said Tommy, 'that they made him the Prince's elephant.'" Chunee is reluctant to agree: "'So another elephant told me once, but it couldn't be, I tell you, it's [whiteness in elephants] a great deformity. Oh, dear me, here comes my driver and the spiky thing in his hand.'"[122] The story uses the pigmentation of elephants to instruct children on the late Victorian social order, suggesting that whiteness grants privilege and blackness destines inferiority. At the same time, the story perpetuates the anxieties fostered by the exhibition of Barnum's elephant by implying that the privileges of whiteness are contextual and situational, and can be acquired quite by chance through an accident of birth whereby one brother is white and the other is an ordinary grey.

The direct association of Barnum with white elephants was also enduring. In 1894 a famous romance novel, *Dodo, a Detail of the Day*, contained the following two references:

> Jack, come and see us this evening; we're having a sort of Barnum's Show, and I'm to be the white elephant. Come and be a white elephant too. Oh, no, you can't Chesterford's the other. The elephant is an amiable beast, and I am going to be remarkably amiable.
>
> Dodo was playing the amiable white elephant to some purpose. She was standing under a large chandelier in the centre of the room, with Chesterford beside her, receiving congratulations with the utmost grace and talking nonsense at the highest possible speed.[123]

At this point in the story, Dodo, as the white elephant, plays the part of a superficial society woman. Clearly, as the quotations demonstrate, ten years after the exhibition in the Zoological Gardens, Barnum's name remained linked to the figurative meaning of a white elephant in the English language.

This chapter has shown how an elephant exhibited in the London Zoological Gardens in 1884 became an object of controversy and fantasy. The elephant was the showpiece of Phineaus Taylor Barnum, the American trickster, who set out to exploit the mythology of these creatures in a period of mounting Anglo-Burmese tension. Visitors came to the London Zoological Gardens to inspect the creature that was the subject of so much publicity. White elephants had been described in memoirs recounting voyages to Siam and Burma. These accounts articulated orientalist fantasies about these beasts. The worship of whiteness, particularly when it was manifested across the body of an animal, seemed to confirm notions of British superiority in relation to the peoples of Siam and Burma, territories that were a focus of British imperial ambition. Disappointment with the lacklustre appearance of the elephant provoked a debate over the authenticity of the animal. In the process, British imperial status and white supremacy were called into question.

The staging of the exhibition was a trick drawing on travelogues of adventurers to enact the definition of a white elephant. Barnum was particularly adept at staging shows which dramatized ideologies of race. The exhibition of Toung Taloung provided a unique challenge. He set out to enact the definition of "white elephant" in the English language. This was a derogatory term referring to something that was expensive, but worthless. It was also supposedly a beast venerated in Asia. As the authenticity of the elephant was questioned, visitors to the Zoological Gardens, scientists, newspaper editorialists, and many others played roles in verifying the status of the animal. Questions of racial definition, financial worth, and religious significance were raised and disputed. The creature's splotchy colouration was considered dissatisfying to the British public seeking confirmation of their racial supremacy.

As an object of widespread interest and debate, the animal became a consumer good linked to soap and concerns of racial hygiene. Using the image of the elephant and drawing on controversies associated with its exhibition, advertisements for Pears' soap exploited anxieties about racial purity articulated during Barnum's exhibition of Toung Taloung. The ads established the tropes for an advertisement figuring the whitewashing of a black child. Paradoxically, just like Barnum's exhibition of Toung Taloung, these images called into question British imperial status. They suggested that whiteness was an impermanent condition in need of regeneration and offered soap as the means of both staying white and becoming more white. The advertisement figuring the children ran periodically in the British press until the early twentieth century, suggesting the extent to which anxieties about racial degeneracy remained linked to a Barnumesque form of humour and trickery.[124]

Though Toung Taloung is long forgotten, white elephants became enduring symbols of excess in the English language. The expression is frequently used in the twenty-first century and the connotations of racism and white supremacy, so evident during Barnum's exhibition of the elephant and the circulation of the Pears' advertisements, still linger.

Chapter Five

Dead Things: The Afterlives of Animals

Some years ago I received a postcard, which inspired the writing of this book (figure 0.2). The postcard featured the "The Kittens' Wedding," a diorama of eighteen stuffed kittens enacting a wedding.[1] The animals have been entirely transformed into anthropomorphized objects: they are positioned upright and lavishly dressed to take on human posturing and comportment. Though the stitching and stuffing are crude and the animals seem malformed, there is an illusion of animation. Inserting the kittens into a white, middle-class Victorian drama, the vignette shows a kitten bride, wearing brocade, meeting her groom, also clothed, in front of the pulpit. Bridesmaids flank the couple in outfits of pink and cream, their finery enhanced by jewellery of blue and red beads. A kitten parson presides over the ceremony with his prayer book open at the marriage service. Other guests, clad in similarly opulent attire, look on stoically. Produced around 1890 by Walter Potter (1835–1918), an "amateur" English taxidermist, the tableau became the main attraction to Potter's museum, which featured this and other examples of anthropomorphic taxidermy. In 2001, "The Kittens' Wedding" was featured in an exhibition at the Victoria and Albert Museum;[2] in 2003, Potter's collection was sold at auction, and "The Kittens' Wedding" fetched an unexpectedly high sum, suggesting, perhaps, enduring fascination with Victorian taxidermy and nostalgia for the Victorian era. Potter's creations seemed to me worth investigating further, as vestiges of Victorian sensibilities, consumer practices, and the diverse meanings Victorians ascribed to taxidermy.

This chapter, which also serves as the conclusion to this book, works its way back to an analysis of "The Kittens' Wedding" by discussing examples of taxidermy produced in nineteenth- and early twentieth-century Britain that were located in homes and different kinds of museums. While previous scholars have examined taxidermy as spectacle, offering interpretations of its visual qualities and showing how taxidermy conveyed ambitions for colonial conquest and power over nature, I focus on the materiality of taxidermy and the ways it encapsulated contradictory ideas about the relationships between animals, objects, and people.[3] Any animal, including a pet, could become taxidermy, and the same or similar taxidermy might be used as a household ornament and then a museum exhibition. As taxidermy, animals were transformed into manufactured objects and different kinds of commodities that journeyed across empires, through zoos, and between households, taxidermists' workshops, department stores, and museums. Stuffed animals were put into human situations, integrated into human society, and subjected to the imagination in ways not possible with living animals. Made into taxidermy, animals were fashioned into possessions of surprising diversity, such as chairs, lamps, ornaments, monuments, trophies, clothing, scientific specimens, and a variety of museum installations. These objects reflected the Victorian and Edwardian belief that animals should be useful to humans, even in death. At the same time, taxidermy extended the biographies of animals and granted them diverse afterlives as dead things.

To expand on these points, I trace attitudes towards after-death treatments of humans and animals by examining the exceptional case of the utilitarian philosopher Jeremy Bentham (1748–1832). Bentham willed his own remains to be dissected and displayed, and aspired to a future in which all human corpses would serve science and remain present among the living. His vision was realized by taxidermy, through which Victorians granted animals a paradoxically animated and provocative afterlife. Given nineteenth-century beliefs about the sanctity of the human body, this could not be done to human corpses. Humans were considered higher beings and spiritual entities, and these notions were upheld through burial, while dead animals were subjected to modification and transformed into objects for everyday use and display. (There were notable exceptions to this rule, based on perceived deformity and racial difference. Those humans perceived to have abnormal bodies were sometimes treated like animals and natural history specimens, anatomized after death and preserved for future study and display. This was the final stage in a process of dehumanization.)[4] Taxidermy made visible and tangible distinctions between human, animals, and objects, and in so doing, invited consideration of those differences. Turning to Victorian beliefs about the possibility of animal afterlife and resurrection, the second part of the chapter focuses on pets and discusses taxidermy as a material manifestation of the ways Victorians managed the boundary between animal and human. The third section examines the uses and meanings ascribed to taxidermy in the home, and here I look at stuffed pets and exotic creatures. I then show that similar purposes and significations were assigned to taxidermy in museums. Even large-scale habitat dioramas, which were praised at their origin as innovations, were similar to the taxidermic displays that preceded them. Taxidermy in the home and museum brought the outside inside and distorted divisions between wild and pet, artificial and natural, and human and animal. Finally we return to the taxidermy of Walter Potter and examine it in the context of Victorian taxidermic production, as well as broader scope of human-animal relations about which this book is concerned.

The Auto-Icon

To understand the various meanings ascribed to dead animal bodies in the nineteenth century, it is helpful to consider objectifications of the human body and treatments of the human corpse at death. For this purpose we will examine the Auto-Icon of Jeremy Bentham, a highly public embodiment of one of the most significant figures of British history. The term "Auto-Icon" was a neologism Bentham invented to connote a man who becomes after death "his own statue," his "own monument," and entirely "his own image."[5] As a philosopher, jurist, and founder of modern utilitarianism, Bentham stood for efficient and responsible government, and his happiness principle, the greatest happiness for the greatest number, arguably shaped many governmental reforms in the nineteenth century.[6] Bentham was at the forefront of the intellectual and political currents of his time; he invented the panopticon, and influenced the liberalism espoused by James Mill, Edwin Chadwick, and John Stuart Mill.

Bentham's writing about the Auto-Icon offers us a way to understand the diverse meanings Victorians assigned to taxidermy. Ever the rationalist, Bentham viewed burial as a waste of resources, and saw the corpse as useful material. As early as 1796, he began to consider alternative posthumous treatments for his body. His essay, "Auto-Icon; or Further Uses of the Dead to the Living," written between 1820 and 1832, was a sustained meditation on this subject, suggesting ways that human cadavers might benefit the living. Throughout the treatise, Bentham presents a vision that is practical, maudlin and boastful, and riddled with assumptions derived from unabated confidence in his own achievements, as well as in English civilization, science, justice, and mechanization. By proposing ways for the dead to remain present among the living, he demonstrates a wish to advance medical knowledge while remaining stalwartly attached to life. His vision is fascinating for the ways it suggests diverse uses for the corpse that are scientific, educational, moral, animated, and affective. First, Bentham advocates the donation of human corpses to anatomists for dissection, a radical suggestion at the time when only the bodies of murderers consigned to the gallows could be used for this purpose. Because execution did not occur with enough frequency to ensure an adequate supply of corpses, body snatching and murder became a means of securing cadavers. Bentham's writing was consistent with his efforts to promote legislative reform that would ensure a steady supply of cadavers to anatomists in order to advance medical training.[7] Second, he promotes the preservation of human heads following mummification procedures he claims to have learned from the Maori.[8] He then specifies eleven functions of Auto-Icons, which he summarizes as follows: "1. Moral, including 2. Political; 3. Honorific; 4. Dehonorific; 5. Economical, or money-saving; 6. Lucrative, or money-getting; 7. Commemorational, including 8. Genealogical; 9. Architectural; 10. Theatrical; and 11. Phrenological."[9] Insisting that this list does not proceed in order of priority, Bentham debates each point and presents his readers with a startling vision in which the dead remain physically present among the living, imparting morality and wisdom, and inspiring action in a variety of pedagogical, ornamental, theatrical, and profitable ways. His contemporaries, and those who came after, used taxidermy for many of the same purposes.

By permitting his body to be publicly dissected, Bentham hoped to inspire his peers to abandon their religious beliefs about the inviolability of the human corpse and bequeath their bodies to science. In the eighteenth and nineteenth centuries, the handling of human bodies at death involved complicated preparations for burial. Before interment, great care was taken in cleaning, dressing, positioning, laying out, and watching over the body. The purpose of these rituals was to assist the dead in their journey to the afterlife.[10] Interment was the final measure to ensure the sanctity of the body. It was feared that violation of the corpse might sever the connection between body and soul, thereby jeopardizing the possibility of resurrection.[11] At the time, the only legal supply of corpses for anatomization came from the gallows. By denying them the possibility of resurrection, dissection was a final punishment for murderers. Anatomization was widely feared through the nineteenth century, and became even more so with the passing of Warburton's Anatomy Act in 1832, shortly after Bentham's death. The Act created a cheap, legal, and institutionalized source of bodies and led to the collapse of the body-snatching trade by permitting the unclaimed bodies of paupers who died in hospitals and workhouses to be dissected with impunity. Anatomization, which had been a final posthumous punishment for murder, now became a punishment for poverty at a time when even the very poor considered it important to bury their dead through elaborate and often expensive funerary rituals in order to maintain and assert respectability.[12] Bentham's request for posthumous dissection was a deliberate rejection of these beliefs and funerary practices in an attempt to assist scientific knowledge. Bentham denied himself the possibility of life after death according to the common sense of his times, and gave himself instead a new form of secular and utilitarian afterlife through posthumous display.[13]

In having his body preserved as an Auto-Icon, Bentham willed the transformation of his remains after dissection into an object for everyday use, much like nineteenth-century taxidermy. Indeed, the similarity between "Auto-Iconism" and taxidermy was not lost on Bentham and was presumably important for the conception of his plans. The first line of the "Auto-Icon" essay refers to the preservation of animals and provides a framework for his discussion of human preservation: "Various are the means by which animal bodies have been preserved from ages."[14] Consider the image of the Auto-Icon, which makes this connection clear (figure 5.1). Bentham's Auto-Icon rests inside a mahogany box, which is essentially a museum display case fashioned to contain his remains, and today the box is located in the South Cloisters of the main building of University College London. Bentham is seated, according to his wishes, in what is meant to be understood as a philosophical repose, a posturing of static activity and quiet contemplation. Wearing Bentham's clothes and holding his walking stick, the Auto-Icon is adorned by material culture carefully chosen to represent the deceased. The face is made of wax. In an ironic twist, Bentham's head was horribly blackened and misshapen during the preservation process (as happened to many taxidermic specimens that rotted or came apart).[15] It was judged too ghoulish to adorn his skeleton. Bentham looks deformed because he is stuffed in a similar manner to a nineteenth-century taxidermic mount – except his clothing functions as a skin. (After dissection, most of his skin was gone, though some was

5.1. Jeremy Bentham's Auto-Icon. Photograph by Cassel Busse

preserved and is now in the collection of the Wellcome Institute.)[16] His skeleton was surrounded by wire, tow, hay, cotton wool, wood, and paper ribbon, which were the same substances that gave shape to many nineteenth-century stuffed animals, and his clothes hold everything together.[17] The Auto-Icon was assembled under the supervision of an anatomist, Dr Southwood Smith, explicitly chosen by Bentham to carry out his wishes for public dissection and display.[18]

What Smith did with the Auto-Icon strengthens the connection between it and other nineteenth-century taxidermy. At first the Auto-Icon was installed in Smith's London home, where it was seen by many visitors. Later it was loaned to the artist Margaret Gillies and then donated to University College London in 1850. Until 1897 the Auto-Icon was kept from public view, presumably because it was a source of embarrassment, and then moved to the University's Anatomical Museum. It was relocated to the Library in 1926. It spent a brief period in the Professors' Common Room and was eventually moved to its present location in the South Cloisters of the University's main building.[19] In 1939 and 1981 it was reassembled and cleaned for conservation.[20] Through all this, Bentham became a dead thing kept for decorative use, didactic enlightenment, intellectual interest, and sentimental purposes. All this suggests that Bentham's Auto-Icon was similar to taxidermy and put to diverse uses – as a parlour ornament and museum specimen, at various times as an object of science, affect, and pedagogy, and in all other guises as an object of curiosity.

The philosopher, it should be noted, would not have been displeased with this outcome, though it does not quite fulfil the grander edifying or scientific aspects of his vision. The Auto-Icon essay indicates that Bentham imagined a diverse use-value for the Auto-Icon, which was alternately moral, animated, affective, scientific, or educational, and always provocative. He wanted it to serve as a tactile and mnemonic device capable of recalling his greatest accomplishments and inspiring others to similar action. Placed in a museum or lecture hall, for example, it might serve as a phrenological specimen that could be compared to other heads and supposedly prove the superiority of white men. He also describes his Auto-Icon serving future Benthamites by acting as the chairman of his own fan club. He writes, "But when Bentham has ceased to live, (in memory will he never cease to live!) whom shall the Bentham Club have for its chairman? Whom but Bentham himself? On him will all eyes be turned – to him will all speeches be addressed."[21] He also crafts dialogues between his

Auto-Icon and important politicians, ideologues, and philosophers to occur as performances. He envisions these as puppet shows staged for the "moral edification of the lower orders." In a curious application of automata, he suggests his Auto-Icon could be rigged to appear lifelike by "means of strings or wires, by persons under the stage" and "made to move in so far as needful or conducive to keeping up the illusion, the hands and feet, one, more or all." The voice would be supplied and "made to appear from the vocal organs of the figure; the body, if necessary, might, by obvious contrivances, be made to appear to breathe."[22] Through this theatricality, the Auto-Icon would become a monument to Bentham's achievements in life and an inspirational legacy of his social and intellectual status.

Other Auto-Icons were not granted the same glory in Bentham's fantasy of after-death embodiment.[23] Rather like taxidermy, these other heads might be displayed anywhere: inside apartments, cupboards, mausoleums, temples, museums, or lecture rooms. Decay and discolouration would not hinder their exhibition, since they could be occasionally repaired and "varnished as pictures are varnished [with paint], and thus perpetually renovated."[24] Exhibited wherever people spend time, Auto-Icons would supervise the living and set a moral example. The heads, for instance, might serve justice by inspiring confessions from the guilty; they could police lines of genealogy by providing physical evidence of lineage; they might show evolutionary progress as museum specimens or be called to account on behalf of the dead through the creation of an Auto-Icon statute law.[25] The living could in turn pass judgment on the dead by displaying the Auto-Icon toppled or resting upright according to changes of opinion.[26] Bentham anticipated a future in which preserved heads would preside over every aspect of daily life and interact with the living.

Perhaps not surprisingly, this vision held little appeal for Bentham's contemporaries. People did not heed his call to preserve themselves in this way (though responses to Gunther von Hangens's "Body Worlds" exhibitions might mark a shift in this trend). Many were appalled by the scope of Bentham's fantasy and the prospect of self-objectification that it implied. Though the authenticity of the essay is not in doubt, some of Bentham's friends and associates suspected it of being forged. Others were embarrassed by its contents and thought it detracted from his legacy.[27] As a result, the Auto-Icon essay was excluded from a compendium of Bentham's writings compiled after his death and virtually ignored for the next hundred years.[28] For many years, the Auto-Icon itself was hidden from view and consigned to storage in University College London. Given the strength of popular beliefs about the inviolability of the human body at death, in all probability it could not have been otherwise. In his own century, it seems, Bentham's vision, with all its contradictory rationality, sentimentality, and egotism, could only be realized across the bodies of animals preserved as mnemonic furnishings, moral lessons, didactic instruments, affective embodiments, and purposeful provocations.

Animal Afterlives

The ways Victorians handled the bodies of dead animals reveal a strong contrast between perceptions of humans and animals. Whereas Victorians went to great lengths to ensure that most human bodies remained intact at death, they directly interfered with animal corpses to create taxidermy. As Katherine Grier points out, taxidermy posits a particular kind of connection between animals and objects, whereby the animal is transformed into an artefact but remains recognizably embodied as its animal self[29] – unlike, for example, a leather coat, whose material origins are disembodied, abstracted, and recalled through the mental effort of associating the coat to the cow. To create taxidermy, the skin of the animal was removed, stuffed, and mounted in a lifelike position – though early techniques varied and sometimes skeletons were wrapped in material to provide the structure of the mount. Taxidermy transformed animals into manufactured objects. One set of directions, for example, described the processes of using animal remains as craft materials in great detail:

> The skin of the monkey being extended on the table, we take the end of the nose with the left hand; thrusting it again into the skin, we receive the bony head with the right hand, which we have introduced into the neck. We anoint it with the preservative, and then introduce some chopped flax, with pincers or forceps, about every part of the head where flesh or muscles existed. After which we pass the long piece of iron wire into the middle of the skull, anoint the skin of the head with a small brush, and restore it to its place.[30]

Though the description is quite graphic, nineteenth-century taxidermists seem to have been indifferent to the gory aspects of their craft, and only one author itemized "1 good stomach and a clear head" as the final entry on a list of essential equipment for the job.[31] The point of these efforts was to produce some semblance of naturalness, and successful specimens hid the immense efforts involved in their manufacture to appear whole and fleshy – as alive or naturally dead as possible. The best taxidermy was thus a conceit that erased all traces of making, while badly executed specimens were bloated or saggy, showed stitch marks, and could be coming apart at the seams.[32]

Good taxidermy was difficult to produce and required equipment, technique, technological savvy, persistence, and imagination. While some Victorians became accomplished taxidermists, others acknowledged that they lacked the skill to create lifelike specimens. Many middle- or upper-class hunters, collectors, adventurers, and ordinary pet keepers created their own specimens and also called on the services of tradesmen who were taxidermists. When bagging exotic game, the hunter's adventures were often supported by indigenous locals who undertook the initial steps to preserve the animal for transport.[33] Animals from zoos, menageries, and circuses were also preserved as taxidermy. Tradesmen-taxidermists offered customers a variety of services including the stuffing of dead pets, the fashioning of animal furniture, and the preservation of specimens collected on scientific voyages and hunting expeditions. The difference between the dilettante and the tradesman-taxidermist was one of class, and by the late eighteenth century, taxidermy had become a business venture and consumer service. Though some taxidermists became highly acclaimed and worked collaboratively in large workshops, most were only marginally successful and needed to supplement their incomes with other trades. This resulted in various combinations, such as "Barber and Taxidermist" or "Hairdresser, Perfumer, Bird Preserver, Tobacconist, Stationer, Jeweller and seller of Berlin Wool and Fancy Goods."[34] By the 1880s, nearly every village had its own resident taxidermist, who was such a stock figure that the *Illustrated London News* described him as the "simple village practitioner of pretty and pleasing art" (figure 5.2). In 1891, nearly a thousand men and women were pursuing the trade.[35] In London, there were as many as 122 women and 247 men employed as animal and bird preservers.[36] At the turn of the twentieth century, department stores also offered services to mount big game, smaller animals, and pets as "Trophies, Museum Specimens, or useful and ornamental" household articles. One ad in the catalogue for Harrod's Department Store provides a set of "Directions to Customer" on how to cure the skins of these animals in preparation for transport to the taxidermist.[37] This suggests that even when individuals procured the services of taxidermists, they often performed the initial anatomization of the animals themselves. We can also infer from the widespread availability of equipment and advice on the best way to produce taxidermy that many Victorians, including men, women, and some children, had experience of crafting taxidermic artefacts.[38]

Taxidermy was not a controversial treatment of the animal corpse in the Victorian era. Unlike human bodies after death, animals could be anatomized and preserved with few qualms, suggesting, perhaps, that animals were viewed as things, or as thing-like, while people were distinct from the animal world and ensouled. These beliefs, though widespread, were occasionally contested, and alternative views were put forward.

A minority of people in fact believed in the animal soul. In the late eighteenth century, the Methodist leader John Wesley (1703–1791) preached the existence of the animal soul as part of his campaign for the humane treatment of animals as fellow beings.[39] By the mid-nineteenth century, religious leaders, writers, and activists who wrote on this subject tended to be an exclusive group with exceptional talent and dedication to philanthropic causes, including, in many cases, animal rights and anti-vivisection. For these individuals, the notion that animals were ensouled was important in making the case that beasts, like humans, had the capacity to experience pain.[40] Some ordinary pet keepers also believed that their pets had souls, but it is unlikely that they were in the majority. The work of John George Wood (1827–1889), a popular science writer, sheds light on this matter. In 1874 Wood published a two-volume work, titled *Man and Beast: Here and Hereafter*, in which he argued for the possibility of an animal afterlife. This book included an anecdote about reactions to Wood's previous writings on the subject. Wood notes that most periodicals approved of his opinions, with the exception of those that were published by religious societies. He was also "inundated with letters" from individuals expressing various reactions to his arguments. This correspondence expressed a mix of opinions:

> Many of them were written by persons who had possessed favourite animals, and who cordially welcomed an idea which they had long held in their hearts, but had been afraid to express. Many were from persons who were seriously shocked at the idea that any animal lower than themselves could live after the death of the body.

5.2. "The Bird-Stuffer," *Illustrated London News*, 15 November 1884

> Some were full of grave rebuke, while others were couched in sarcastic
> terms.[41]

Some commentators dismissed Wood's ideas, though others expressed eagerness to be reunited with animals in the next stage of existence. While the samples Wood provides may not be representative of the Victorian population at large, they suggest that speculation about the existence of an animal soul was topical in the latter half of the nineteenth century, and that opinion on the matter was divided – especially when it came to discussions of pets. Yet these beliefs had very little impact on posthumous treatments of most animals, including pets, used as materials for tanneries, glues, and leatherworks, or discarded, buried, or preserved as taxidermy.

When pets died, pet keepers articulated their grief in various ways. Towards the end of the century, animal obituaries, published in newspapers, announced grief and offers of condolence. Some notices were quite heart-wrenching in their anonymity. In a column titled "In Remembrance Of," *Household Pets* published brief epithets such as "Faithful Bob, homely, but true, died July 3," or "Little Dick, whose song was hushed June 30."[42] The newspaper *Fur and Feather* particularly mourned the demise of animals that had won prizes at shows: "We are sorry to hear that Mrs. Greenwood has lost her handsome little smoke queen Lady Southampton, who died some weeks back."[43] Pets may have been interred in gardens or local environs, but pet cemeteries were not a widespread phenomenon in nineteenth-century Britain. The first pet cemetery in England was located in Hyde Park, London and founded in 1881.[44] When it closed in 1915, the Hyde Park cemetery contained three hundred graves, mostly of dogs, though some cats, canaries, and monkeys were also buried there (figure 5.3). The stones marking the graves were decorated with epitaphs, as moving as the animal obituaries, stating, for example, "Here lies 'Tip,' Sept. 8, 1888" or "'Mona,' born 2nd November, 1878, died 15th August, 1892. Loved, mourned, and missed."[45] These dedications memorialized affection for deceased pets, and some revealed hope that pet owners would be reunited with their pets in the afterlife.[46] According to newspaper reports, Victorians were enthralled with these messages and the "beautiful … devotion [to dead pets] one sees" there.[47] We should nevertheless be careful about over-emphasizing the importance of the Hyde Park cemetery as emblematic of Victorian attitudes towards animal death. The existence of this establishment was exceptional, probably because for most of the

THE DOGS' CEMETERY
(HYDE PARK).

5.3. "The Dogs' Cemetery (Hyde Park)." From Frances Simpson,
"Cat and Dog London," 258

century there were severe shortages of urban graveyard space.[48] More-over, the animals interred in this cemetery had upper-class owners who could afford the luxury of burying their pets. Taxidermy may have been a more popular option for grieving pet owners, and pet-keeping manuals, such as the *Book of Home Pets*, included a chapter on "Preparing and Stuffing Birds and Animals," indicating that preservation as taxidermy was a routine of pet keeping. Even less prestigious pets, associated with the working classes, such as rabbits, could be preserved in this way, as the following joke published in a penny newspaper makes clear:

"A nice husband you are!" said madam, in a passion. "You care less about me than about those pet animals of yours. Look what you did when your lop, Azor, died." Husband (quietly): "Well, I had him stuffed." Wife (exasperated): "You wouldn't have gone to that expense for me – not you, indeed!"[49]

The humour in the joke relies on distinctions between treatments of humans and animals after death. Jealous of her husband's affection for his rabbits and the ways this affection has been materialized through taxidermy, the wife accuses him of caring more for his pets than he does for her. The husband responds by implying a distinction between the posthumous treatment of human and animal bodies.

Pet keepers demanded that any affection they demonstrated towards pet animals be reciprocated in extreme ways, even after the animal's death. Preserving pets as taxidermy was a common practice, even discussed in a lecture at the London Mechanics' Institute in 1859, an association composed of "respectable" working-class men and women. This lecture on pet keeping was a component of the curriculum offered by the Institute. Taxidermy was considered a (final) routine of pet keeping and one of the ways a pet could serve its owner.[50] Once stuffed, the dead pet could remain present in the household as a useful monument or ornament. One observer commented in 1896, as if this was evident, "Of course the idea of turning into useful articles pets that have died from natural causes or old age is at once ingenious and praiseworthy."[51] Similarly, a taxidermist claimed in 1912, "An animal that has been a faithful friend and companion to man during its lifetime, may in this way [as taxidermy] claim a fuller recompense in death than mere burial and subsequent oblivion."[52] For these reasons, perhaps, pet-keeping manuals, including *The Book of Home Pets*, gave instructions on preparing and stuffing birds and animals.[53]

From Pet to Furniture

Pets could be transformed into taxidermy for various purposes, and sometimes to provide an outlet for mourning. Pets resurrected as taxidermy could function as mnemonic furnishings commemorating the past life of the animal. As in Bentham's vision for Auto-Icons, taxidermy allowed the living to interact with the dead as part of domestic routine. For example, we can infer that the owner of a cat named Oliver, transformed into taxidermy between 1896 and 1905, grieved his passing, but also wanted the cat to remain present after his death (figure 5.4). As taxidermy, Oliver is carefully seated, well groomed, and seemingly alert; he is carefully positioned next to a small silver slipper and

5.4. "Oliver," cat under dome, no: 2002.134, Museum of London,
© Museum of London

the remains of a floral bouquet, now badly decomposed, under a glass dome with an oval wooden base. In life, Oliver was the pet and companion of a woman living in Charlton; as taxidermy, he became a material memory and household furnishing – and remained present in the very spaces where he had lived his life. Kept even after the death of his owner, Oliver was donated to the Museum of London in 2002, and became a remnant of London's social history. Through his long afterlife, it seems, Oliver has been a provocative object.

Other pet keepers were perhaps not as appreciative of their stuffed pets, and rejected the material memories created by taxidermists. Bereaved pet owners wanted taxidermists to somehow create specimens that conveyed the personality of the living pet.[54] Many had unrealistic expectations of the taxidermist's craft and sometimes sought literal resurrection of their pets, which taxidermy could not provide.

Transformed into objects, dead pets could provoke a variety of emotional responses, including humour. One photograph of a Victorian family demonstrates how taxidermy could be a source of amusement (figure 5.5). This photograph shows women and children seated in a plush parlour or drawing room. Two children open the door and peer in on the scene, quite possibly with mischievous intent. The attention of the group is monopolized by a cat perched on the table with one paw extended threateningly over the lip of a rather large fishbowl. Though captured by the photograph in a pose of animation, the cat, as Jennifer Calder notes, is "ominously stuffed-looking."[55] The stiff posture and ruffled fur provide the animal with a staged quality which is matched only by the theatricality of the photograph: this is not the austere portrait of Victorian domestic life to which we are accustomed. The stuffed cat provides the focal point of the scene to represent domestic harmony through merriment. This cat is no less affective than Oliver, but the feelings it inspires are entirely different. In this scene, taxidermy provides humour. Part of the humour, perhaps, was the implicit acknowledgment that taxidermy entailed a thorough and permanent domestication of the animal and its unruly nature. Taxidermy provided opportunities for Victorians to make animals submit to human needs, wants, and fashions.

In other moments, the transformation of the pet into taxidermy allowed pet keepers to innovatively use the pet's body, as the case of the "Pet Monkey Holding Candelabra" indicates (figure 5.6). This creation was part of a late nineteenth-century trend in which animals and birds were transformed into lamps. According to one source, these objects

5.5. "Family Portrait." From Jennifer Calder, *The Victorian Home*, 24

5.6. "Pet Monkey Holding Candelabra," *Strand Magazine* (July 1896): 274

provoked such a craze that "defunct simians from the Zoo" were eagerly bought up, and Charles Jamrach, a famous wild beast importer, "was vexed with orders for *dead* monkeys." Anyone desiring to keep up with the latest fashions could therefore commission one of these furnishings – once again using commodity chains, between home, taxidermist zoo, and empire. By these means, wealthy Britons could purchase trophies and decorate their homes with spoils of empire, even if they did not kill the creatures themselves. The monkey used to make this lamp had apparently been a favoured pet. In her grief, the owner "resolved to have her dead darling turned into something useful as well as ornamental." She "couldn't bear to think of the poor little thing as a mere stuffed specimen grinning idiotically beneath a glass case." As exotic furniture, the monkey continued to serve its owner, caught forever in a pose of subservience. This positioning was ironically commemorative and deliberately comical, like the cat in the photograph discussed above, since apparently in life the monkey "had been phenomenally active – tweaking the noses of dignified people" in a most irritating way.[56] The transformation of the monkey into candelabra was therefore also an act of conquest through which the owner asserted final control over the animal and its rascally nature.

Exotic Objects

A variety of exotic specimens could also be refashioned for domestic use, and these objects, like the monkey candelabra, suggest that when it came to taxidermy, pets and even wild animals could be brought inside and treated as household furnishings, made into trophies, decoration, and objects of edification, utility, and affect.[57] This taxidermy could be freestanding and exposed to the air, used to upholster furniture, or mounted on wood blocks, panels, and shields, as well as placed under glass domes and cabinets. Panels and shields holding dismembered heads and sometimes feet were considered elegant frames for home décor, while glass domes and cabinets kept animal bodies pristine by guarding against dust and insect attacks.[58] (By the 1890s, according to the satirical novel *Diary of a Nobody*, stags' heads were such popular household décor that those with limited means and aspiring to middle-class status purchased imitations made out of plaster-of-Paris and coloured brown!)[59] Cases could be designed to permit viewing from a variety of vantage points and elaborately carved to add to the ornamentation.[60] Animals inside cases were artistically arranged and often placed on foliage manufactured out of bits of grass, flowers, cardboard, crumpled newspaper, and papier-mâché and set against a painted background. In crafting these tableaux, many taxidermists attempted to imitate the work of animal illustrators and painters, such as Harrison Weir and Edwin Landseer.[61] (Painters, in turn, relied on taxidermy to achieve realism, sometimes with disastrous results such that painted animals looked dead and deformed.)[62] Some taxidermists were also inspired to create household ornaments which resembled still life paintings. In this spirit, one manual advised its readers as follows:

> One of the finest ways to display a bird to be represented as *dead* is on a panel. Bunches of snipe, duck, geese and grouse prepared in this way make handsome dining room ornaments. Squirrels, rabbits and other small mammals may be arranged in the same manner. Be sure that your specimen looks *dead*.[63]

The emphasis on death made this taxidermy a boldly expressive celebration of bounty, sacrifice, and predation – and conveyed similar iconography to that found on other dining-room furnishings, such as ceramic tableware, sideboards, and paintings. By decorating the dining room in artful ways, these objects showed the earthly origins of food and the predatory means of acquiring it.[64] Such elaborate displays drew attention to the preserved animal, but also made taxidermy part of and consistent with other items of domestic furnishings made out of ceramics, textiles, glass, and wood.

Taxidermy could be didactic as well as decorative, and contemporaries were aware of connections between taxidermy in middle-class homes and the growing enthusiasm for natural history. In 1840, for example, William Swainson (1789–1855), the ornithologist, botanist, and entomologist, described the pedagogical benefits of filling drawing rooms and windowsills with beautiful specimens:

> In nothing has the growing taste for natural history so much manifested itself as in the prevalent fashion of placing glass cases of beautiful birds and splendid insects on the mantel pieces or the side-table. The attention of the most indolent is attracted, the curiosity of the inquisitive awakened; and thus a first impulse may be given, particularly to youthful minds, to tastes and studies which may prove the solace and delight of after years.[65]

These comments articulate the belief, shared by other authors of manuals on taxidermy, that the display in domestic spaces promoted enthusiasm for natural history and even influenced the development of this science. Moreover, taxidermy was believed to enhance appreciation for living animals, "arous[ing] in the mind of youth an intelligent interest in the beautiful and wonderful varieties of the animated creation, and do as much to refine and elevate the popular taste."[66]

Displayed in spaces where Victorians lived and worked, taxidermy could convey general impressions of nature, brought indoors and domesticated, as well as moments of personal triumph. Trophies made from "whole animals and parts of animals" were lauded as particularly respectable "articles of furniture and general utility."[67] Consider, for example, the "Chair Made from a Baby Giraffe" (figure 5.7). This is a hunting trophy, probably owned by an aristocrat, made "useful" as a chair; like the monkey lamp, it encapsulates a multifaceted narrative of intimate human-animal relations. The giraffe has been hunted, dismembered, and fashioned into a domestic object, now used to upholster and adorn a chair. Each time the wealthy hunter reclines in this seat, sitting on and within the giraffe, he once again partakes in the conquest of the animal. (Anyone else who sits in the chair will also share the experience.) In the photograph we see an unusual pairing that would never occur in nature. The hunter's Scotch terrier is seated on the chair, ensconced within the giraffe. The pet and chair are objects of conspicuous consumption; together they represent the domestication of animals and their absent owner. In this way, trophies collected during hunting expeditions or purchased from taxidermists became especially noteworthy household furnishings. Such objects make evident the ways Victorians inscribed human histories onto animal bodies.

Other items had similarly tall tales attached to them, which, whether true or not, endowed the killing of the beast with moral purpose and magnified the esteem of the owner who presented himself as noble hunter. For example, a tiger chair in which the seat is covered by "the beautifully-marked skin, and the head and paws are so arranged as to give an impression that the terrible animal is about to spring," was made for a gentleman in the Indian Civil Service. The chair was apparently "particularly interesting from the fact that the tiger was a dreaded man-eater, which had devastated and appalled several villages in Travancore."[68] The narrative cast the white hunter as a saviour: by

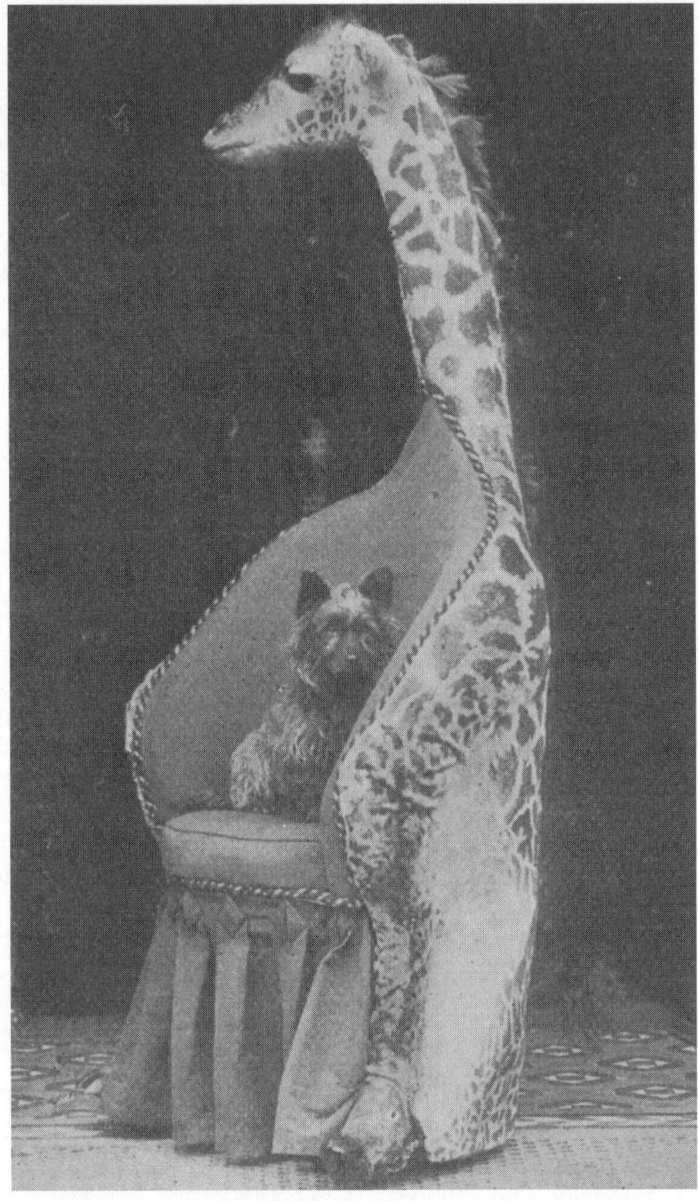

5.7. "Chair Made from a Baby Giraffe." From Fitzgerald, "Animal Furniture,"
Strand Magazine (July 1896): 274

killing the animal, he freed the village from the tiger's scourge. The hunter could relive this feat every time he reclined in the chair. Recollection of imperial adventure could be taken even further, as occurred with the transformation of an "accommodating" baby elephant, shot in Ceylon. The animal is seated "in a perfectly natural position, but adapted for the use of the hall porter. The hall porter asleep in this singular chair, by the way, should make an interesting picture."[69] This chair was apparently designed to be the seat of a servant and functioned as a conspicuous symbol of hunting prowess, wealth, and class dominance (figure 5.8). Similar items produced out of the hides of exotic animals were made for wealthy clientele, including boxes, candlesticks, and photograph frames.[70] These items presumably took on new meanings as they were used by different individuals (or species): aristocratic owners, hunters, ladies, porters or other servants, and pets. The same item could be affective in different ways by imparting lessons, materializing memory, or representing accomplishment, aspiration, morality, humour, wealth, servitude, and fashion. As taxidermy, hunted game and exotic animals took on paradoxically animated afterlives, consistent with Bentham's vision in which the dead provide perpetual service to the living. Similar purposes were assigned to taxidermy in Victorian museums.

Inside Museums

Nineteenth-century museums of natural history contained taxidermy that was as diverse as that in the home, and sometimes the same taxidermy might be used as a household ornament and then a museum exhibition, as one classified advertisement in the *Bazaar, Exchange and Mart* makes clear: "Fine stuffed seal, right for museum or gentleman's hall. Price 10s. 6d."[71] Through taxidermy, museums presented visions of the natural world that were highly stylized and similar to those found in Victorian homes. Like taxidermy in the home, taxidermy in museums could be simultaneously or alternately mnemonic, moral, didactic, affective, and provocative – indeed, these were its purposes. Museums brought the outside inside for public consumption and created artificial visions of animal life that were paradoxically praised as realistic and natural.

Connections between domestic and museum taxidermy were not coincidental because museums were formed out of private collections, and sometimes homes of the wealthy became museums, displaying

5.8. "Small Elephant Made into a Hall-Porter's Chair,"
Strand Magazine (July 1896): 279

diverse objects that were amassed according to the tastes of an individual collector. This was the case, for example, with the collections of tea merchant Frederick John Horniman (1835–1906), which were originally exhibited in his home in Surrey House, Forest Hill. Horniman started collecting in the 1860s and opened his house to the public as "The Horniman Free Museum" in 1891.[72] Most of the collection was acquired by missionaries, hunters, dealers, friends, and other travellers who collected on Horniman's behalf, and the collection represented Horniman's idiosyncrasies and interests, but it was also intended to be entertaining and educational to a broader public. The geographical range of the collection represented the expanding British Empire and associated conquests, such that several months after the sack of Benin in 1897, for example, several objects from the Benin palace were displayed in the museum. Rooms mixed taxidermy, including anthropomorphic taxidermy, with ethnographic objects. By presenting a complex vision of "marvels from many lands," the Horniman Free Museum encouraged visitors to reflect on their place in the broad order of nature and expanding empire.[73] In one room, for example, visitors might encounter a stuffed African lion; porcelain from Dresden, Japan, and France; a case of "Marine Monsters," including starfish and two examples of mermaids and mermen; a case of hummingbirds; weaponry and hukkas from India; and "articles" from New Guinea. Other rooms contained "freaks," such as three-legged animals, and portraits of eminent Victorians. The collection eventually expanded to such an extent that the Horniman family moved out of the house, and in 1898 the house was pulled down and a new museum was built on the site, donated to the Corporation of London and opened in 1901. At the closing of the Horniman Free Museum, one million visitors had been through its rooms.[74]

These displays offered Victorians uniquely close encounters with foreign and fierce animals; as such they could also be entertaining, inspiring illicit fun – especially when the animals were not displayed under glass. Thus, in one photograph, possibly from the Horniman Free Museum, we see a young boy sitting astride a polar bear, while a young girl stands by its hindquarters on the fake rockery holding on to what looks like a snowshoe (figure 5.9).[75] (These are the children of the curator Richard Quick, and the photograph may have been taken after hours or during renovations of the museum.) This photographic moment, like the picture of the dog sitting in the giraffe chair, makes evident the ways taxidermy involved a form of domestication by taming beasts in death; it also shows the extent to which it was possible to

5.9. Photograph of curator Richard Quick's children with polar bear
before the bear was transferred to the new museum circa 1901.
© Horniman Museum and Gardens

partake in the conquest of animals preserved as taxidermy – and incorporate animals, now dead, into personal histories and experiences.[76]
(These children likely never forgot their encounter with the Arctic bear.)
The moment captured by the photograph reminds us that taxidermy
rendered even the fiercest beasts inert, touchable, and subject to human
whim in ways aspired to, but not possible, in spaces like the Zoo, where
fierce animals could and did injure visitors who sought such close encounters. Moreover, the temptation to touch some stuffed creatures was
clearly impossible to resist.

The transition away from antiquarian display in the new Horniman Museum entailed a reorganization of the collection for pedagogical purposes, and many of the animals were now displayed under glass. The collection was more rigorously divided into categories of "Art" and "Nature," separating the anthropological and zoological artefacts. The zoological displays underwent considerable transformation so that by 1903 they were explicitly scientific and intended to educate museum visitors about evolution, as the guidebook stated:

> To be understood thoroughly the labels should be read in due order from the beginning. The subjects dealt with are – Terms used in classification, Variation, Sexual Differences, Struggle for Existence, Natural Selection including Adaptation and Mimicry, Life History of the Species and Races, and similar parts in Different Animals.[77]

A photograph of the natural history gallery from 1913 illustrates this description, showing displays of smaller animals that are fairly staid, each animal presented against a blank background (without representation of flora) and next to others.[78] Presumably such arrangements encouraged visitors to compare the animals presented together on a single shelf and were intended to be more pedagogical than entertaining.[79] Such arrangements displayed each animal as an exemplar of its species, in much the same way as animals were displayed in the Zoo. In contrast, the large cases in the centre of the room contained large animals – polar bear, walrus, reindeer, moose, sheep, deer, and lion – in poses that are more suggestive of liveliness. By 1913, the animals were presented under glass and no longer accessible to touch, yet theatricality remained: the polar bear featured in the photograph with the children was still standing on top of chunks of ice, presumably made from papier-mâché; the animal's left paw speared a seal, and its expression was fierce, with teeth bared.

The drama of the display is created by the positioning of the animal, which makes the beast seem lively and dangerous. In this display, the bear looks animated, possibly because it was first featured in a collection of the explorer J.H. Hubbard at the Canadian Court of the Colonial and Indian Exhibition of 1886 and was intended to convey a contrived impression of the animal as it might behave in nature. Horniman purchased the bear, as well as other specimens displayed at the Exhibition, including a large walrus, from Hubbard.[80] Like other acquisitions, these animal-objects circulated through imperial networks of exchange, and Horniman's Museum offered visitors glimpses of distant lands and peoples within the British Empire.[81]

Several international exhibitions in the second half of the nineteenth century provided opportunities for British collectors and taxidermists to purchase specimens and learn taxidermic techniques from foreign colleagues. By developing their methods of exhibition, taxidermists from the 1860s onwards sought to imitate the artistry of the tableaux mounted in these exhibitions, which were often very large in scale and designed to draw attention. The taxidermy created by Hermann Ploucquet and displayed at the Great Exhibition of 1851 had a particular influence on British taxidermists.[82] Ploucquet exhibited a diverse array of taxidermy, including pieces that "represented a boar-hunt and a stag-hunt of the natural size, and the same in miniature; groups and nests of different birds of prey; several hawks pouncing upon their prey; [and] numerous groups, in which stuffed animals are made to imitate the attitudes and actions of men, with such an expression of comic intelligence."[83]

Ploucquet's displays received rave reviews in nineteenth-century English newspapers, and allegorical and sensational taxidermy, similar to Ploucquet's stag-hunt and boar-hunt, remained popular in subsequent decades, influencing the production of other dioramas.[84] For example, specimens mounted between 1860 and 1876 by Rowland Ward, who created the giraffe chair, tiger chair, and elephant hall-porter's chair, were lauded as particularly good. A sensational piece designed by Jules Verneaux in 1867, in which a mannequin of an Arab courier riding a camel is attacked by lions, was similarly celebrated as inspiration for a new generation of taxidermists.[85] The India Court of the Colonial and Indian Exhibition of 1886 also featured large-scale taxidermy, once again by Rowland Ward, which showed a "superb realistic model of an elephant being attacked in the tall grass by tigers, while startled peahens seek flight above."[86] Though often of colossal size, all of these pieces used taxidermy to provide theatrical views of nature and were therefore similar to the trophies displayed in the home that allowed individuals to interact with, partake in, or aspire to the conquest of exotic creatures and the lands from which they came. In so doing, these tableaux were consistent with the didactic, scientific, educational, and provocative aspects of Bentham's vision.

The influence of international exhibitions was also evident in the desire to reform displays of taxidermy in some natural history museums.[87] Writing in 1869, for example, Alfred Russel Wallace (1823–1913), best known for arriving at the theory of evolution by natural selection independently from Charles Darwin, argued that most museums of natural history did not produce the right effects on their visitors – they were neither entertaining, educating, nor uplifting. According to Wallace, the taxidermy in these institutions was particularly problematic:

> Let any one look at an artistically mounted group of fine and perfect quadruped or bird skins, which represent the living animals in perfect health and vigour, and by their characteristic attitudes and accessories tell the history of the creature's life and habits; and compare this with the immature, ragged, mangy-looking specimens one often sees in museums, stuck up in stiff and unnatural attitudes, and resembling only mummies or scarecrows. The one is both instructive and pleasing, and we return again and again to gaze upon it with delight. The other is positively repellent, and we feel that we never want to look upon it again.[88]

To improve the state of museum taxidermy, Wallace suggests better methods of organizing and displaying specimens. In so doing, he envisions the formation of a large institution with several departments, along the lines of the Natural History Museum in South Kensington, which opened in 1881.

Wallace was not unique in calling for improvements to museums of natural history; experts had been making suggestions on how to rectify these problems since the early nineteenth century.[89] Contemporaries were well aware of the poor conditions of museum collections and described natural history museums as morbid palaces, filled to the rafters with disorganized, badly stuffed, and sometimes rotting specimens. Some specimens moved from the British Museum to the new Natural History Museum of South Kensington between 1881 and 1883 were described as "unfit to exhibit to the public" and "had never been properly skinned, and with the exception of the extraction of the entrails, the bones and flesh of the birds had been left entire, and apparently without an attempt to further preserve the specimens."[90] At the time of their manufacture, however, the methods by which these animals were stuffed was praised in guidebooks to the British Museum, which assured readers that every effort was made to "impart some idea of the living being itself."[91] As techniques of preservation changed, experts decried the taxidermy of previous eras, and through to the late nineteenth century taxidermists liked to horrify each other with descriptions of earlier productions, some of which showed preserved skin "stretched to its utmost tension, as it is in drowned and bloated things."[92]

By the 1880s, curators in large museums were removing duplicate and rotting specimens in the hopes of simplifying museum displays and showing only "the leading types [of each species] which are really all that are necessary for the instruction of the public."[93] They also began to create taxidermy that was increasingly large in scale and organized into "habitat groups," like that displayed in international exhibitions. In the late nineteenth century, natural history museums in Sweden and the United States were the first to mount exhibitions of habitat dioramas.[94] Habitat dioramas often contained large animals and were designed to achieve a *trompe l'œil* effect, inspiring the momentary illusion of animals living in their habitats.[95] As Montagu Browne (1837–1923), one leading British proponent of this method who became curator of the Leicester Museum in 1881, stated, the objective was "to carry the eye and mind to the actual localities in which the various species of animals or birds are found."[96] These vignettes were intended to provide a glimpse of animal life rarely witnessed to educate the general public about nature.

In constructing habitat dioramas, considerable artistry was employed to produce simulations of natural settings. This process, called "artistic taxidermy," required the creation of anatomically correct specimens set against elaborate backdrops, complete with foliage, rockery, and sometimes fake blood in order to produce dramatic effects. Though the intention was to provide a spectacle of realism, specimens had to be articulated in a way that accorded with popular perceptions of how animals had behaved when alive, even if these ideas were highly imaginative and sometimes anthropomorphic. Experts advised that the facial expressions of tigers, for example, be rendered so as "to make the animal grin and not smile, and to lend the eyes the flash of anger." This required that the taxidermist use "his best judgment, knowledge, skill, and what is more, his infinite patience." Zebras, perceived as "vicious horses," had to be fashioned accordingly, so that a zebra seemed about to "make an attack" with the short mane "semi-erect," the ears "thrown-back," the lips "quivering and nearly rigid drawn apart [to] show the glistening upper 'nippers' and the crowns of the lower ones."[97] Most Victorians had not seen these animals in the wild, and it was considered important to satisfy audience expectations, some of which were created through information conveyed in guidebooks to the London Zoological Gardens that described typical behaviours of beasts in anthropocentric ways. When the expressions of resurrected animals did not meet expectation, these "monstrosities" were heavily criticized. One article, for example, described several specimens as follows:

One of these had the plumage of an eagle, but its body was almost parallel to the ground, and its drooping wings expressed ignoble indolence. These are the attributes of the vulture, not of the eagle, whose very name symbolizes dignity, courage, and grace. Another had the plumage of a magpie, but the man who stuffed and mounted it was ignorant of the craftiness and sprightliness of the magpie, or he would not have allowed it to assume such a heavy hang-dog appearance. There was also the skin of a fox, but the taxidermist had not been happy in catching its cunning expression, and if you could pardon this, closer scrutiny would prove that he had given Reynard round or dog's eyes, whereas, being nocturnal, the fox has elliptical or cat's eyes.[98]

As the quotation makes clear, taxidermy had to accord with popular understandings of an animal's character, which could entail personification – such that eagles had to seem noble, magpies crafty, and foxes cunning. These expectations were similar to the demands of pet keepers, when they insisted that taxidermists represent the personality of the living pet.

Because museum taxidermy had to convey common impressions of the animal's behaviour while alive, a measure of artificiality was permitted. Consider, for example, the tableau of two tigers struggling over the carcass of an elephant – which is very similar to the taxidermy exhibited in the international exhibitions created by Ploucquet, Ward, and Verneaux (figure 5.10). The scene was constructed by long and laborious processes, using wood, wax, plaster, tube-oil pigments (to represent blood and torn flesh), papier-mâché, and animal skins – the human hand moulding animal bodies to its purpose. The technological savvy involved in the construction of the scene was considered an integral component of its effect, as Montagu Browne, its creator, explained:

The case of the fighting tigers … may, perhaps, be considered somewhat sensational and out of place as a museum object, but it was primarily executed to show that such things could be set up, not on weighty "manikins" loaded with clay, but on light paper models, and also with some material (*not* putty and paint) which should faithfully and naturally imitate the flesh …[99]

The tableau was an illusion, made of light materials to evoke the heavy flesh of the elephant and the clash of tigers. By appearing lifelike, these resurrected animals paradoxically evinced the power and ingenuity of human craftsmanship. As seamless specimens, they hid the efforts

5.10. "Group of Fighting Tigers with Elephant." From Montagu Browne,
Artistic and Scientific Taxidermy and Modelling, plate VI

involved in their manufacture and showed a highly contrived vision of nature that was dramatic and therefore provocative.

Construction of habitat dioramas was celebrated as bringing artistry into the museum and implied a shift in the operation and function of some natural history museums towards public pedagogy and entertainment.[100] This was considered a vexatious issue, and one article, marshalling arguments against the diorama, declared, "The scene-painter must not interfere with the scientist. A museum is a palace of truth before it is a palace of art."[101] Less controversial was the demand made by some experts in the making of dioramas that taxidermists develop competencies in a variety of fields, including topography, botany, and art, and distance their work from that of amateurs, collectors, and huntsmen, who were accused of lacking specialized knowledge.[102] These qualifications were considered necessary to achieve a simulation of realism, showing the dead animal brought back to life and interacting with its environment.[103] In the call for professionalization and the praise for artistic taxidermy, there was both a class dimension and a desire for exclusivity so that some institutions would be set apart from others. In the second half of the nineteenth century, a number of smaller museums featured displays which were similar in style, though not scale, to dioramas, but most did not receive acclaim for their efforts because they were owned and run by taxidermist-tradesmen.

The collection of Edward Hart (1847–1928) in Christchurch, Hampshire provides an example of taxidermy that has not been celebrated as a precursor to the diorama, though Hart's cases of taxidermy provided audiences with simulated views of nature and elaborate backdrops which depicted the landscape. Hart was the son of a taxidermist who worked at his father's taxidermy shop for several years before opening his own establishment. He prepared birds and animals for local sportsmen and eventually started his own collection, which contained only birds captured in the environs around Christchurch in the Hampshire woodlands. Hart hunted most and mounted all of the birds in his collection, and created the cases in which the birds were displayed. Eventually he opened his own museum, which became renowned and attracted a variety of visitors, including the Princess of Wales in the early twentieth century.[104]

Hart viewed the amassing of his collection as an act of conservation and saw no contradiction in hunting birds for this purpose, though he deplored the disappearance of birdlife that resulted from the encroachment of industry and tourism in Hampshire. In the guidebook to his museum, he articulates disdain for visitors who bring with them "brazen throated gramophones and music-hall songs" that disrupt the lives of birds.[105] Hart's displays provided visitors with encounters with "Nature" – each case portrays the Hampshire landscape of the late nineteenth century and is striking for its beauty. The painstaking efforts to create these displays are evident in Hart's records. Very often the completion of a case took decades as he slowly found and hunted the birds; the purpose was to display different plumages of each sex, and often even an albino. For instance, six bullfinches were acquired between 1862 and 1884 for one case. Hart records that they were "[a]ll shot by me either in Grove wood or Bosley Wood, Christchurch."[106] The birds are displayed on branches which merge seamlessly with the painted background conveying grassland, distant trees, and sky.[107] The purpose of these display cases was to "foster [in visitors to the museum] a new sentiment of love for Nature and for Nature's God."[108]

Walking through Hart's museum, visitors would encounter multiple cases, most offering views of animals in the "wild," and in one example a view of pets. Hart's taxidermy, like Bentham's Auto-Icon, was intended to educate, amuse, astonish, and impart moral lessons. Visitors to Hart's museum would likely have enjoyed the impressions of birdlife on offer, but would also have reflected on human interactions with these animals. Of the surviving display cases and records, several examples suggest that Hart drew visitors' attention to human encounters with birdlife around Christchurch. One case shows two swallows returning to a nest, which is situated in a tower; here birds are using the built environment to their advantage. While showing the birds flying through a tower opening, the case conveys perspectives of height and distance by offering views of distant sky, lake, and roadway.[109] In another case, Hart displays two robins, one with a ring on its leg, which were his pets, nesting in a "curious site" – an old boot – in a garden. Hart's notes suggest his interest in these creatures and his attachment to them as pets. He feeds the birds and places a ring on one of their legs to signify ownership. Describing the robin as "the labourer's bird," Hart writes about "that bond of sympathy which exists between the son of toil and this sweet companion of his labour." He tells readers, "All the adult birds in cases 213a and b were pets of mine, but the one in case 213b exceeded them all in attachment to me. Fortunately it had a fairly long life before 1909 when I placed a silver ring on its leg, it remained with me till 1914, ere an accident befell it in the adjoining garden."[110] Hart's actions were consistent with working-class beliefs that the caging of robins was unlucky, as discussed in the first chapter. Moreover, by displaying pets alongside other birds, Hart's museum was another site where distinctions between wild and pet, outside and inside, artificial and natural were not sharply defined.

This brings us finally to the taxidermy of Walter Potter, whose museum most explicitly offered Victorians views of themselves. Like all other taxidermists of his era, Potter staged human histories with animal bodies, but his taxidermy made this obvious by inserting animals into human situations.

Curiosity Killed the Cat

Potter was a hotel proprietor in Bramber, Sussex. He used his wages to support his hobby of taxidermy. Like many would-be taxidermists, he began by stuffing birds; his first mount was a framed yellow canary. In 1861 he exhibited his first large-scale tableau of humanized animals, which depicted the nursery rhyme "The Death and Burial of Cock Robin," a popular subject of taxidermy in the nineteenth century.[111] The poem told the story of a wren and robin, happily married, that are killed under separate circumstances by a hawk and a sparrow. The other animals bury the robin in an elaborate funeral. Potter's montage took seven years to prepare and was composed of ninety-eight specimens of British birds.[112]

The success with which Potter exhibited "The Death and Burial of Cock Robin" led to the design and exhibition of other vignettes that eventually became the displays in his museum. Potter's museum was a nineteenth-century curiosity cabinet, a hodgepodge of wonders, housing thousands of curios, including miniature newspapers, dollhouses, a cannibal's fork, and Chinese spectacles. The taxidermy was conventional and fantastical, as well as scientific and sentimental. Potter displayed natural history tableaux of different flora and fauna from Britain and the empire, in addition to a number of freakish specimens, such as a two-headed lamb, a six-legged cat, and a four-legged chicken. His museum also contained hunted trophies, such as giraffes, rhinos, and lions, stuffed animals that had formerly been his pets, and personified beasts. In this regard, Potter's museum was similar to Horniman's original museum, in that both presented a complex vision of a natural world inhabited by freaks, exotics, and common pets. Most of this taxidermy was produced by Potter, while other pieces were slowly acquired after his death by subsequent curators of the collection. Over time the collection expanded to include minerals, antiquities, and travel souvenirs donated by the public.[113] Victorians who visited Potter's museum could gawk at the haphazard and beautiful creations resurrected by the taxidermist's craft.

As an example of Victoriana, Walter Potter's collection was continuously displayed from 1861 until 2003. In 1918, after Potter died, the museum passed to his daughter and then to his grandson. The collection was moved to Brighton in 1972 and then to Arundel. Along the way, various curators acquired additional objects, including some taxidermy and other Victorian bric-a-brac. In its final manifestation as the Museum of Curiosities, at Jamaica Inn on Bodmin Moor, the collections delighted as many as thirty thousand visitors per year.[114] It housed ten thousand curiosities, of which approximately six thousand were stuffed specimens. In September 2003 the contents of the museum were sold at auction for enormous sums. It was hoped, for example, that "The Kittens' Wedding" would sell for between £4,000 and £6,000, but it was purchased for £21,150.[115]

Of all the artefacts in the collection, by all accounts it was the anthropomorphic taxidermy which held visitors most in thrall. Potter created these specimens out of the bodies of common pets, including birds, cats, cavies, toads, squirrels, rabbits, and rats – animals that resided in close proximity to humans and were easily acquired in the local environs. As pets, these animals could be incorporated into human culture and were already somewhat personified. Potter took this humanization further and used these specimens, rather like puppets, to create tableaux of an idealized Victorian society. At the same time, he demonstrated the versatility of his skill as a taxidermist, resurrecting the dead animals to eternally perform human tasks. For example, a tableau titled "The Lower Five or Rat's Den" showed fifteen large brown rats gambling in a lower-class establishment.[116] The details of the scene are remarkable, and it is described in a guidebook to the museum as follows:

> Four large rats are playing dominoes, while two more look on. The money on the table shows quite clearly that they are gambling. One player with upraised "hands" is exclaiming loudly because his opponent has just laid down the double-six, which will enable him to peg out on the board. In other parts of the room some are sleeping, reading or arguing, while more than one has had a "drop too much", one member is hobbling along on crutches, with a bandaged foot. As yet unobserved by the occupants are the two policemen, entering quietly by the doors at the back. A small notice on the table says that "no money will be returned", but another notice on the mantelpiece observes that the constables have never been known to make a charge! Most of the furniture was made from cigar boxes and the matches actually "strike."[117]

The vignette offered viewers a portrait of rural life that was overtly Arcadian.

"The Lower Five or Rat's Den" was intended to contrast with another vignette of eighteen squirrels gambling, drinking, reading the newspaper, and smoking in "The Upper Ten or Squirrels' Club."[118] Described by the guidebook as a "countryman's vision of the refined pleasures of the town," this vignette shows a loftier establishment.[119] The room is decorated with country scenes and even miniature taxidermy. A waiter enters to serve port, and a younger squirrel rushes about to offer nuts. In other scenes, which also used the bodies of pets, guinea pigs play cricket, rabbits learn in a classroom, and kittens sit down to dinner. These tableaux employed the bodies of animals to show Victorians humorous views of their daily life that were highly stylized. Potter offered visions of little classed worlds in which the daily realities of life in the late nineteenth century are absent and replaced by images of an idyll. His vignettes show no signs of industrialism, poverty, class struggle, political strife, or imperial expansion; instead his animals all seem to know and enjoy their place in the social order.[120]

Potter's vignettes of personified animals were not unusual in Victorian popular culture. The propensity to put animals in human situations was also evident in other Victorian artistic and literary productions, which Potter may have known. Michelle Henning, for example, situates Potter's taxidermy in the context of English rural folk culture. She suggests analogies between Potter's taxidermy and the work of Beatrix Potter as well as *Aesop's Fables*.[121] Walter Potter was also likely inspired by illustrations of personified animals, and he owned prints of animals in human situations by Louis Wain.[122] Wain, a highly regarded animal fancier, was famous for his chromolithographs showing humorous personifications of domestic animals, including one of cats. His images were reproduced in the Victorian illustrated press, as well as on Christmas and Valentine cards.[123]

This brings us finally to "The Kittens' Wedding," Potter's vignette of stuffed kittens performing nuptials (figure 0.2). The vignette was most likely a copy of a similar tableau, also of cats, produced by Hermann Ploucquet and displayed at the Great Exhibition of 1851.[124] Potter, it seems, imitated many of Ploucquet's works.[125] Ploucquet was particularly skilled at a branch of taxidermy which endowed animals with human traits. At the Great Exhibition of 1851, Ploucquet exhibited montages of animals "engaged in human actions," including "a party of tabbies drinking tea, a number of large animals of the weasel tribe as sportsmen, with beaters of smaller species, hunting an unfortunate flock of hares, weasels fighting duels; frogs walking genteelly out with umbrellas; rabbits trying in vain to do sums on a slates; and cats singing and playing the piano." Reporters were infatuated with Ploucquet's ability "to gift brutes with human intelligence, and to make them parts in the long, and sometimes exceedingly droll histories, just like men and women."[126] Although it is not known if Walter Potter visited the Great Exhibition, he would likely have been exposed to the newspaper reports commenting on its displays.

The creation of Potter's tableau involved the euthanizing of kittens, so as to obtain eighteen animals of the same age, size, and type.[127] In the Victorian era this would not have been considered cruelty. Killing cats on this scale has historical antecedents, and calls to mind a massacre of cats by printers in the rue Saint-Severin that took place in Paris in 1740. The "Great Cat Massacre" was a spontaneous and elaborate proceeding in which the printers rounded up and bludgeoned cats, staged a mock-trial, hung several of the animal corpses, and later reenacted the scene in mime. The historian Robert Darnton interprets the episode as an articulation of class conflict and discontent that drew on longstanding ceremonies and symbols involving cats. In early modern Europe, there was nothing unusual about the ritual killing of cats, and the torture of cats was a popular amusement in carnivals, ceremonies, and everyday life. Cats were complex symbols, associated with witchcraft and devilry, female sexuality, cuckolding, and fertility, and they figured as ingredients in folk medicines; cats could harm members of a household or bring protection if enclosed within its walls – and some of these significations were still current in the Victorian era.[128] For example, in the late nineteenth century, cats were still being walled up, sometimes already dead, inside new buildings, perhaps to ward off evil spirits or keep away rats and mice.[129] As we have seen, cats remained symbols of women and female sexuality – but became particularly associated with bourgeois propriety; they were considered difficult pets and too independent to submit to human management. Potter disciplined the cats by making them enact matrimony in perpetuity. Given their attitudes towards cats, most Victorians would have understood the vignette as instructive and amusing because it drew on and inverted their understanding of feline nature.[130] Via taxidermy, the kittens are now artefacts representing bourgeois propriety and domesticity, ideals that were the touchstones of the Victorian social order and broader imperial edifice.

In fascinating ways, Potter's taxidermy also evokes the "cute," identified and theorized by Lori Merish as "an aesthetic marked by race, class and gender, as well as by sexuality" that "transforms transgressive subjects into beloved objects."[131] Cute is generally associated with the child (and the childlike body) and often takes the form of the small or miniature.[132] Merish's analysis explains the uncomfortable and enduring power of Potter's vignettes – especially the puzzling use of kittens and other young animals. Potter uses kittens, never cats, and his rabbits and other animals are always very young. Cuteness, Merish argues, emerged as a distinct cultural phenomenon in late nineteenth-century America as a discourse related to P.T. Barnum's exhibition of Tom Thumb, and reached its heyday in the racialized adoration of Shirley Temple in the 1930s. At the same time, cuteness evokes the politics of race by depicting diminutive white bodies as especially worthy of emotional attachment, identification, and possession. For Merish, cuteness, especially in its nineteenth- and early twentieth-century formulation, presents itself as a commodity that is trafficked to white, middle-class audiences who identify with it and wish to own it. Cuteness desexualizes and assimilates the Other – in this case the kittens – into white middle-class cultural fantasies. As an articulation of the cute, the marriage ceremony, Merish points out, becomes a particularly powerful drama through which the diminutive body is assimilated into adult mores and "situated within the nexus of social and property relations." Once married, the cute body is no longer sexually available. The domestication implied by marriage symbolically curtails rampant sexual desire and the implied possibilities of promiscuity.[133] This symbolism is powerfully conveyed across Potter's vignettes. Though the term "cute" is not used by nineteenth-century British Victorians to describe Potter's taxidermy, his productions are examples of this aesthetic – suggesting, perhaps, its transatlantic emergence in various commercial amusements, if not in the actual use of the term. Standing upright and dressed in lavish clothing, the kittens confound distinctions between humans, animals, and objects. Potter's vignette invites participation by offering spectators opportunities to play the parts of wedding guest and watchful audience. Like Bentham's Auto-Icon, "The Kittens' Wedding" was a provocation to moral contemplation and affect – in this case, hilarity. For, in a punning gesture, curiosity had killed the cat to create a materialization of Victorian sensibilities towards animals and their own complex social relations.

Conclusion

To explain the taxidermy of Walter Potter, this book has taken a circuitous route, through which we have witnessed a variety of attitudes as well as social and consumer practices. We have seen animals assigned multiple social roles, transformed into pets, zoo captives, representations, and moral exemplars. In each chapter we witnessed how Victorians strove to incorporate animals as companions and sources of erudition in their daily lives, and this often entailed reforming the habits of both animals and people. We have examined the intertwined lives of animals and people, and witnessed how joyous, fraught, and political these relationships could be. Telling us much about the textures of everyday life for humans and animals in nineteenth-century Britain, these relationships always shed light on broader societal concerns.

This chapter has reflected on the materiality of Victorian taxidermy, showing the diverse ways stuffed animals were put into human situations, integrated into human society, and subjected to the Victorian imagination. Jeremy Bentham's writings about his Auto-Icon have provided a framework for understanding some of the meanings and purposes of Victorian taxidermy. Bentham intended his corpse to become an instrument of science, scientific comparison, and public pedagogy, as well as a posthumous materialization of his lifetime achievements. He envisioned his Auto-Icon as useful to the living by serving as a mnemonic furnishing, moral lesson, didactic instrument, and affective embodiment. The Auto-Icon was created in defiance of conventional treatments of the human body at death. Given Victorian beliefs about the sanctity of the human corpse, Bentham's vision could not be realized with other human bodies, but it could be accomplished using the bodies of animals. Since Victorians were divided on beliefs about the possibility of animal resurrection and the existence of an animal afterlife, dead animals could be transformed into diverse objects for use in homes and museums.

Treatments of animal corpses show that Victorians ascribed different meanings to human and animal bodies. While dead animals were regarded as raw material for human craftsmanship into diverse objects, this was not the case with human cadavers. Humans were considered higher beings and spiritual entities, and these notions were upheld through burial. When it came to after-death treatment, animals could be humanized, thereby drawing attention to human-animal relations, but white Victorians of proper social standing with "normal bodies" could not be animalized and preserved as taxidermy. Dead animals were transformed into household furnishings and reintegrated into the routines of the living as material memories, trophies, moral embodiments, household decoration, and other useful artefacts. Similar purposes were assigned to taxidermy in Victorian museums, where taxidermy was used to interpret the lives of animals for public education and entertainment. By changing their practices, some taxidermists working in and for British museums attempted to create increasingly lifelike specimens in large-scale habitat dioramas which were paradoxically highly artificial and provocative. Even lesser-known taxidermists, producing smaller display cases, used taxidermy to inform, amuse, astonish, and moralize. Much like the taxidermy produced for household use, museum taxidermy blurred distinctions between wild and pet, artificial and natural, and human and animal.

Walter Potter's taxidermy amplified the anthropomorphic tendencies that were evident in all Victorian taxidermy. He presented Victorians with a view of their social order in which personified animals know their place and are happy to occupy their assigned positions. In his own time, Potter's vignettes were considered amusing and instructive; they drew attention to the human qualities of animals and the animal in men and women. Viewed in this context, Potter's taxidermy reflected and refracted the world view that the Victorians made, for his creations are surely relics of Victorian sensibilities, class, gender, and imperial relations, material and consumer culture, and the history of human-animal interactions.

Notes

Introduction

1 Simpson, "Cat and Dog London," 260.

2 Fitzgerald, "'Animal' Furniture."

3 Kearton, "The Zoological Gardens," 330.

4 *Bazaar, Exchange and Mart*, 3 January 1872.

5 Woman's Suffrage Collection Propaganda Postcards SC/5, Museum of London.

6 Kean, *Animal Rights*, 54–8.

7 In "Does the Animal Exist?" Pearson and Weismantel also discuss the notion of animal social lives, arguing that historians should consider the social and physical spaces people in the past have shared with animals.

8 For a theorization of the meanings that accrue to objects (including living beings) as commodities, see Appadurai, "Introduction, Commodities and the Politics of Value," in *The Social Life of Things*, 3–65; and Kopytoff, "The Cultural Biography of Things," in ibid., 64–94.

9 On the CDA, see Walkowitz, *Prostitution and Victorian Society* and Levine, *Prostitution, Race and Politics*.

10 Davidoff and Hall, *Family Fortunes*.

11 Kenneth L. Ames, *Death in the Dining Room and Other Tales of Victorian Culture*, 77.

12 For a sampling of this literature, see Bowler, *The Non-Darwinian Revolution*, and James A. Secord, *Victorian Sensation*. On Victorian visual culture and Darwin, see Donald and Munro, eds., *Endless Forms*; Prodger, *Darwin's Camera*.

13 Levine, *The British Empire*, 82.

14 For information on the fountain, see Kean, *Animal Rights*, 55; Kean, "Traces and Representations," 56n16.

15 See, for example, Rappaport, *Shopping for Pleasure*; de Grazia and Furlough, eds., *The Sex of Things*; Finn, "Men's Things"; Scanlon, ed., *The Gender and Consumer Culture Reader*.

16 The literature on consumer processes is vast. Important foundational works include Appadurai, ed., *The Social Life of Things*; Douglas and Isherwood, *The World of Goods*; Smart Martin, "Makers, Buyers, Users"; McCracken, *Culture and Consumption*, 71–91; Daniel Miller, *Material Culture and Mass Consumption*; Schudson, "Historical Roots of Consumer Culture."

17 See, for example, Brewer and Porter, eds., *Consumption and the World of Goods*; McKendrick, Brewer, and Plumb, *The Birth of a Consumer Society*.

18 On British consumer culture, see Benson and Ugolini, "Introduction," in *Cultures of Selling*, 1–29; and de Groot, "Metropolitan Desires and Colonial Connections."

19 John Benson, *The Rise of Consumer Society in Britain, 1880–1990*, 4.

20 Stearns, "Stages of Consumerism," 105–6.

21 Johnson, "Conspicuous Consumption and Working-Class Culture in Late Victorian and Edwardian Britain," 29.

22 Ibid., 31–7.

23 On Victorian leisure and London entertainments see Altick, *The Shows of London*; Bailey, *Leisure and Class in Victorian England*; Flanders, *Consuming Passions*; Qureshi, *Peoples on Parade*; Walvin, *Leisure and Society*.

24 Briggs, *Victorian Things*. See also Cohen, *Household Gods*; Logan, *The Victorian Parlour*; Vickery, *Behind Closed Doors*.

25 The exception is Sarah Cheang's article, "Women, Pets and Imperialism," examining the display of Pekingese dogs as objects of conspicuous consumption and imperial nostalgia.

26 See, for example, Lemire, *The Business of Everyday Life*" and "Shifting Currency"; Ross, *Love and Toil*, 81–4; Stallybrass, "Marx's Coat"; Tebbutt, *Making Ends Meet*.

27 Ibid., 20n49.

28 On the social changes brought by the railway, see Bagwell, *The Transport Revolution*, 112–22; Shivelbusch, *The Railway Journey*, 19–23, 54.

29 Clipping from an unidentified newspaper of 1832 in vol. VII–VIII of the Fillinham Collection, British Library.

30 On the role of the Great Exhibition in Victorian commodity culture, see Thomas Richards, *The Commodity Culture of Victorian England*.

31 On Victorian advertisements, see ibid; Loeb, *Consuming Angels*; Ramamurthy, *Imperial Persuaders*.

32 Simpson, "Cat and Dog London," 256.

33 For a survey of developments in the Victorian newspaper industry, see Aled Jones, "The Press and the Printed Word."

34 For analyses of the shape of the field, see essays in Henninger-Voss, ed., *Animals in Human Histories*; Kete, ed., *A Cultural History of Animals*; Philo and Wilbert, *Animal Spaces, Beastly Places*; Ritvo, "On the Animal Turn"; Rothfels, ed., *Representing Animals*.

35 Fudge, *The History of Animals*; *Animals, Rationality, and Humanity in Early Modern England*; and *Perceiving Animals*.

36 Thomas, *Man and the Natural World*, 16.

37 Ritvo, *The Animal Estate*, 4.

38 On the development of attitudes towards animal cruelty and welfare in the eighteenth and nineteenth centuries, see James Turner, *Reckoning with the Beast*, and Donald, "'Beastly Sights.'" On the history of animal rights legislation and various campaigns, see Brian Harrison, "Animals and the State in Nineteenth-Century England"; Perkins, *Romanticism and Animal Rights*; E.S. Turner, *All Heaven in a Rage*. On animal advocacy and non-canonical women writers, see Ferguson, *Animal Advocacy and Englishwomen, 1780–1900*. On anti-vivisection campaigns, see French, *Antivivisection and Medical Science in Victorian Society*; Lansbury, *The Old Brown Dog*; Walkowitz, *City of Dreadful Delight*, 6–7, 91–210.

39 Morse and Danahay, eds., *Victorian Animal Dreams*.

40 Kean, *Animal Rights*.

41 Kete, *The Beast in the Boudoir*. On Parisian relations with animals in the eighteenth century, see Robbins, *Elephant Slaves and Pampered Parrots*.

42 Ritvo, *The Animal Estate*, 82–121, and "Pride and Pedigree," 234–45.

43 Grier, "Material Culture as Rhetoric" and *Pets in America*.

44 Rothfels, "Catching Animals" and *Savages and Beasts*.

45 Cohen, *Household Gods*, 215n20; Davidoff and Hall, *Family Fortunes*; Loeb, *Consuming Angels*, 3.

46 See, for example, Swart, "'The World the Horses Made.'"

47 Three recent volumes notably frame their discussion in these terms: Branz, ed., *Beastly Natures*; Daston and Mitman, eds., *Thinking with Animals*; Landes, Lee, and Youngquist, eds., *Gorgeous Beasts*. See also Kean, "Traces and Representations."

48 Grier, "Material Culture as Rhetoric."

49 Grier, *Pets in America*, *At Home with Animals*, and "The Material Culture of Pet Keeping.".

50 Auslander, "Beyond Words"; Hood, "Material Culture – The Object"; Giorgio Riello, "Things That Shape History"; Prown, "Mind in Matter."

51 *Kittens' Wedding Tableau* (detail) on postcard produced by the Victoria and
   Albert Museum in the possession of the author. For a similar image, see
   Atterbury and Cooper, *Victorians at Home and Abroad*, 60.

52 Henning, "Anthropomorphic Taxidermy and the Death of Nature,"
   664–70; Milgrom, *Still Life*, 160–90; Morris, *Walter Potter's Curious World of
   Taxidermy*; Rachel Poliquin, *The Breathless Zoo*, 182–90.

53 Kate Carter, "The Curious World of Walter Potter – in Pictures," *Guardian*,
   13 September 2013.

1. The Social Lives of Pets

1 Stillman, "Billy and Hans: A True History."

2 *Beeton's Book of Poultry and Domestic Animals*, 540–3.

3 Leigh, *Pets a Paper*, 14–15; "Railway Accommodation for Dogs," *Dog
   Owners' Supplement to the Bazaar*, 25 February 1895; "Dog Ticket, Miss,"
   Illustrated London News, Christmas, 1882.

4 Appadurai, "Introduction," in *The Social Life of Things*, 3–65.

5 Thomas, *Man and the Natural World*, 112–17.

6 Grier, *Pets in America*, 6–7.

7 Scherren, "Bird-Land and Pet-Land in London," 328.

8 *Household Pets*, 1 October 1910.

9 Patterson, *Notes on Pet Monkeys and How to Manage Them; Parrots and
   Monkeys by the Author of "the Knights of the Frozen Sea," Etc., with Twenty-Six
   Illustrations*.

10 Patterson, *Notes on Pet Monkeys*, 68–9.

11 *Oxford English Dictionary Online*, "fancy," available at http://www.oed
   .com.myaccess.library.utoronto.ca/. Accessed 12 October 2012.

12 Mayhew, *London Labour and the London Poor by Henry Mayhew with a New
   Introduction by John D. Rosenberg*, 2:48. Mayhew was commissioned by the
   Morning Chronicle to investigate the working conditions of the London
   poor. He published a series of weekly articles on the topic between 1849
   and 1850, and later compiled the articles into book form.

13 *Illustrated Sporting and Dramatic News*, 17 January 1880.

14 Crompton et al., *Home Pets*, 10.

15 On connections between the dog fancy and middle-class social aspirations,
   see Ritvo, *The Animal Estate*, 82–121. Ritvo discusses the evolution of Victorian dog breeding in "Pride and Pedigree," 234–45. See also Jaquet, *The Kennel
   Club*. On bourgeois dog keeping in France, see Kete, *The Beast in the Boudoir*.

16 Mayhew, *London Labour and the London Poor*, 2:64.

17 Hudson, *The Book of a Naturalist*, 249–50.

18 Kean notes that the Spitalfields weavers organized a society for breeding fancy pigeons and canaries and reported to the Royal Commission of
   Handloom Weavers in 1840 (*Animal Rights*, 119).

19 Avis, *The Canary and Its History, Varieties, Management and Breeding*, 91;
   The British Aviary, and Bird Breeder's Companion, 14.

20 Francis Smith, *The Canary*, 31–2. See also Robert L. Wallace, *The Canary
   Book*, 193–5.

21 Smith, *The Canary*, 20.

22 *The Canary, Goldfinch, Greenfinch, Nightingale, Lark, Titmouse, Redbreast,
   Linnet, Yellowhammer, Wren*, 161, 171.

23 Mayhew, *London Labour and the London Poor*, 2:64; for a similar comment
   see *The Canary, Goldfinch, Greenfinch*, 171.

24 Mayhew, *London Labour and the London Poor*, 2:64.

25 This association is mentioned in the *Fancier's Chronicle*, 25 July 1890.

26 *The Canary, Goldfinch, Greenfinch*, 200–1; Trimmer, *The History of Robins*.

27 For a discussion of the robin, see *The British Aviary, and Bird Breeder's
   Companion*, 54; *The Canary, Goldfinch, Greenfinch*, 193–201; Mayhew, *London
   Labour and the London Poor*, 2:60.

28 Edward Hart, 15 April 1927, writing about Edward Hart case NH.83.3/93,
   Horniman Museum and Gardens.

29 *The Canary, Goldfinch, Greenfinch*, 200–1.

30 On Victorian attitudes towards cats, see Kean, *Animal Rights*, 157–62.

31 Ibid., 160–1.

32 C.H. Lane, *Rabbits, Cats, and Cavies*, 220.

33 *Exchange and Mart*, 12 May 1869.

34 On the Angora cat as a luxury good, see Veblen, *Theory of the Leisure Class*,
   chapter 6, available at http://xroads.virginia.edu/~HYPER/VEBLEN/
   chap06.html.

35 *The Lady: A Journal for Gentlewomen*, 3 January 1889.

36 *Household Pets*, 10 December 1910.

37 See, for example, Lane, *Rabbits, Cats and Cavies*; *Fur and Feather: A Weekly
   Journal devoted to Rabbits, Cage Birds, Cats, Cavies and Pet Stock, for Exhibition
   and Fancy*; *Fur Fanciers' Journal: A Journal Devoted to the Interests of Rabbits,
   Cats & Cavies*.

38 *Fur Fanciers' Journal*, 18 January 1892. Ritvo notes that the dog fancy
   influenced decisions to exhibit working men's cats in a separate category.
   See Ritvo, *The Animal Estate*, 17.

39 *Our Cats*, November 1899.

40 *The Book of Home Pets*, 682.

41 Blake and Williams, *Fancy Mice*, 2.

42 Davies, *Fancy Mice Their Varieties and Management as Pets or for Show*, 1.

43 Maxey, *Fancy Mice and Rats, How to Breed and Exhibit*, 76.

44 Ibid., 57.

45 Ibid., 8. On the virtues of keeping fancy mice, see *Fur Fanciers' Journal*, 18 January 1892.

46 Crompton et al., *Home Pets*, 54–64; "Girls' Pets and How to Manage Them: Fowls," *Girl's Empire* 1 (1902): 142–4, "Girls' Pets and How to Manage Them: Pigeons II," *Girl's Empire* 1 (1902): 58–9.

47 "The Pleasures of Poultry Keeping," *Ladies' Kennel Journal* (February– March 1901): 1454.

48 Kean, *Animal Rights*, 47; see also note 52.

49 *Fur and Feather: A Weekly Journal*, 24 December 1890.

50 Crompton et al., *Home Pets*, 68–9, 72.

51 Ibid., 78; "Girls' Pets and How to Manage Them. By a Well-Known Breeder and Exhibitor. General Management and Breeding of Rabbits," *Girl's Empire* 1 (1901): 479.

52 Crompton et al., *Home Pets*, 66. Working-class fanciers and pet keepers continued to breed rabbits until at least the middle of the twentieth century. See Monica Dickens, *The Fancy*, first published in 1943.

53 *Bazaar, Exchange and Mart*, 3 April 1901.

54 Ibid.

55 "Girls' Pets and How to Manage Them," 480.

56 Charles Cumberland, "The Guinea Pig, for Food, Fur and Fancy," *Bazaar, Exchange and Mart*, 9 January 1885.

57 Charles Cumberland, "The Guinea Pig, for Food, Fur and Fancy," *Bazaar, Exchange and Mart*, 30 January 1895.

58 Cumberland, *The Guinea Pig, or Domestic Cavy for Food, Fur, and Fancy*, 41–4.

59 *Beeton's Book of Poultry and Domestic Animals*, in contrast, classed the guinea pig as a "Home Pet" and its flesh "unfit for food" (698).

60 Cumberland, *The Guinea Pig*, 89–94.

61 Ibid., 14; "A Chat on Cavies," *Fur Fanciers' Journal: A Journal Devoted to the Interests of Rabbits, Cats & Cavies*, 1 May 1891.

62 "The Fancy – Fact, Fiction, Past and Present," *Fur Fanciers' Journal: A Weekly Paper Devoted to Exhibitors of Pet Stock & c*, 28 December 1892.

63 G.A. Johnson, "Girls' Pets. The Grass-Snake," *Girl's Empire* 1 (1902): 188; "A Queer Pet," *Girl's Empire* 1 (1902): 333.

64 Mayhew, *London Labour and the London Poor*, 2:47.

65 Smith, *The Canary*, 31–3. On working-class canary fancying, see also Robert L. Wallace, *The Canary Book*, 193–4.

66 Leigh, *Pets a Paper*, 20–2.

67 *The British Aviary, and Bird Breeder's Companion*, iv; "The Morning Toilet, Seven Dials," *Illustrated London News*, 5 September 1874.

68 Mayhew, *London Labour and the London Poor*, 2:47–81.

69 Scherren, "Bird-Land and Pet-Land in London," 326–7.

70 Ibid., 327.

71 Kean, *Animal Rights*, 119.

72 *Fur and Feather*, 1 April 1890; *Canary and Cage Bird Life*, 20 October 1905.

73 *Bazaar, Exchange and Mart*, 17 February 1890.

74 Ibid., 3 June 1868.

75 Ibid., 18 April 1871.

76 Ibid., 9 January 1875.

77 *The Lady: A Journal for Gentlewomen*, 17 September 1885.

78 *Bazaar, Exchange and Mart*, 1 January 1886.

79 Ibid., 3 May 1880.

80 Ibid., 2 January 1880.

81 Ibid., 3 January 1890.

82 *Fur and Feather*, 21 February 1895.

83 Ibid., 8 May 1890; for additional legal advice, see "Two Dead Canaries," *Bazaar, Exchange and Mart*, 24 January 1890.

84 *Bazaar, Exchange and Mart*, 3 January 1890.

85 For this advertisement and others, see back of Blake and Williams, *Fancy Mice*.

86 *Fancier's Chronicle*, October 1880.

87 *Bazaar, Exchange and Mart*, 8 January 1886.

88 "Answers to Correspondents," *Fur and Feather*, 8 May 1890.

89 *Household Pets*, 15 October 1910.

90 Blakston, Swaysland, and Wiener, *The Illustrated Book of Canaries and Cage-Birds*, 5.

91 Leigh, *Pets a Paper*, 6.

92 *The Canary, Goldfinch, Greenfinch*, 149.

93 Patterson, *Notes on Pet Monkeys*, 26.

94 Jennings, *Domestic and Fancy Cats*, 31–2, 38.

95 "Girls' Pets and How to Manage Them. The Fox Terrier," *Girl's Empire* 1 (1902): 200.

96 Scherren, "Bird-Land and Pet-Land in London," 327.

97 *Fancier's Chronicle*, 26 November 1880.

98 See *Pattern Book of General Wire Goods, including G.B.'s Patent Machine Made Brass and Iron Chain … Manufactured by Geo. Baker, Cecil Street Wire Mills and Wire Works, Late of Chaster Street, Birmingham*, in Domestic Pets, Box 2, John Johnson Collection of Printed Ephemera. For advice on the caging of mice, see Maxey, *Fancy Mice and Rats*, 8.

99 Robert L. Wallace, *The Canary Book*, 16.

100 Scherren, "Bird-Land and Pet-Land in London," 328.

101 Ibid.

102 Jennings, *Domestic and Fancy Cats*, 58.

103 *Fur and Feather*, 19 December 1895.

104 "Girls' Pets and How to Manage Them. A Goldfish Aquarium," *Girl's Empire* 1 (1902): 106.

105 See advertisement for dog collars by Silber and Fleming, 56, Wood Street, London, EC, and for George Towell, Cage Manufacturer and Naturalist, 19, Old Millgate, Market Place, Manchester, in Domestic Pets, Box 1, John Johnson Collection of Printed Ephemera.

106 Mayhew, *London Labour and the London Poor*, 1:358–61.

107 "Dog Collar Department," *Harrod's General Catalogue*, 1910, 160–1.

108 Crompton et al., *Home Pets*, 78; Lytton, *Toy Dogs and Their Ancestors*; Avis, *The Canary and Its History*.

109 Spicer, *Toy Dogs*, 72–3.

110 Thomas Richards, "The Image of Victoria in the Year of the Jubilee," 14–15.

111 For advertisements endorsing Spratt's, Clarke's Buffalo Biscuits, Melox, Victoria Dog Biscuits, and Gilbertson & Page Biscuits, see Domestic Pets, Box 1, John Johnson Collection of Printed Ephemera. The same box contains advertisements for various types of bird seed. See also advertisements for Victoria Dog's Biscuits in Advertisements: Scrapbook B2, Museum of London.

112 See back of Blake and Williams, *Fancy Mice*.

113 See the back of Cooper and Clarke, *Bull-Dogs and Bull-Dog Breeding and Toy Bull-Dogs*.

114 Orline Gates, "Canaries, and How to Keep Them," *Girl's Empire* 2 (1903): 265; "Tricks for Canaries," *Girl's Empire* 2 (1903): 239.

115 Lytton, *Toy Dogs and Their Ancestors*, 330.

116 See advertisements for these books in *Fancier's Chronicle*, 4 January 1895.

117 *Bazaar, Exchange and Mart*, 5 March 1890.

118 On taming monkeys, see Patterson, *Notes on Pet Monkeys*, 46, 96–7.

119 Ibid., 96.

120 "That Monkey!" *Illustrated London News*, 4 July 1885; "Things Are Not Always What They Seem," *Illustrated London News*, 27 July 1889, 123; Clifford, *Yoppy*. Parrots were similarly believed to manifest fits and were also frequently abandoned. See *Parrots and Monkeys*, 63–4; Russ, *The Speaking Parrots*, 35.

121 "Girls' Pets and How to Manage Them: The Fox Terrier," *Girl's Empire* 1 (1902): 200. See also Lytton, *Toy Dogs and Their Ancestors*, 330.

122 "Some Don'ts for Pet Lovers," *Household Pets*, 8 October 1910; "Some Don'ts for Dog Owners," *Our Home Pets: An Illustrated Monthly* (January 1903).

123 "Tricks for Canaries," *Girl's Empire* 2 (1903): 239.

124 Winslow, *Concerning Cats*, 265. Kean discusses the ways Methodism fostered these attitudes in *Animal Rights*, 19–27. Lansbury discusses the humanitarism of working-class residents of Battersea in *The Old Brown Dog*, 31–46.

125 *Our Home Pets: An Illustrated Monthly* (October 1902).

126 Mrs L.S. Baker, "Girls' Pets and How to Manage Them," *Girl's Empire* 1 (1901): 427.

127 *Household Pets*, 24 September 1910.

128 Stables, *"Cats" Their Points and Characteristics, with Curiosities of Cat Life, and Chapter on Feline Ailments*, 357.

129 On class and the Victorian animal welfare movement, see Ritvo, *The Animal Estate*, 125–67.

130 *The Canary and Other Song Birds*, 8.

131 Brian Harrison, "Animals and the State in Nineteenth-Century England"; Ritvo, *The Animal Estate*, 125–66.

132 For a discussion of the ways animal welfare influenced British culture in the nineteenth and twentieth centuries, see Kean, *Animal Rights*.

133 Pollock, *Animals That Have Owned Us*, 1.

134 See, for example, Chance, *A Book of Cats*.

135 Stables, *"Cats" Their Points and Characteristics*.

136 *Household Pets*, 15 October 1910.

137 For products such as "Gillard's Compound for Distemper in Dogs," see Domestic Pets, Box 1, John Johnson Collection of Printed Ephemera; the back of Cooper and Clarke, *Bull-Dogs and Bull-Dog Breeding*, as well as the back pages of Jaquet, *The Kennel Club*.

138 Ad for "St. Jacob's Oil," Advertisements: Scrapbook B3, Museum of London.

139 For this ad, see Domestic Pets, Box 1, John Johnson Collection of Printed Ephemera.

140 *Fur and Feather*, 19 December 1895.

141 Ibid.

142 Early gatherings of wealthy gentlemen dog fanciers were informal and often took place in pubs. For a discussion of paintings representing these recreations, see William Secord, *Dog Painting 1840–1940*, 159–63.

143 For a discussion of pigeon fancying, see James A. Secord, "Nature's Fancy" and "Darwin and the Breeders."

144 See Jaquet, *The Kennel Club*.

145 *Fur Fanciers' Journal: A Journal devoted to the Interests of Rabbits, Cats & Cavies*, 1 July 1891.

146 Crompton et al., *Home Pets*, 65.

147 For reports on shows held at the Crystal Palace, see *Illustrated Sporting and Dramatic News*, 20 June 1874 (dogs); 17 January 1880 (pigeons); 6 March 1880 (birds); 26 January 1884 (dogs); 18 February 1884 (birds); 1 November 1884 (cats). These events were also covered in the *Illustrated London News*: 17 February 1887 (birds); 22 October 1887 (cats); 2 November 1889 (cats); 1 November 1890 (cats); 8 November 1890 (dogs); 18 January 1892 (dogs); 9 April 1892 (pigeons).

148 Cards produced by Chocolat Lombard, Player's Cigarettes, and Spratts can be found in Domestic Pets, Box 1, John Johnson Collection of Printed Ephemera. They are not dated.

149 *Fur Fanciers' Journal: A Weekly Paper devoted to Exhibitors of Pet Stock & c*, 1 January 1892; 14 December 1892.

150 *Bazaar, Exchange and Mart*, 1 January 1890 (cat); 3 January 1890 (cat); 10 February 1890 (dog); and *Fur and Feather*, 1 April 1890 (rabbits); 14 April 1890 (rabbits and cats); *Fur and Feather*, 21 February 1895 (rabbits, cats, dogs).

151 See back pages of Cooper and Clarke, *Bull-Dogs and Bull-Dog Breeding*, and Jaquet, *The Kennel Club*.

152 *Fur and Feather*, 1 April 1890; *Fancier's Chronicle*, 15 October 1880.

153 Cooper and Clarke, *Bull-Dogs and Bull-Dog Breeding*, 55.

154 Jennings, *Domestic and Fancy Cats*, 49.

155 "Selecting a Foster Mother," *The Dog Owners' Supplement to the Bazaar*, 25 February 1895.

156 Cooper and Clarke, *Bull-Dogs and Bull-Dog Breeding*, 55.

157 For an advertisement seeking a foster mother for poultry, see *Bazaar, Exchange and Mart*, 3 January 1890.

158 Lyell, *Fancy Pigeons*, 50.

159 George Earl, *Going North at King's Cross Station*, 1893, oil on canvas, reproduced as plate 31 in William Secord, *Dog Painting: The European Breeds*, 44.

160 *Ladies' Kennel Journal* (January 1895): 204.

161 "A Cheap Travelling Dog-Box," *The Dog Owners' Supplement to the Bazaar*, 25 February 1895.

162 *Bazaar, Exchange and Mart*, 26 March 1890.

163 *Fur and Feather*, 3 January 1895.

164 Stables, *Our Friend the Dog*, 63–4.

165 *Fur and Feather*, 21 February 1895.

166 "Railway Rates and Dog Insurance," *Ladies' Kennel Journal* (January 1895); for another complaint, see "Delay in Transit," *Bazaar, Exchange and Mart*, 24 January 1890.

167 "Railway Accommodation for Dogs," *The Dog Owners' Supplement to the Bazaar*, 25 February 1895.

168 Jennings, *Domestic and Fancy Cats*, 58.

169 *Fur and Feather*, 25 July 1895, 52.

170 Bliss, *Every Inch a King*; Stables, *Sable and White*.

171 Avis, *The Canary and Its History*, 89.

172 *Our Cats*, 2 May 1903.

173 Jennings, *Domestic and Fancy Cats*, 50.

174 "Buying Dogs with a View to Breeding," *Bazaar, Exchange and Mart*, 14 March 1890; see also inquiries in *The Dog Owners' Supplement to the Bazaar*, 25 February 1895.

175 *Our Cats*, 14 February 1903.

176 *Canary and Cage Bird Life*, 7 January 1910.

177 Cooper and Clarke, *Bull-Dogs and Bull-Dog Breeding*, 15.

2. Sexy Beasts, Fallen Felines, and Pampered Pomeranians

1 "Of Poodledom," *Vanity Fair*, 11 May 1899; 18 May 1899; 25 May 1899; 1 June 1899; 22 June 1899.

2 *Vanity Fair*, 11 May 1899.

3 Ibid. Mrs Grundy is a famous literary allusion from Thomas Morton's *Speed the Plough: A Comedy in Five Acts* (1798). Her name evokes the censoriousness of conventional opinion.

4 "Of Poodledom," *Vanity Fair*, 1 June 1899.

5 In defining gender, I have drawn upon the ideas of Susan Kingsley Kent, *Gender and Power in Britain, 1640–1990*, xi, and of Joan Wallach Scott, *Gender and the Politics of History*, 42–5.

6 Ritvo, "Sex and the Single Animal."

7 For Judith Butler, daily *"stylized repetition of acts,"* informing and informed by cultural representations, are integral to the making of gender identities. Gender, Butler argues, is "a constructed identity, [and] a performative accomplishment." According to Butler, one is always in the process of becoming a gender – of willfully creating oneself as a man or a woman by putting on certain gender signifiers that are generated, displayed and contested everywhere in society ("Performative Acts and Gender Constitution," 270–1).

8　On feminist campaigns, see Caine, *English Feminism, 1780–1980*. On the Contagious Diseases Acts, see Walkowitz, *Prostitution and Victorian Society*, and Levine, *Prostitution, Race and Politics*.

9　For an analysis of the ways scientific interpretation of nature became a masculine endeavour and women were conceptualized as the passive recipients of scientific manipulation, see Brown and Jordanova, "Oppressive Dichotomies," and Gates, *Kindred Nature*.

10　For a selection of nineteenth-century debates on the innate differences between men and women, see Rowold, ed., *Gender and Science*.

11　"Annual Costs of England's Cats," *Our Cats*, 21 March 1903.

12　On the cat fancy, see Ritvo, *The Animal Estate*, 115–20.

13　See chapter on cats in Crompton et al., *Home Pets*.

14　*Our Cats*, 27 December 1899, 73. Similar sentiments are expressed in "Our Cats: A Domestic History," *Illustrated London News*, 18 October 1884.

15　Winslow, *Concerning Cats*, 88–9.

16　Dedication found in ibid.

17　Though I focus on cats, all female animals were portrayed as sexually rapacious in discourses on animal breeding. For more on this subject, see Ritvo, "Sex and the Single Animal," 130–4.

18　Jennings, *Domestic and Fancy Cats*, 3.

19　*Our Cats*, 3 January 1890.

20　"How Happy Could I Be with Either!" *Illustrated London News*, 18 June 1887.

21　*Fur and Feather: An Illustrated Weekly Journal for Town and Country*, 30 May 1895; Stables, *"Cats" Their Points and Characteristics*, 210.

22　Davies, *Fancy Mice*, 21; Jennings, *Domestic and Fancy Cats*, 3.

23　Lane, *Rabbits, Cats and Cavies*, 248; Stables, *"Cats" Their Points and Characteristics*, 211–20; "Scientific Jottings," *Illustrated London News*, 5 January 1889.

24　*Fur and Feather*, 30 May 1895.

25　Stables, *"Cats" Their Points and Characteristics*, 210.

26　In the eighteenth century, the term was also used to mean "hare" or "rabbit." In the twentieth century, it became slang for an effeminate man. See *Oxford English Dictionary Online*, "pussy," thttp://www.chass.utoronto.ca.myaccess.library.utoronto.ca, accessed 12 October 2012. On the historical symbolism of cats, see Darnton, 92–6.

27　Stables, *"Cats" Their Points and Characteristics*, 190.

28　Stables, *The Domestic Cat*, 139–40.

29　James Turner, *Reckoning with the Beast*, 63.

30 "The Two Pets," *Illustrated London News*, Christmas 1881; for accompanying poem, see p. 32. See also "A Merry Christmas to You!" *Illustrated London News*, 22 December 1883.

31 "We Wish You a Merry Christmas," *Illustrated London News*, Christmas 1882. For accompanying narrative, see p. 34. "A Garden Party," *Illustrated London News*, 19 July 1884; "Carriage Folk," *Illustrated London News*, 15 May 1886, illustrated supplement; "In Disgrace," *Illustrated London News*, 1 August 1891.

32 "Pussy's Perquisite," *Illustrated London News*, Christmas 1882. For accompanying narrative, see p. 35.

33 For a discussion of similar images, see Higonnet, *Pictures of Innocence*, 34; Paul, "Beatrix Potter and John Everett Millais."

34 Carroll, *Through the Looking Glass*, 4–6.

35 "The Favourite," *Illustrated London News*, Christmas 1881. For similar pictures, see "La Jeunesse," *Illustrated London News*, 28 June 1890; "Love Me, Love My Cat," *Illustrated London News*, 16 May 1891.

36 Walkowitz, *City of Dreadful Delight*, 3, 87–97.

37 "Some Don'ts for Pet Lovers," *Household Pets*, 8 October 1910; "Practical Hints," *Our Cats*, 14 February 1903, 29 August 1903; "A Home for Derelict Cats and Dogs," *Household Pets*, 24 September 1910, 10 December 1910; Stables, *"Cats" Their Points and Characteristics*, 340.

38 Ibid., 343–4.

39 "A Plea for Poor Pussy: The Many-Sided Character of the London Cat," *Our Cats*, 17 January 1903.

40 *Our Cats*, 29 August 1903.

41 Stables, *"Cats" Their Points and Characteristics*, 365; Winslow, *Concerning Cats*, 262–3.

42 Stables, *"Cats" Their Points and Characteristics*, 44; *Our Cats*, 29 August 1903.

43 "Frowned Upon by Fortune: A Tale of Feline Love and Suicide," *Vanity Fair*, 10 September 1903.

44 "Don't Forget Your Cats!" *Illustrated London News*, 3 September 1892.

45 "Sketches of the Cat Show," *Illustrated London News*, 1 November 1890.

46 For complaints against this tendency, see *Our Cats*, 29 November 1899.

47 "Terrier Show at the Aquarium," *Illustrated London News*, 20 March 1886.

48 On Victorian masculinity, see Tosh and Roper, eds., *Manful Assertions*; Tosh, *Manliness and Masculinities in Nineteenth-Century Britain*; Tosh, "Masculinities in Industrializing Society."

49 Playbills in vol. IV and VI of the Fillinham Collection, British Library.

50 *Household Pets*, 8 October 1910.

51 See, for example, "Looking Out," *Illustrated London News*, 28 June 1856.

52 "'Erebus and Terror' By J.W. Bottomley," *Illustrated London News*,
    8 February 1873.

53 See, for example, "The St. Bernard Show," *Illustrated London News*,
    10 November 1883. See also Kete, *The Beast in the Boudoir*, 71–3.

54 "Bashaw, The Faithful Friend of Man, Trampling Underfoot His Most
    Insidious Enemy," by Matthew Cotes Wyatt, England, UK, 1831–4.
    Museum no. A.4-1960, Victoria and Albert Museum. For more informa-
    tion: http://www.vam.ac.uk/content/articles/b/bashaw/.

55 "Old Chums," *Illustrated London News*, 22 March 1890; "His Only Friend,"
    Illustrated London News, 18 September 1875.

56 One story about a Skye terrier's loyalty to an impoverished policeman in
    Edinburgh is still popular today. See MacGregor, *Greyfriars Bobby*.

57 "Sanctuary," *Illustrated London News*, 27 January 1883.

58 "High Life," *Illustrated London News*, 31 January 1874, extra supplement;
    "Low Life," *Illustrated London News*, 14 February 1874, extra supple-
    ment. For similar commentary, see also "Bothered," *Illustrated London
    News*, 24 February 1872; "The Morning Toilet, Seven Dials," *Illustrated
    London News*, 5 September 1874. For analyses of Landseer's paintings, see
    Cowling, *The Artist as Anthropologist*, 161–3; Lippencott and Bluhm, *Fierce
    Friends*, 88–9.

59 Stables, *Our Friend the Dog*, 76.

60 "High Life," *Illustrated London News*, 31 January 1874.

61 Crompton et al., *Home Pets*, 24–33.

62 Stonehenge, *The Dog in Health and Disease*, 134.

63 Cooper and Clarke, *Bull-Dogs and Bull-Dog Breeding*, 14.

64 Crompton et al., *Home Pets*, 16.

65 For more on the nineteenth-century bulldog fad, see Ritvo, *The Animal
    Estate*, 107–13.

66 MacInnes, "Mastiffs and Spaniels."

67 Jenner, "The Great Dog Massacre."

68 Ritvo, *The Animal Estate*, 185. On rabies see ibid., 166–202.

69 For discussion of the ways dogs symbolized masculinity in impressionist
    art, see Rubin, *Impressionist Cats and Dogs*.

70 "The Forest Glade," *Illustrated London News*, 19 December 1874; "A
    Frosty Morning," *Illustrated London News*, 2 March 1889; "The Old Home
    Revisited," *Illustrated London News*, 12 April 1890; "Waiting for the Boat,"
    Illustrated London News, 5 October 1889; "A Woodland Walk," *Illustrated
    London News*, 5 November 1887.

71 "A Nice Family," *Illustrated London News*, 3 December 1887; "Privileged Visitor," *Illustrated London News*, 23 May 1891.

72 "A Disgrace to His Family from the picture by Stanley Berkley in the Institute of Painters in Oil Colours," *Illustrated London News*, 26 December 1885.

73 "Beg!" *Illustrated London News*, 28 January 1882, extra supplement. For accompanying narrative, see p. 83. For a similar image, see advertisement for "Oswego" Biscuits manufactured by Peek, Frean and Co., *Graphic*, 8 December 1884.

74 "The Secret," *Illustrated London News*, 6 December 1884. Similar ideas are expressed in "Secret and Confidential," *Illustrated London News*, 20 June 1885.

75 "Love Me, Love My Dog," *Illustrated London News*, 14 November 1885. Similar ideas are expressed in "Photograph from Life: Our Boys," *Illustrated London News*, 19 December 1885.

76 Postcard, Museum of London, acquisition no: 28.354/189.

77 Postcard, Museum of London, acquisition no: 28.354/337.

78 Postcard, Museum of London, acquisition no: 28.354/45.

79 "People I Have Met by the Author of 'That Artful Vicar,'" *Illustrated London News*, 31 January 1880.

80 "People I Have Met," *Illustrated London News*, 18 November 1882.

81 See, for example, William Fitzgerald, "Dandy Dogs," *Strand Magazine* (January 1896); Mrs Leslie Williams, *A Manual of Toy Dogs*, 3.

82 Crompton et al., *Home Pets*, 18.

83 Travers, *Mary Poppin*, 48–62.

84 Crompton et al., *Home Pets*, 17.

85 "Le Beau Page," *Illustrated London News*, 15 February 1873; "Lucky Dog," *Illustrated London News*, Christmas 1878.

86 "A Shop-Girl in Kensington Gardens," *Vanity Fair*, 9 April 1903.

87 The discourse on animal breeding conveyed a masculine tone and often emphasized ideas about the dominant influence of male animals in the appearance of offspring. Ritvo, "Sex and the Single Animal," 134–5.

88 Darwin, *The Descent of Man*, 662.

89 For a discussion of this analogy, as well as the ways Darwinism was used to support and refute women's campaign for the franchise, see Eveleen Richards, "Darwin and the Descent of Women" and "Redrawing the Boundaries."

90 *Fur Fanciers' Journal*, 1 January 1892.

91 Ritvo, "Sex and the Single Animal," 137–8.

92 *Fur Fanciers' Journal*, 1 May 1891.

93 *Canary and Cage Bird Life*, 15 December 1905.

94 *Our Home Pets: An Illustrated Monthly* (November 1902).
95 See, for example, the description of a disappointed female dog owner in "The Kennel Club Dog Show at the Crystal Palace," *Illustrated London News*, 27 January 1883.
96 Dickens, *The Fancy*, 222.
97 "Sketches at Cat Show at the Crystal Palace," *Illustrated London News*, 27 October 1884; for accompanying narrative, see p. 403. "The Kennel Club Dog Show at the Crystal Palace," *Illustrated London News*, 27 January 1883; for accompanying narrative, see p. 98.
98 Ibid.
99 "The Canary and Cage-Bird Show at the Crystal Palace," *Illustrated London News*, 24 February 1883.
100 "The Pleasures of Poultry Keeping," *Ladies' Kennel Journal* (February–March 1901): 1454.
101 *Ladies' Kennel Journal* (May 1898): 318.
102 *Ladies' Kennel Journal* (April 1898): 191.
103 These affiliations were mentioned in the first publication of the *Ladies' Kennel Journal* (December 1894).
104 *Fancier's Chronicle*, 4 January 1895. See also *Ladies' Kennel Journal* (January 1895): 229.
105 For the objects of the club, see *Ladies' Kennel Journal* (January 1897): 4; (April 1898): 191.
106 Rappaport, *Shopping for Pleasure*, 74–107.
107 On the ways in which working-class women experienced the campaign for female suffrage "outside suffragism," see Boussahba-Bravard, ed., *Suffrage outside Suffragism*.
108 For the views of suffragists on feminine virtue and moral superiority, see Caine, *English Feminism, 1780–1980*.
109 *Ladies' Kennel Journal* (April 1898): 295.
110 Tickner, *The Spectacle of Women*.
111 *Ladies' Kennel Journal* (July 1898): 7.
112 Cheang, "Women, Pets and Imperialism," 377–81.
113 In this the LKA is consistent with the activities of other Edwardian feminist movements. See Burton, *The Burdens of History* for a discussion of how British feminism came of age while steeped in and reinforcing the imperial ethos.
114 *Ladies' Kennel Journal* (June 1898): 381.
115 *Ladies' Kennel Journal* (July–August 1896): 35.
116 *Ladies' Kennel Journal* (January 1897): 20.
117 *Ladies' Kennel Journal* (August–September 1896): 145.

118 *Ladies' Kennel Journal* (October–November 1895): 156. The journal also published twenty-eight portraits of Queen Victoria's dogs. See ibid. (March 1896): 141–54.

119 *Ladies' Kennel Journal* (January–February 1901): 1430.

120 Ibid.

121 See, for example, *Ladies' Kennel Journal* (October–November 1895): 289; (May 1898): 285.

122 *Ladies' Kennel Journal* (May 1898): 318. These conflicts did not abate in the subsequent decade, and Cheang documents a similar conflict between the *Ladies' Field* newspaper and the Kennel Club in 1908. Cheang, "Women, Pets and Imperialism," 370.

123 *Kennel Gazette*, 23 September 1895.

124 *Fancier's Chronicle*, 24 June 1895. For positive responses to the *Ladies' Kennel Journal*, see *Fancier's Chronicle*, 1 February 1895.

125 *Fancier's Chronicle*, 12 July 1895.

126 "The Woman's Dog," *Saturday Review*, 29 November 1913.

127 Kean, *Animal Rights*, 82.

128 Postcard, acquisition no: 78.6/2, Museum of London.

129 Postcard, acquisition no: 50.82.858, Museum of London. Another postcard dated December 1908, also sent by someone sympathetic to women's suffrage, stated on the back, "Wishing you a merry Xmas time and most happy New Year + may it bring you what you want, + what I want too. H.G.R." This postcard has no acquisition number, but can be found in box of Women's Suffrage Collection Propaganda Postcards SC/5, Museum of London.

130 Postcard, acquisition no: 50.82/1706, Museum of London. For a very similar image, see acquisition no: 50.82/1698, Museum of London.

131 Postcard, acquisition no: 50.82/1702, Museum of London. For another pro-suffrage image featuring a cat, see Kean, *Animal Rights*, 145–6.

132 Tickner, *The Spectacle of Women*, 10.

133 Postcard, Women's Suffrage Collection Propaganda Postcards SC/5, Museum of London.

134 Poster "The Cat and Mouse Act Passed by the Liberal Government," acquisition no: 50.82/1113a, Museum of London. In *The Spectacle of Women*, Tickner speculates that the poster was created by Pearse (27).

3. In the Zoo: Civilizing Animals and Displaying People

1 The Zoo might also be compared to other venues which exhibited animal and human novelties through the nineteenth century. See the work of

Durbach, *Spectacle of Deformity*; Peacock, *The Great Farini*; Qureshi, *Peoples on Parade*; and Altick, *The Shows of London*.

2 *The Leisure Hour* (September 1859), from Collection of Newspaper Clippings 1843–53, ZSL Archives.

3 Doré and Jerrold, *London*, 107–8.

4 On the connection between the Zoological Gardens of London and Empire, see Robert W. Jones, "The Sight of Creatures Strange to Our Clime"; Murray, "Lives of the Zoo"; Ritvo, *The Animal Estate*, 205–32; Ritvo, "The Order of Nature"; Ritvo, "Zoological Nomenclature and the Empire of Victorian Science"; Schneer, *London 1900*, 97–106.

5 My analysis of the Zoo privileges the tactile and material experiences of visitors, while also discussing the Zoo as a visual experience. Perhaps the most famous essay on zoos as spectacle is John Berger's *About Looking*. Berger suggests that, as a consequence of changes wrought by nineteenth-century capitalism, we are no longer able to authentically and directly relate to animals. Nigel Rothfels considers Berger's arguments and offers a discussion of touching animals in zoos, in "Touching Animals."

6 Ritvo, *The Animal Estate*, 205–32; Ritvo, "The Order of Nature," 43–4.

7 See, for example, Peacock, *The Great Farini*; Altick, *The Shows of London*; Ritvo, *The Animal Estate*, 205–42; Neil, "White Wings and Six-Legged Muttons"; John M. Turner, *Victorian Arena*; Assael, *The Circus and Victorian Society*.

8 The founding of the Zoological Society is discussed in Adrian Desmond, "The Making of Institutional Zoology in London, 1822–1836."

9 *Picturesque Guide to Regent's Park*, 42–3. Also quoted in Scherren, *The Zoological Society of London*, 13.

10 Ritvo, "The Order of Nature," 44.

11 Veltre, "Menageries, Metaphors and Meanings," 19.

12 *Literary Gazette*, quoted in Scherren, *The Zoological Society of London*, 22.

13 Endersby, *A Guinea Pig's History of Biology*, especially 1–127 on the nineteenth century.

14 Murray, "Lives of the Zoo," 21; Ritvo, "The Order of Nature," 44.

15 Scherren, *The Zoological Society of London*, 43. See also Report of the Council at the Anniversary Meeting, 3 May 1830, 14–15, ZSL Archives.

16 Report of the Committee of Science and Correspondence to the Council, 22 March 1831, 3, ZSL Archives.

17 Report of Council, 29 April 1833, 16, ZSL Archives.

18 Sclater, *Guide to the Gardens of the Zoological Society of London*, 13th ed., 3, 53.

19 Scherren, *The Zoological Society of London*, 109.

20 Report of Council, 29 April 1859, 25, ZSL Archives. Enthusiasm for these endeavours was also conveyed in guidebooks. See Mitchell, *Guide to the Gardens of the Zoological Society*, 57.

21 *The Times*, 21 January 1859. One author even bemoaned the Englishman's lack of interest in exotic foods. See Simmonds, *The Curiosities of Food*.

22 *Saturday Review*, 3 August 1861.

23 Clipping from *Pall Mall Gazette*, 4 December 1867. For a discussion of eland in private menageries, see Ritvo, *The Animal Estate*, 238–9. For a discussion about eating zoo animals during the siege of Paris as an expression of upper-class boredom and pleasure-seeking, see Spang, "'And They Ate the Zoo.'"

24 Ritvo, *The Animal Estate*, 206.

25 This definition approximates that suggested by Belk et al., "Collectors and Collecting." For a sampling of the literature on collecting, see Clifford, "On Collecting Art and Culture"; Belk, *Collecting in a Consumer Society*; Elsner and Cardinal, eds, *The Cultures of Collecting*; Akin, "Passionate Possession"; Pearce, ed., *Interpreting Objects and Collections*.

26 On institutional collecting, see Michael Ames, *Cannibal Tours and Glass Boxes*; Nicks, "Dr. Oronhyatekha's History Lessons"; Amato, "The Quai Branly Museum." Harriet Ritvo analyses the collection practices of the London Zoo in terms of science and imperial ideologies in "Zoological Nomenclature and the Empire of Victorian Science."

27 Report of Council, 29 April 1833, 11, ZSL Archives.

28 Ritvo, "The Order of Nature," 46–7.

29 Anderson, "Climates of Opinion," 148.

30 Report of Council, 29 April 1851, 14, ZSL Archives.

31 For example, the costs of attempts to procure a giraffe are discussed in Report of Council, 29 April 1836, 13–14. The Zoological Society also frequently purchased animals from Charles Jamrach, a renowned local animal dealer. See Report of Council, 29 April 1873, ZSL Archives.

32 Report of Council, 3 May 1830, 5, ZSL Archives.

33 Ibid., 7–12.

34 For another example, see Minutes of Council Meeting, 14 July 1847, 11–14, ZSL Archives.

35 Report of Council, 29 April 1858, 17, ZSL Archives.

36 Robert W. Jones analyses this "diplomacy" (my term) by recounting the visits of Cetshwayo, King of the Zulus, to Britain in 1882. During his stay, the King was taken to a number of London venues that were symbolic of British power: to Bond Street for a shopping expedition and to the Zoological Gardens ("The Sight of Creatures Strange to Our Clime," 2–4).

37 Initially, European traders only obtained animals at the coast or at inland trading stations and were completely dependent on indigenous animal catchers and middlemen. The business soon became "whitened and professionalized" as Europeans took over the management of each stage. See Rothfels, "Catching Animals," 190–204.

38 Report of Council, 29 April 1831, 13, ZSL Archives.

39 Report of Council, 29 April 1870, 26–37, ZSL Archives.

40 Report of Council, 29 April 1885, 26, ZSL Archives.

41 On the civilizing mission, see Levine, *The British Empire*, 100, 105–6; Wenzel, "Literacy and Futurity."

42 Clipping from *The Leisure Hour* (September 1859), ZSL Archives.

43 *Mirror*, 16 June 1832, 387.

44 Clipping from *Daily News*, 17 August 1880, ZSL Archives. Robert W. Jones uses Edward Said's notion of "imperial geography" to analyse how such descriptions created impressions of the Zoo as an imperial space ("The Sight of Creatures Strange to Our Clime," 8–9).

45 Clipping from unidentified newspaper, 8 July 1835, ZSL Archives.

46 Mitchell, *Centenary History of the Zoological Society of London*, 134–5.

47 Guillery, *The Buildings of the London Zoo*, 8.

48 See discussion of this problem in Report of Council, 29 April 1829, 17–18, ZSL Archives.

49 Report of Council, 29 April 1845, 12; Report of Council, 29 April 1858, 10; Report of Council, 29 April 1885, 26; as well as the remarks of President Flower in the Appendix to the Report of Council, 29 April 1887, 65–6, ZSL Archives.

50 Report of Council, 29 April 1886, 26, ZSL Archives.

51 Edwards, *London Zoo from Old Photographs, 1852–1914*, 79; Guillery, *The Buildings of the London Zoo*, 29.

52 Veltre, "Menageries, Metaphors and Meanings," 16.

53 Report of Council, 29 April 1851, 11, ZSL Archives.

54 Report of Council, 29 April 1867, 17, ZSL Archives.

55 Guillery, *The Buildings of the London Zoo*, 2. Because most of Burton's buildings were thatched-roof structures, only the clock tower (originally the camel house), an aviary, and part of the giraffe house survive today.

56 *Picturesque Guide to Regent's Park*, 18.

57 Guillery, *The Buildings of the London Zoo*, 2–8.

58 Ibid., 6–7. An image of the monkey house can be found in *Illustrated London News*, 23 July 1864. For an image of the elephant and rhinoceros house, see *Illustrated London News*, 26 June 1869.

59 See image of the reptile house, *Illustrated London News*, 2 June 1849.

60 See, for example, *The Zoological Gardens*; Sclater, *Guide to the Gardens of the Zoological Society of London*, 6th ed.; Mitchell, *Official Guide to the Gardens of the Zoological Society of London. With a Plan of the Gardens …*; Huxley, *Official Guide to the Gardens and Aquarium of the Zoological Society of London.*

61 One unofficial guidebook aimed at children stated that its purpose was to inform those "who do visit the Gardens, and [to be] an acceptable present to those who have not the means of seeing this delightful place of recreation and fashionable resort." In this way, even those unable to visit the Zoo could vicariously participate in its projects. Bishop, *Henry and Emma's Visit to the Zoological Gardens, Regent's Park*, 1.

62 This length of time is suggested in *The Zoological Gardens*, 32.

63 Sclater, *Guide to the Gardens of the Zoological Society of London*, 6th ed., 14.

64 Tony Bennett explains how walking is necessary for the comprehension of museum exhibitions. As visitors walk through exhibit areas, they follow and create a narrative chronology step by step (*The Birth of the Museum*, 44–7, 77).

65 Undated clipping of a guide to the Zoological Gardens from an unidentified newspaper in vol. IV of the Fillinham Collection, British Library.

66 C. Williams, *The Zoological Gardens Regent's Park*; Bishop, *A Visit to the Zoological Gardens, in Regent's Park* and *Henry and Emma's Visit to the Zoological Gardens, Regent's Park*; Barnicoat, *The Animals at the Zoo*.

67 *A Day in the Zoo, Realistic Pictures of the Birds, Beasts and Fishes.*

68 Edwards, *London Zoo from Old Photographs*, 49.

69 See, for example, "The Bears and Buns," *Illustrated London News*, 19 April 1873. The article mentions that an ostrich died from being fed money.

70 Clipping of 2 October 1836 from an unidentified newspaper in vol. IV of the Fillinham Collection, British Library.

71 *The Times*, 29 September 1852.

72 Mitchell, *Official Guide to the Gardens of the Zoological Society*, 13th ed. (London: Zoological Society of London, 1915), 4. Children's guidebooks seem to have cautioned against feeding dangerous substances to the animals somewhat earlier. Barnicoat, for example, advised children as follows: "I hope that no boy or girl who reads this book will ever tease an animal, either inside the Zoo or out of it. And when you go to the Zoo, don't feed the animals without looking first to see whether feeding them is permitted. Even then be quite sure you give them the right food" (*The Animals at the Zoo*, 1).

73 17 April 1881, from unidentified newspaper clipping, ZSL Archives.

74 *Daily News*, 17 August 1880, newspaper clipping, ZSL Archives.
75 Robert P. Lawere, "Feeding the Reptiles," *The Times*, 19 August 1880; H.E. Murrell, "Feeding the Reptiles," *The Times*, 23 August 1880; *The Times*, 18 May 1887; 20 May 1887, newspaper clippings, ZSL Archives.
76 Mitchell, *Official Guide to the Gardens of the Zoological Society of London*, 6th ed. (London: Zoological Society of London, 1908), 18. I am grateful to Kristina Paukens for this reference.
77 "The Chimpanzee at the Zoological Gardens," *Illustrated London News*, 12 September 1891.
78 Kearton, "The Zoological Gardens,"348.
79 "The Gorilla 'Pongo' at the Royal Aquarium, Westminster," *Illustrated London News*, 18 August 1877. Pongo apparently drank wine and water out of a glass and politely handed it back to its keeper. See also Mitchell, *Official Guide to the Gardens*, 6th ed., 18; Ritvo, *Animal Estate*, 228–9; Rothfels, *Savages and Beasts*, 189–93; Peacock, *The Great Farini*, 238.
80 Mrs Owen, *The Life of Richard Owen*, quoted in Scherren, *The Zoological Society of London*, 85.
81 Åkerberg, "Knowledge and Pleasure at Regent's Park," 113.
82 *Mirror*, 25 February 1832, 114.
83 Stables, *The Domestic Cat*, 9.
84 Hart-Scott, *True Stories of the London Zoo from the Westminster Gazette*, 49.
85 "The Hippopotamus in a New Character," *Punch*, 31 August 1850.
86 Undated from *Observer*, newspaper clippings 1843–53, ZSL Archives.
87 "Come along Fido!" and "The Diary of a Hippopotamus," *Punch*, 6 July 1850.
88 Edwards, "The Value of Old Photographs of Zoological Collections," 143–4.
89 *Observer*, 11 August 1861; 20 August 1861, newspaper clipping, ZSL Archives.
90 Clipping from an unidentified newspaper dated 1839 in vol. IV of the Fillinham Collection, British Library. See also Bishop, *A Visit to the Zoological Gardens, in Regent's Park*, 34.
91 Scherren, *The Zoological Society of London*, 57.
92 J.G.S., "The Nature of Bears," *The Times*, 2 July 1867.
93 *Illustrated Police News*, 6 July 1867; *Penny Illustrated Paper*, 13 July 1867.
94 *Illustrated Police News*, 21 September 1867.
95 *Daily News*, 17 January 1876, newspaper clipping, ZSL Archives.
96 "The Zoological Society's Gardens," *The Times*, 17 January 1876.
97 *The Times*, 30 December 1875.
98 Clipping from *Court Circular*, 7 April 1866, ZSL Archives.
99 See admittance cards, vol. IV, Fillinham Collection, British Library.

100 "Beware!" *Punch*, 2 May 1863.

101 Clippings from *Observer*, 11 August 1861; 20 August 1861, ZSL Archives.

102 *Daily Telegraph*, 7 May 1879.

103 Ibid.

104 "Odd Sketches at the Zoological Gardens," *Illustrated London News*, 20 November 1880.

105 "Odd Sketches at the Zoological Gardens," *Illustrated London News*, 19 June 1880,.

106 "Odd Sketches at the Zoological Gardens," *Illustrated London News*, 20 November 1880; see also "Odd Sketches at the Zoological Gardens," *Illustrated London News*, 15 August 1881.

107 The *Illustrated London News* referenced physiognomy in one of the articles accompanying these illustrations. See "Odd Zoological Sketches," *Illustrated London News*, 20 November 1880.

108 Cowling, *The Artist as Anthropologist*, especially 121–81 for a discussion on class. See also Pearl, *About Faces*, especially 148–85 on dress, posture, and hairstyle in photography. On the ways theories on physiognomy were applied to the Irish, likening Irishmen to apes, see Curtis, *Apes and Angels*.

109 Oliver Hochadel examines satirical drawings, comparing people and monkeys in Viennese and German zoological gardens and shows how the images used humour and entertainment to encourage speculation on Darwin's theories ("Darwin in the Monkey Cage," 89–92).

110 "Odd Sketches at the Zoological Society," *Illustrated London News*, 15 August 1881.

111 On the Westminster Royal Aquarium and prostitution, see Durbach, *Spectacle of Deformity*, 90. Tracy C. Davis discusses the efforts of the National Vigilance Association to regulate advertisements for entertainments in the Aquarium that were deemed problematically sexual in "Sex in Public Places."

112 "Beasts at the Zoo," *Punch*, 16 June 1866, 10.

113 Edwards, *London Zoo from Old Photographs*, 31.

114 Kearton, "The Zoological Gardens," 350.

115 Åkerberg, *Knowledge and Pleasure at Regent's Park*, 78.

116 Kearton, "The Zoological Gardens," 344.

117 See Edwards, *London Zoo from Old Photographs*.

118 Simms, *Living London*, 25.

119 Kearton, "The Zoological Gardens," 344–50.

120 For an analysis of uniforms and the ways they convey and inspire performances of masculine docility, status, rank, role, character, and occupation, see Craik, "The Cultural Politics of the Uniform."

121 Letter quoted in Scherren, *The Zoological Society of London*, 57.
122 *Morning Herald*, 26 May 1836, quoted in ibid., 63.
123 For these images, see Scherren, *The Zoological Society of London*, plate 11, plate 12.
124 "The Hippopotamus in the Gardens of the Zoological Society Regent's Park," *Illustrated London News*, 1 June 1850.
125 "The Hippopotamus at the Zoological Gardens," *The Times*, 6 June 1850; see also "The Mediterranean," *The Times*, 27 May 1850.
126 Garnett, *A Man in the Zoo*, 33.
127 Ibid., 6–7.
128 Ibid., 9–11.
129 Ibid., 12–13.
130 Ibid., 13.
131 Ibid., 13–14.
132 Ibid., 15.
133 Ibid., 21.
134 Ibid., 20.
135 Ibid., 78.
136 Ibid., 79–84.
137 Ibid., 84, 87–8.
138 Ibid., 92.
139 Ibid., 94.
140 John MacKenzie, "The Imperial Exhibitions of Great Britain," 261, 267.
141 *Oxford English Dictionary Online*, "Zoo," http://www.oed.com.myaccess.library.utoronto.ca/. Accessed 12 October 2012.
142 *Webster's Dictionary Online*, "Zoo," http://www.merriam-webster.com/dictionary/zoo. Accessed 12 October 2012.
143 Galsworthy, *The White Monkey*, 15.

4. The White Elephant in London: On Trickery, Racism, and Advertising

1 *The Times*, 22 December 1883.
2 *The Times*, 17 January 1884.
3 For an overview of this argument, see Hall and Rose, "Introduction"; Thompson, *The Empire Strikes Back?*.
4 The literature on the ways ordinary citizens were implicated in imperial ideologies is vast. See MacKenzie, ed., *Imperialism and Popular Culture*. For a discussion of the ways museum collections conveyed imperialist ideologies in Britain, see Bennett, *The Birth of the Museum*; Coombes, *Reinventing Africa*. For a discussion of the ways advertising conveyed

imperialist ideologies, see McClintock, *Imperial Leather*; Ramamurthy, *Imperial Persuaders*; Thomas Richards, *The Commodity Culture of Victorian England*.

5 Lola Young, "Hybridity's Discontents," 158. On the connection between evolutionary thought and racism, see Brantlinger, "Victorians and Africans," 182–7.

6 Durbach, *Spectacle of Deformity*, 147–70.

7 This imagery became particularly powerful in the second half of the nineteenth century. In the 1880s, anxieties about city dwelling were connected to concerns about physical appearance, British racial degeneration, and imperial competition from other European powers. Durbach, *Spectacle of Deformity*, 154–8; Gareth Stedman Jones, *Outcast London*; Koven, *Slumming*; Pick, *Faces of Degeneration*, 189–203; Ross, *Love and Toil*, 11; Walkowitz, *City of Dreadful Delight*, 15–39.

8 Durbach, *Spectacle of Deformity*, 158. On the ways animals were exhibited as novelties and their features compared to human traits, see Neil, "White Wings and Six-Legged Muttons."

9 See Adams, *E Pluribus Barnum*; James W. Cook, *The Arts of Deception*; Reiss, *The Showman and the Slave*.

10 Martin, *The White African American Body*, 58–70.

11 Tagliacozzo, "Ambiguous Commodities, Unstable Frontiers."

12 Boyer, "Picturing the Other."

13 Myint-U, *The Making of Modern Burma*, 1–7, 178–85, 87–98; Pollak, *Empires in Collision*, 1–8.

14 For a discussion of nationalism in Thailand and competing cosmological concepts of mapping, see Winichakul, *Siam Mapped*. See also Peleggi, *Thailand*, 13–15, 59–61.

15 Bowring, *The Kingdom and People of Siam*, 1:475.

16 Ibid., 476. Preserving parts of the skin of deceased white elephants was a common custom, and many specimens remain on display in the ivory room of the National Museum in Bangkok. Ringis, *Elephants of Thailand in Myth, Art and Reality*, 108–9.

17 Ibid., 94.

18 Ibid., 110. For a more complete ethno-history of white elephants in Thailand, see 96–104.

19 Pratt, *Imperial Eyes*, 2.

20 Finlayson, *The Mission to Siam and Hue, 1821–22*.

21 Neale, *Narrative of a Residence at the Capital of the Kingdom of Siam, with a Description of the Manners, Customs and Laws of the Modern Siamese*.

22 Vincent, *The Land of the White Elephant*.

23 Finlayson, *The Mission to Siam and Hue*, 151. Sir John Bowring, another sympathetic observer, described the colour of the white elephant he encountered as "really a light mahogany, the eye that of an albino." Bowring, *The Kingdom and People of Siam*, 2:312.

24 Finlayson, *The Mission to Siam and Hue*, 153.

25 Neale, *Narrative of a Residence at the Capital of the Kingdom of Siam*, 98–9. See also 100–1, 125.

26 See, for example, Graham, *Siam*, 526–7; Leonowens, *The English Governess at the Siamese Court*, 139–45; Sir Yule, *Narrative of the Mission Sent by the Governor-General of India to the Court of Ava in 1855*, 133–5; Winston, *Four Years in Upper Burma*, 26–7. For an earlier account of a missionary's residence in Ava and Rangoon between 1783 and 1806, see Jardine and Wiseman, eds., *The Burmese Empire a Hundred Years Ago as Described by Father Sangermano*, 76–80.

27 The same point is raised in Ringis, *Elephants of Thailand in Myth, Art and Reality*, 96.

28 For the exact definition see *Oxford English Dictionary Online*, "White Elephant," http://www.oed.com.myaccess.library.utoronto.ca/. Accessed 7 October 2013.

29 *Illustrated Sporting and Dramatic News*, 17 January 1880.

30 Bock, *Temples and Elephants*, 32–3.

31 For extensive references to Bock, see "Mr. Barnum's White Elephant," *Pall Mall Gazette*, 14 January 1884, and "Carl Bock and Barnum's White Elephant," *Penny Illustrated Paper*, 19 January 1884.

32 F.E.W., "Mr. Barnum's White Elephant," *The Times*, 22 January 1884.

33 Charles E. Fryer, *The Times*, 25 January 1884.

34 Nai Pleng, "The White Elephant," *The Times*, 29 January 1884.

35 For an examination of the style of Barnum's showmanship, see James W. Cook, *The Arts of Deception*.

36 Adams, *E Pluribus Barnum*, 1.

37 For other analyses of Barnum's showmanship, see Dennett, *Weird and Wonderful*; Durant and Durant, *Pictorial History of the American Circus*; Fitzsimons, *Barnum in London*; Harding, *Elephant Story*; Harris, *Humbug*; Kunhardt, Kunhardt, and Kunhardt, *P.T. Barnum*; Saxon, *P.T. Barnum*; Irving Wallace, *The Fabulous Showman*; Werner, *Barnum*.

38 For visitor statistics during each day of the elephant's residency, see *The Occurrences in the Gardens*, 17 January to 12 March 1884, ZSL Archives.

39 These visitor numbers were reported in *The Times*, 28 February 1884 and *The Occurrences in the Gardens*, ZSL Archives.

40 See, for example, the *Graphic, Illustrated Police News, Pall Mall Gazette, Penny Illustrated Paper, Penny Pictorial News, Pictorial World,* and *Spectator* between January and March 1884.

41 For the effects of Barnum's early showmanship on Englishmen, see Fitzsimons, *Barnum in London.*

42 Durbach, *Spectacle of Deformity,* 100.

43 Barnum, *Struggles and Triumphs,* 338.

44 Barnum, quoted in Harding, *Elephant Story,* 110.

45 Barnum, *Struggles and Triumphs,* 338.

46 Balmanno Squire, "To the Editor of the Times," *The Times,* 23 January 1884.

47 Benjamin Hill Evans, letter to Zoological Society of London, 30 January 1884, ZSL Archives.

48 See "The White Elephant," *The Times,* 21 January 1884; "The White Elephant," *The Times,* 23 January 1884 and *The Times,* 28 February 1884.

49 John Guy Laverick, letter to Philip Lutley Sclater, 22 February 1884, ZSL Archives.

50 William Henry Flower, "Letter to the Editor," *The Times,* 26 January 1884.

51 See *The Times,* 18 January 1885 and *Illustrated London News,* 26 January 1884. For a description of the ways the hill tribes were imagined and represented by the British in India, see Kennedy, *The Magic Mountains.*

52 "The White Elephant," *The Times,* 21 January 1884.

53 *The Times,* 21 January 1884.

54 "The White Elephant," *The Times,* 21 January 1884.

55 *The Times,* 22 January 1884.

56 "The White Elephant," *The Times,* 23 January 1884.

57 Ibid.

58 As McClintock argues, clean, white bodies were markers of identity, distinguishing the upper classes from the dirty and implicitly racialized poor. See McClintock, *Imperial Leather,* 211. Koven also examines representations and meanings of dirt in London's slums in *Slumming,* 183–227.

59 "Priests of the Burmese 'White Elephant' at the Zoological Gardens," *Illustrated London News,* 2 February 1884. Here the *ILN* is quoting the comments of G.P. Sanderson in the pages of the *The Times* on 22 January. Sanderson was an authority on elephants and had been put in charge of the Bengal Elephant Catching Establishment in 1875. He wrote a book on his observations and adventures titled *Thirteen Years among the Wild Beasts of India* (1878).

60 "The 'White' Elephant at the Zoological Gardens," *Illustrated Sporting and Dramatic News,* 26 January 1884.

61 *Spectator*, 19 January 1884.

62 W.H. Flower, "Letter to the Editor," *The Times*, 21 January 1884.

63 Balmanno Squire, "To the Editor of the Times," *The Times*, 23 January 1884.

64 W. Dommett Stone, "Letter to the Editor," *The Times*, 23 January 1884,

65 "Arrival of the White Elephant from Burmah," *Illustrated London News*, 26 January 1884.

66 "The White Elephant," *British Medical Journal*, 26 January 1884.

67 "The White Elephant," *The Times*, 21 January 1884.

68 "The White Elephant," *The Times*, 25 January 1884.

69 *Animal World*, 1 February 1884, quoted in Jolly, *Jumbo*, 144.

70 "The Purchase of the White Elephant," *The Times*, 24 January 1884.

71 "The White Elephant," *The Times*, 21 January 1884.

72 "Mr. Barnum's Burmese Priests," *The Times*, 26 January 1884.

73 Robert Gordon, *The Times*, 24 January 1884.

74 C.[*sic*]P. Sanderson, *The Times*, 22 January 1884. This is presumably the same Sanderson mentioned in note 59 above.

75 Durant and Durant claim that Barnum bought the elephant for $75,000 in *Pictorial History of the American Circus*, 95. The most accurate assessment is provided by Saxon, who states that Barnum's official accountant entered the figure of £6000 in the office diary (*P.T. Barnum*, 304). The same amount is quoted in Kunhardt, Kunhardt, and Kunhardt, *P.T. Barnum*, 295.

76 "City and Suburban News," *New York Times*, 28 March 1884.

77 Barnum, *Struggles and Triumphs*, 339.

78 Saxon, *P.T. Barnum*, 303–5.

79 Durbach, *Spectacle of Deformity*, 100.

80 Barnum encouraged this opinion among American audiences by sponsoring a poetry competition. The winning entry articulated Western sentiment towards the idea of animal worship: "To tyrants on returning East: *We worship neither man nor beast.*" See Joaquin Miller "The Sacred White Elephant – Toung Taloung," quoted in Werner, *Barnum*, 351.

81 Ayaybain, "To the Editor of the Times," *The Times*, 21 January 1884. The anecdote comes from Vincent, *The Land of the White Elephant*, 66.

82 Ayaybain, "To the Editor of the Times," *The Times*, 21 January 1884.

83 T.W. Rhys Davids, "The Buddhists at the Zoological Gardens," *The Times*, 29 January 1884.

84 T.W. Rhys Davids, "To the Editor of the Times," *The Times*, 7 February 1884.

85 "Mr. Barnum's Burmese 'Priests,'" *The Times*, 28 January 1884.

86 Ibid. See also "Priests of the Burmese 'White Elephant' at the Zoological Gardens," *Illustrated London News*, 2 February 1884.

87 Frederick Brine, letter to Philip Lutley Sclater, 31 January 1884, ZSL
    Archives.

88 Benjamin Hill Evans, letter to the Zoological Society of London,
    30 January 1884, ZSL Archives.

89 Joseph Charlton Parr, letter to the Zoological Society of London,
    26 January 1884, ZSL Archives.

90 Sir John, letter to the Zoological Society of London, 31 January 1884, ZSL
    Archives.

91 Anglo-Indian, "Letter to the Editor," *The Times*, 24 January 1884.

92 Sir Edwin Ray Lankester, letter to Philip Lutley Sclater, 28 January 1884,
    ZSL Archives. See also E. Ray Lankester, "To the Editor of the Pall Mall
    Gazette," *Pall Mall Gazette*, 28 January 1884.

93 See listings for "Arrivals" on 17 January 1884 and "Departures" on
    12 March 1884, in *The Occurrences in the Gardens*, ZSL Archives.

94 W.H. Flower, "Letter to the Editor," *The Times*, 26 January 1884.

95 Philip Lutley Sclater to J.R. Davis (Barnum's agent), 28 January 1884, ZSL
    Archives.

96 The terms of agreement between Barnum's agent and the secretary of the
    Zoological Society were not recorded. See Zoological Society Minutes of
    Council, Vol. XVII, 16 January 1884, 201–2 and 5 March 1884, 223–4, ZSL
    Archives.

97 On Jumbo, see Harding, *Elephant Story*; Jolly, *Jumbo*; Murray, "Lives of the
    Zoo," 194–205; Ritvo, *The Animal Estate*, 232.

98 "The White Elephant," *The Field, The Country Gentleman's Newspaper*,
    26 January 1884. For a lengthier discussion, see Murray, "Lives of the
    Zoo," 224–5.

99 Throughout late January 1884, *The Times* reported an increased number
    of visitors to the London Zoological Gardens. See *The Times*, 22 January
    1884; 23 January 1884; 24 January 1884. This is corroborated by records
    kept in *Occurrences at the Gardens*, ZSL Archives.

100 Sir Spencer, letter to the Zoological Society of London, 2 February 1884,
    ZSL Archives.

101 "Mr. Barnum's "White Elephant," *Pall Mall Gazette*, 11 March 1884.

102 Schudson, "Historical Roots of Consumer Culture," 61–81.

103 For more information, see "Bubbles; A Child's
    World," http://collections.vam.ac.uk/item/O75697/
    bubbles-a-childs-world-print-millais-john-everett/.

104 McClintock, "Soft-Soaping Empire," 133. On the history of Victorian adver-
    tising agencies, see Hindley and Hindley, *Advertising in Victorian England*.
    For a comprehensive analysis of Victorian advertising iconography, see

Loeb, *Consuming Angels*. For an analysis of advertising representing empire, see Thomas Richards, *The Commodity Culture of Victorian England*.

105 Another full-page advertisement appeared in *Illustrated Sporting and Dramatic News*, 22 March 1884.

106 See Advertisements: Scrapbook B2, Museum of London.

107 McClintock, *Imperial Leather*, 210–14.

108 Ramamurthy, *Imperial Persuaders*, 26–30.

109 de Groot, "Metropolitan Desires and Colonial Connections," 189. For a book analysing how similar imagery created a complicated formulation of white identity, see Pieterse, *White on Black*, 196.

110 Ramamurthy also discusses this advertisement in *Imperial Persuaders*, 44.

111 On "poke your head through" backdrops featuring the "You Dirty Boy!" advertisement, see Linkman, *The Victorians*, 179–80.

112 The first announcement of Adam Forepaugh's white elephant in the *New York Times* occurred on 16 March 1884. See "Siam and the Elephants," *New York Times*, 16 March 1884.

113 For exposure of the hoax by one of the elephant's keepers, see "A Whitewashed Elephant; Forepaugh's 'Light of Asia' a Fraud on the American People," *New York Times*, 11 April 1884.

114 "A Very Sea-Sick Elephant: A Beast with Brown Eyes and Grey Skin. The Stranger Who Arrived on the City of Chester Yesterday and What Is Said of His Claims," *New York Times*, 21 March 1884. For a report of the arrival of Barnum's elephant stateside, see "The Sacred Beast Here; From Burmah to the Great Moral Show. Mr. Barnum's Anxious Trip to the Lydian Monarch and a Satisfactory Examination of the White Elephant," *New York Times*, 29 March 1884.

115 For a copy of Forepaugh's playbill see Kunhardt, Kunhardt, and Kunhardt, *P.T. Barnum*, 294.

116 For a copy of Barnum's playbill, see ibid., 295.

117 "An Interesting Experiment," *New York Times*, 21 April 1884.

118 For an analysis of anxieties about the bodies of African Americans with white or gradually whitening skin, see Martin, *The White African American Body*.

119 Ibid., 168–9.

120 One exception is a brief report from Burma by Mr Alfred E. Rimmer, an officer of the Irrawaddy Flotilla Company, who reports in the *Illustrated London News* that a "'white elephant' has been caught, and there have been palace rejoicings for a month. I went to see it and it was as great a fraud as Barnum's 'white elephant.' There were a few muddy patches on its skin, and some white hairs, probably from age; but the King is wild with joy." *Illustrated London News*, 5 December 1885.

121 "The White Elephant," *Punch*, 27 October 1892.

122 "A Great Mistake," in *Fur Coats and Feathered Frocks*.

123 Edward F. Benson, *Dodo, a Detail of the Day*, 19 and 31.

124 The image appeared on the back cover of a Pears' Christmas Annual in the first decade of the twentieth century. Ramamurthy, *Imperial Persuaders*, 28.

5. Dead Things: The Afterlives of Animals

1 Kittens' Wedding Tableau (detail) on postcard produced by the Victoria and Albert Museum in the possession of the author. For a similar image, see Atterbury and Cooper, *Victorians at Home and Abroad*, 60.

2 "Inventing New Britain: The Victorian Vision," exhibition at the Victoria and Albert Museum, 2001.

3 My examination of nineteenth-century taxidermy augments a developing historiography on representations of animal death: Kenneth L. Ames, *Death in the Dining Room*; Haraway, "Teddy Bear Patriarchy"; Poliquin, *The Breathless Zoo*; Wonders, *Habitat Dioramas*; Alberti, ed., *The Afterlives of Animals*.

4 See, for example, Asma, *Stuffed Animals and Pickled Heads*; Durbach, *Spectacle of Deformity*; Qureshi, "Displaying Sara Baartman, the Hottentot Venus."

5 See Bentham, "Auto-Icon; or Further Uses of the Dead to the Living."

6 The extent of Bentham's influence on social reform in England in the 1830s is still being debated. The question of whether the men who crafted legislation were friends of Bentham, had read Bentham, or ever even heard of him, remains unresolved. It seems clear, nevertheless, that legislation instituting changes to the Poor Law, factory inspections, police and prisons, public health, and education, among others, was consistent with Bentham's ideas articulated in a prodigious output of writing over the course of his life. See Perkin, *Origins of Modern English Society*, 267–70.

7 For a discussion of Bentham's involvement in drafting the 1832 Anatomy Act, see Richardson, "Bentham and Bodies for Dissection."

8 Bentham, "Auto-Icon," 2.

9 Ibid., 3.

10 For a discussion of popular beliefs about the corpse, see Richardson, *Death, Dissection and the Destitute*, 3–29.

11 For a discussion of nineteenth-century beliefs about death and afterlife, see Jalland, "Victorian Death and Its Decline"; Rugg, "From Reason to Regulation."

12 For a discussion of the Anatomy Act, see Richardson, *Death, Dissection and the Destitute*. For discussions of the social shame attached to

dissection and the effect this had on working-class funerary practices, see Richardson, "Why Was Death So Big in Victorian Britain?"; Rugg, "From Reason to Regulation," 225. There is extensive debate about these burial and mourning rituals: some historians have condemned them as overly ostentatious, while others have interpreted them as healthy responses to grief. For a sample of this literature, see Cannadine, "War and Death, Grief and Mourning in Modern Britain," 189–96; Jalland, "Death, Grief, and Mourning in the Upper-Class Family, 1860–1914"; Laqueur, "Bodies, Death and Pauper Funerals"; Strange, *Death, Grief and Poverty in Britain, 1870–1914*, 1–26.

13 Richardson, *Death, Dissection and the Destitute*, 159–61.

14 Bentham, "Auto-Icon," 1.

15 In Southwood Smith's words, "I endeavoured to preserve the head untouched, merely drawing away the fluids by placing it under an air pump over sulphuric acid. By this means the head was rendered as hard as the skulls of the New Zealanders, but all expression was of course gone. Seeing this would not do for exhibition, I had a model made in wax by a distinguished artist … one of the most admirable likenesses ever seen." T.S. Smith to William Munk, quoted in Marmoy, "The Auto-Icon of Jeremy Bentham at University College, London," 82.

16 Museum no: A44694, Wellcome Collection. No information has been found to account for how and when the piece of skin came into the possession of Henry Wellcome. See "Bentham's Skin," http://www.ucl.ac.uk/Bentham-Project/news/benthamiana/odds_ends/skin. Access date 14 December 2014.

17 For details on the original mounting of the Auto-Icon, as well as subsequent repairs, see Richardson and Hurwitz, "Jeremy Bentham's Self Image," 196.

18 Smith's views on anatomical dissection were consistent with Bentham's. Smith had published an influential article, "Use of the Dead to the Living," which appeared in the *Westminster Review* in 1824.

19 See Crimmins, ed., *Bentham's Auto-Icon and Related Writings*, xlv–li; Marmoy, "The 'Auto-Icon' of Jeremy Bentham at University College, London." For more details on the Auto-Icon, see UCL Bentham Project, "The Auto-Icon," available from http://www.ucl.ac.uk/Bentham-Project/who/autoicon.

20 For images of this process, see Richardson and Hurwitz, "Jeremy Bentham's Self Image," 197.

21 Bentham, "Auto-Icon," 5.

22 Ibid., 12–13.

23 In discussing Bentham's essay, Richardson and Hurwitz suggest that a "powerful narcissistic impulse reverberates through this last manuscript" ("Jeremy Bentham's Self Image," 197).

24 Bentham, "Auto-Icon," 4, 9.

25 Ibid., 5, 7, 8.

26 Ibid., 6, 7.

27 Smith recognized that Bentham's requests for dissection and posthumous display might be ridiculed. See Thomas Southwood Smith, "A Lecture Delivered over the Remains of Jeremy Bentham, Esq. (1832)," 73.

28 Marmoy, "The 'Auto-Icon' of Jeremy Bentham at University College, London," 78–9.

29 Grier, "Material Culture as Rhetoric."

30 Bowdich, *Taxidermy*, 30. For similar instructions on how to create a fire screen out of pigeon bodies, see *Cassell's Household Guide, Being a Complete Encyclopedia of Domestic and Social Economy and forming a Guide to Every Department of Practical Life*, 1:289–91, quoted in Logan, *The Victorian Parlour*, 172–3.

31 Davie, *Methods in the Art of Taxidermy*, 7, 3. For other discussions of equipment, see Bowdich, *Taxidermy*, 15–17; *Birds' Nests and Eggs*, 335. For information on how available materials, including equipment, determined the techniques of preservation and the development of natural science in England until 1845, see Larson, "Equipment for the Field," , 358–63, 370–2. For a discussion of the major technical problems confronting taxidermists in the eighteenth century and the development of various methods, see Farber, "The Development of Taxidermy and the History of Ornithology."

32 For an image of "Willy the Lion" with saggy skin and stitch marks stuffed by Edward Gerrard, see *The Contents of Mr. Potter's Museum of Curiosities*, 64.

33 In advertisements for taxidermic services, these efforts of locals were sometimes disparaged. The *Harrod's General Catalogue* suggested that the tradesmen's services were needed because "many [specimens] which have been dressed by natives, &c., do not always turn out so satisfactory" (*Harrod's General Catalogue*, 1910, 639).

34 These descriptions were quoted in Herriott, *British Taxidermists*, 7. Christopher Frost's *History of British Taxidermy* also catalogues advertisements by many nineteenth-century British taxidermists.

35 For statistics, see Kean, *Animal Rights*, 120; MacKenzie, *The Empire of Nature*, 41.

36 Ibid.

37 *Harrod's General Catalogue*, 1910, 639–40.

38 For inquiries on how to stuff birds and preserve the skins of cats, see
   Exchange and Mart, 11 January 1871; 2 January 1880. For advertisements selling equipment, see "Taxidermist's Companions," *Harrod's
   General Catalogue*, 1910, 643. One taxidermist discusses how he learned
   to preserve a mouse as a child: "The Art of Stuffing," *Natural Science: A
   Monthly Review of Scientific Progress* 5, no. 30 (1894): 58. For a discussion
   of women manufacturing taxidermy for parlour decoration in Britain,
   see Logan, *The Victorian Parlour*, 147. For a discussion of women manufacturing taxidermy in Victorian Canada, see Jenny Cook, "Bringing
   the Outside In," 41. Cook asserts that women were motivated to produce taxidermy by studies of science and religion. They introduced
   nature into the home to explain Christian social values. For a discussion of women manufacturing taxidermy for the decoration of hats and
   other items of fashion, see Tolini, "'Beetle Abominations' and Birds on
   Bonnets." For a discussion of female taxidermists in France, see Carole E.
   Harrison, "Citizens and Scientists."
39 Kean, *Animal Rights*, 18–21.
40 French, *Antivivisection and Medical Science in Victorian Society*, 376–8;
   Thomas, *Man and the Natural World*, 137–42n31; James Turner, *Reckoning
   with the Beast*, 79–95.
41 Wood, *Man and Beast*, 14.
42 "In Remembrance Of," *Household Pets*, 24 September 1910, 14.
43 *Fur and Feather. A Weekly Journal devoted to Rabbits, Cage Birds, Cats, Cavies
   and Pet Stock, for Exhibition and Fancy*, 21 August 1890; 5 January 1895.
44 In contrast, by the 1870s pet cemeteries were established in France and
   already common in Germany. In America the oldest pet cemetery was
   founded no earlier than 1896. See Gillis, *A World of Their Own Making*, 76;
   Howell, "A Place for the Animal Dead," 10; Kete, *The Beast in the Boudoir*,
   33–5, 90.
45 E.A. Brayley Hodgetts, "A Cemetery for Dogs," *Strand Magazine* (July–
   December 1893): 626–7.
46 Philip Howell discusses dedications on the gravestones in the Hyde Park
   Cemetery in "A Place for the Animal Dead," 8; Teresa Magnum discusses
   these epitaphs and other memorials to dead dogs in "Animal Angst."
47 "Pets at Rest," *Household Pets*, 8 October 1910.
48 For a discussion of the shortage of sanitary graveyard space and attempts
   to remedy the problem, see Jalland, "Victorian Death and Its Decline,"
   242–5; Rugg, "From Reason to Regulation," 215–21.
49 *Fur and Feather*, 12 June 1890.
50 Leigh, *Pets a Paper*, 30.

51 William Fitzgerald, "Animal' Furniture," *Strand Magazine* (July 1896): 275.

52 Rowland Ward as quoted in Frost, *History of British Taxidermy*, 11.

53 One pet-keeping manual even provided instructions for the preservation of pet monkeys. See Patterson, *Notes on Pet Monkeys*, 102–3.

54 Leigh, *Pets a Paper*, 29.

55 Calder, *The Victorian Home*, 24. Given the state of photographic technology and the lengthy exposure time required to produce a portrait, animal subjects in photographs were usually stuffed. For a fascinating discussion of the use of stuffed animals in Victorian nature photography, see Brower, "'Take Only Photographs.'"

56 Fitzgerald, "'Animal' Furniture," 274.

57 Thad Logan suggests that taxidermy was standard in middle-class Victorian parlours (*The Victorian Parlour*, 141–2).

58 For a lengthy discussion, see Davie, *Methods in the Art of Taxidermy*, 113–17.

59 Grossmith and Grossmith, *Diary of a Nobody*, chapter 7. Available at : http://www.gutenberg.org/files/1026/1026-h/1026-h.htm.

60 For a photograph of a picture frame mount, see Montagu Browne, *Artistic and Scientific Taxidermy and Modelling*, 414.

61 Ibid., 12–13; North, "The Taxidermal Art," 239.

62 For a discussion of the ways stuffed animals in painting and photography evoke the picturesque, see Millard, "Images of Nature," 28. For more examples, see Taylor, *Animal Painting in England*.

63 Davie, *Methods in the Art of Taxidermy*, 136.

64 Dead animals were also a common sculptural motif in dining-room decoration and carved into sideboard furniture. See Kenneth L. Ames, *Death in the Dining Room*, 44–96.

65 Swainson, *Taxidermy*, 81–2. See also Allen, *The Naturalist in Britain*, 40; Allen, "Tastes and Crazes,"394–407.

66 "The Bird-Stuffer," *Illustrated London News*, 15 November 1884.

67 Fitzgerald, "'Animal' Furniture," 273–4.

68 Ibid., 277.

69 Ibid., 279–80. I do not know where the elephant chair was located – it may have been in a home or a club.

70 "An Indian Game Trophy," *The Times*, 3 June 1887.

71 *Bazaar, Exchange and Mart*, 2 January 1885.

72 "Mr. F. Horniman's Museum, Forest Hill," *Illustrated London News*, January 1891.

73 "The Horniman Museum," *Illustrated London News*, 29 June 1901.

74 On the life of Frederick John Horniman and the early years of the Horniman Museum, see "Horniman Museum, Historical Information

Sheet 2: Horniman Family"; Finbarr Whooley, "Frederick Horniman's Centenary – The Life of a Remarkable Man"; Michael Horniman, "The Horniman Family"; "F.J. Horniman and the Museum," from handout at London Showcase ETV Exhibition, July 1973; and Keith Nicklin, "Report on the Establishment and Growth of the Ethnography Collection and Its Use at the Horniman Museum," all located in the Horniman Museum and Gardens.

75 The photograph of curator Richard Quick's children was taken before the polar bear was transferred to the new museum circa 1901- Horniman Museum and Gardens.

76 On stuffed polar bears, see Wilson, *Nanoq*.

77 *A Handbook to the Collection Arranged as an Introduction to the Study of Animal Life*. Price One Penny. London County Council, n.d., Horniman Museum and Gardens.

78 Photograph, "Natural History Gallery," 5 March 1913, Horniman Museum and Gardens.

79 On arrangements of taxidermy in natural history museums and taxonomies, see Poliquin, *The Breathless Zoo*, 126.

80 For records of acquisitions from Hubbard, see Horniman Museum and Gardens. Hubbard's collection is also discussed in David, *The Arctic in the British Imagination*, 171.

81 *Annual Report: The Horniman Museum*, 1895, Horniman Museum and Gardens.

82 For photographs of the work of Hermann Ploucquet, see Beaver, *The Crystal Palace, 1851–1936*, 60.

83 *Birds' Nests and Eggs*, 322.

84 "The Natural History of the Exhibition," *Illustrated London News*, 26 July 1851.

85 The influence of the "Lion and Tiger Struggle" by Edwin Ward, Rowland Ward's "Combat of Red Deer," and Jules Verneaux's "Arab Courier Attacked by Lions" is discussed by Hornaday and Holland, *Taxidermy and Zoological Collecting*, 229. See also Beard, "A New Art," 67.

86 "Colonial and Indian Exhibition," *Illustrated London News*, 8 May 1886.

87 On Charles Darwin's efforts to advocate for changes to the display of natural history departments, see Poliquin, *The Breathless Zoo*, 129–130.

88 Alfred Russel Wallace, "Museums for the People," 247.

89 In 1820, for example, William Swainson introduced the method of storing relaxed specimens in flat drawers as a way to conveniently keep hundreds of museum specimens. Larson, "Equipment for the Field," 370.

90 "Practical Taxidermy," *Nature, a Weekly Illustrated Journal of Science* 30 (1884): 338–9.

91 Clipping of a guidebook to the British Museum in vol. II of the Fillinham
   Collection, British Museum.
92 North, "The Taxidermal Art," 231.
93 "Practical Taxidermy," *Nature, a Weekly Illustrated Journal of Science* 30
   (1884): 338–9.
94 For a detailed examination of the origin of these exhibitions, see
   Wonders, *Habitat Dioramas.*
95 Ibid., 17.
96 Montagu Browne, *Practical Taxidermy: A Manual of Instruction to the
   Amateur in Collecting Preserving and Setting up of Natural History Specimens
   of All Kinds* (London, 1879), quoted in ibid., 45.
97 "Taxidermy as Fine Art," *Natural Science: A Monthly Review of Scientific
   Progress* 5, no. 30 (1894): ii–iii.
98 North, "The Taxidermal Art," 231. These claims of newness were exaggerated. Taxidermists had always striven to render the animal as accurately as possible.
99 Montagu Browne, *Artistic and Scientific Taxidermy and Modelling*, 397.
100 On the competing priorities of scientific research, public pedagogy,
   and entertainment in nineteenth-century British museums, see Alberti,
   "Placing Nature"; "Taxidermy as Fine Art," *Natural Science: A Monthly
   Review of Scientific Progress* 5, no. 30 (1894); Carrol, "The Natural History
   of Visiting"; Sheets-Pyenson, *Cathedrals of Science*; Stearn, *The Natural
   History Museum at South Kensington*; Yanni, *Nature's Museums*. For information on more heterodox exhibitions and their contributions to the
   development of natural history see Altick, *The Shows of London.*
101 "Taxidermy as Fine Art," *Natural Science: A Monthly Review of Scientific
   Progress* 5, no. 30 (1894): iv.
102 "The Art of Stuffing," *Natural Science: A Monthly Review of Scientific
   Progress* 5, no. 30 (1894): 59; Montagu Browne, *Artistic and Scientific
   Taxidermy and Modelling*, 6, 17.
103 See, for example, directions on how to form the shapes of eagles, spar-
   rows, vultures, and doves in Waterton, *Wanderings*, 181.
104 "Hampshire Taxidermist Hart, Edward," http://www3.hants.gov.uk/
   museum/biology/taxidermy/taxidermy-a-to-z/hart-edward.htm, accessed 3 December 2012; newspaper clippings, Edward Hart Collection,
   Horniman Museum and Gardens; correspondence arranging the arrival
   of the Princess of Wales found in envelope IV, acquisition no. 17.11.1953,
   Edward Hart Collection, Horniman Museum and Gardens.
105 Hart, *An Annotated List of the Birds and Animals*, 5.
106 Hart, notes on British bullfinch, case no. 37.H, Edward Hart Collection,
   Horniman Museum and Gardens.

107 Hart, case of bullfinch, acquisition no. NH 83.3/16, Horniman Museum
     and Gardens.
108 Hart, *An Annotated List*, 6.
109 Hart, case of swallows, acquisition no. NH83.3/96, Horniman Museum
     and Gardens.
110 Hart, "Notes on British Robin," case no. 213b. Edward Hart Collection,
     Horniman Museum and Gardens; e-mail from Joanne Hatton to Sarah
     Amato, 2 December 2012. Hart's case displaying the robins can be found
     at aquisition no. NH.83.3/93, Horniman Museum and Gardens.
111 According to Franklin North, a tableau of the death and burial of Cock
     Robin was shown to the Society of American Taxidermists in the early
     1880s. See North, "The Taxidermal Art," 239.
112 Baddeley, "Mr. Potter's Museum of Curiosities,"6.
113 Ibid.
114 Ibid.
115 Grice, "Stuff, Things and Stuffed Things."
116 A photograph of the tableau can be found in *Potter's Museum of Curiosity*,
     9.
117 Ibid., 8.
118 For a photograph, see ibid., 9.
119 Ibid., 10.
120 Potter's taxidermy is a material manifestation of Martin Weiner's argu-
     ment in *English Culture and the Decline of the Industrial Spirit, 1850–1980*
     that the British middle class had become ambivalent about industrialism
     by the second half of the nineteenth century. Weiner argues that the very
     people who created Britain as "the workshop of the world" now found
     the capitalist ethos distasteful and longed for a retreat to the countryside.
121 Henning, "Anthropomorphic Taxidermy and the Death of Nature."
122 A chromolithograph by Louis Wain, "The Naughty Puss," together with
     another print of personified animals, "The Dog's Academy," was offered
     for sale at auction as part of the Walter Potter Collection in September
     2003. *The Contents of Mr. Potter's Museum of Curiosities*, 7.
123 See Greeting Cards/Novelty Postcards and Blotters A5, Museum of
     London; Christmas Cards 4: Animals, Birds, Children, John Johnson
     Collection of Printed Ephemera.
124 For photographs of the work of Hermann Ploucquet, see Beaver,
     The Crystal Palace, 1851–1936, 60.
125 For more examples from the Walter Potter collection, see *Potter's Museum
     of Curiosity*.
126 "The Natural History of the Exhibition," *Illustrated London News*,
     26 July 1851.

127 *Potter's Museum of Curiosity*, 17.
128 Darnton, "Workers Revolt: The Great Cat Massacre of the Rue
      Saint-Severin."
129 See mummified cat from circa 1870–90, acquisition no. 77.142, Museum of
      London.
130 Poliquin, *The Breathless Zoo*, 182–90. Here Poliquin offers a different inter-
      pretation of the Kittens' Wedding, asserting that "[t]here is no moral por-
      trayed, no sense that kittens are somehow like us – or we like them. There
      is no nuance between various character wiles and follies. The animals tell
      us nothing about themselves, and no viewer could pretend otherwise."
      Poliquin argues that the vignettes are miniatures, like dollhouses and toy
      soldiers, offering storybook views of an idealized world. I would add
      that Potter's scenes should be considered in the context of longstanding
      attitudes and the Victorian tendency to feminize cats.
131 Merish, "Cuteness and Commodity Aesthetics," 185, 194.
132 Ibid., 187.
133 Ibid., 192–4.

Bibliography

Archival and Museum Collections

Booth Museum of Natural History
    Visitor Books
    Field Notes
British Library
    Fillinham Collection
Horniman Museum and Gardens
    Edward Hart Collection
Harrod's Knightsbridge
    Harrod's General Catalogue, 1910, 1928–9
    Harrod's News, July–August 1917
John Johnson Collection of Printed Ephemera
    Animals on Show: Box 1, Box 2
    Circuses: Boxes 1–5
    Christmas Cards: Box 4
    Domestic Pets: Box 1, Box 2
    Embroidery Patterns: Box 1
    Entertainments: Box 4
    Greeting Cards/Novelty Postcards and Blotters
    Fancy Work: Box 1
Museum of London
    Advertisements: Scrapbook B2, B3
    Christmas Card Collection
    Collections of Taxidermy
    Collections of Toys
    Printed Ephemera
    Woman's Suffrage Collection Propaganda Postcards SC/5

Wellcome Collection
Zoological Society of London (ZSL) Archives
    Collection of Newspaper Clippings
    Letters
    Minutes of Council, 1847–8
    The Occurrences in the Gardens
    Reports of Council, 1829–1919

Newspapers and Periodicals

The Atheneum
The Bookman
The British Medical Journal
Canary and Cage Bird Life
The Century Illustrated Monthly Magazine
The Dog Owners' Supplement to the Bazaar
Exchange and Mart (after 1872 *Bazaar, Exchange and Mart*)
*The Fancier's Chronicle: A Journal for Poultry, Pigeon, Dog, Pet Stock and
    Bee Fanciers*
The Field, The Country Gentleman's Newspaper
*Fur and Feather. A Weekly Journal Devoted to Rabbits, Cage Birds, Cats, Cavies
    and Pet Stock, for Exhibition and Fancy*
Fur and Feather: An Illustrated Weekly Journal for Town and Country
The Fur Fanciers' Journal: A Weekly Paper Devoted to Exhibitors of Pet Stock & c.
*The Fur Fanciers' Journal: A Journal Devoted to the Interests of Rabbits, Cats &
    Cavies*
The Girl's Empire
The Graphic
The Guardian
Household Pets
Illustrated London News
Illustrated Police News
Illustrated Sporting and Dramatic News
The Kennel Gazette
Ladies' Kennel Journal
The Lady: A Journal for Gentlewomen
The Leisure Hour
*The Midland Fancier and Clubs' Medium: A Journal for Fanciers of Poultry, Pigeons,
    Rabbits, Cage Birds & c.*
The Mirror
The Nation

Natural Science: A Monthly Review of Scientific Progress
Nature, a Weekly Illustrated Journal of Science
The New Age
The New York Times
The New York Times Book Review
Our Cats
Our Home Pets: An Illustrated Monthly
The Pall Mall Gazette
The Penny Illustrated Paper
Penny Pictorial News
Pictorial World
Punch, or The London Charivari
The Saturday Review
The Spectator
The Strand Magazine
The Times (London)
The Times Literary Supplement
Vanity Fair

Primary Sources

Avis, Richard. *The Canary and Its History, Varieties, Management and Breeding.* London: Groombridge and Sons, 1870.

Barnicoat, Constance. *The Animals at the Zoo. Or, the Children's Holiday at the Zoological Gardens.* London: "Book for the Bairns" Office, 1907.

Barnum, P.T. *Struggles and Triumphs, or, Sixty Years' Recollections of P.T. Barnum Including His Golden Rules for Money-Making. Illustrated, and Brought up to 1889.* Buffalo: Courier Co., Printers, 1889.

Batty, Joseph H. *Practical Taxidermy and Home Decoration Together with General Information for Sportsmen.* New York: Ornage Judd Co., 1890.

Beard, J. Carter. "A New Art." *Scribner's Magazine* 20 (1896): 66–72.

Beeton's Book of Poultry and Domestic Animals: Showing How to Rear and Manage Them in Sickness and in Health. London: Ward, Lock and Tyler, n.d.

Benson, Edward F. *Dodo, a Detail of the Day.* London: Hodder and Stoughton, 1894.

Bentham, Jeremy. "Auto-Icon; or Further Uses of the Dead to the Living." In *Bentham's Auto-Icon and Related Writings,* ed. James E. Crimmins. Bristol: Thoemmes Press, 2002.

Birds' Nests and Eggs. Also Directions for Bird Stuffing. With Thirteen Engravings and Designs and Colored Illustration of the Eggs of British Birds. London: Bickers and Bush, 1861.

Bishop, James. *Henry and Emma's Visit to the Zoological Gardens, Regent's Park.* London: Dean and Munday.
– *A Visit to the Zoological Gardens, in Regent's Park.* London: Thos. Dean and Co., 1845.
Blake, Dr Carter, and Mrs Leslie Williams. *Fancy Mice: Their Varieties, Management, and Breeding. Illustrated. Fourth Edition.* London: L. Upcott Gill, 1896.
Blakston, W.A., W. Swaysland, and August F. Wiener. *The Illustrated Book of Canaries and Cage-Birds. British and Foreign.* London: Cassell and Co., 1877.
Bliss, Mrs J. Worthington. *Every Inch a King; or, the Adventures of Rex and His Little Friends. Illustrated by Harrison Weir.* London: Griffith and Farran, 1879.
The Book of Home Pets: Showing How to Rear and Manage in Sickness and in Health, Birds, Poultry, Pigeons, Rabbits, Guinea-Pigs, Dogs, Cats, Squirrels, Fancy Mice, Tortoises, Bees, Silkworms, Ponies, Donkeys, Goats, Inhabitants of the Aquarium, Etc. Etc. With a Chapter on Ferns. London: S.O. Beeton, 1862.
The British Aviary, and Bird Breeder's Companion. London: William Cole, 1840.
Browne, Montagu. *Artistic and Scientific Taxidermy and Modelling.* London: Adam and Charles Black, 1896.
Bock, Carl. *Temples and Elephants: Travels in Siam in 1881–1882.* Oxford, New York, and Toronto: Oxford University Press, 1986.
Bowdich, Sarah. *Taxidermy: or, the Art of Collecting, Preparing and Mounting Objects of Natural History. For the Use of Museums and Travellers. With Plates.* 4th ed. London: Longman, Rees, Orme, Brown, and Green, 1829.
Bowring, Sir John. *The Kingdom and People of Siam: With a Narrative of the Mission to That Country.* Vol. 1. London: J.W. Parker and Son, 1857.
– *The Kingdom and People of Siam: With a Narrative of the Mission to That Country in 1855.* Vol. 2. London: J.W. Parker and Son, 1857.
The Canary and Other Song Birds; Whether Hard-Billed, or Seed-Eating Birds, or Soft-Billed, or Insect and Grain-Eating Birds: Their Management in Health and Treatment in Disease. By a Practical Cage-Bird Keeper. London: Dean and Son, 1870.
The Canary, Goldfinch, Greenfinch, Nightingale, Lark, Titmouse, Redbreast, Linnet, Yellowhammer, Wren. How to Rear and Manage Them, in Sickness and in Health. London: Bickers and Bush, 1861.
Carroll, Lewis. *Through the Looking Glass, and What Alice Found There, With Fifty Illustrations by John Tenniel.* London: Macmillan and Co., 1872.
Chance, Mrs W. *A Book of Cats: Being a Discourse on Cats, with Many Quotations & Original Pencil Drawings.* London: J.M. Dent and Co., 1898.
Clifford, Molly Lee. *Yoppy: The Autobiography of a Monkey.* London: Gay and Bird, 1903.

Cooper, Henry St, and Mrs Carlo F.C. Clarke. *Bull-Dogs and Bull-Dog Breeding and Toy Bull-Dogs*. London: Jarrold and Sons, 1905.

Crompton, Herbert, Gordon Stables, Arthur G. Butler, J.J. Bissell, W.F. Lumley, Meredith Fradd, and Miss Frances Simpson. *Home Pets*. London: Greening and Co., 1907.

Cumberland, Charles. *The Guinea Pig, or Domestic Cavy for Food, Fur, and Fancy*. London: L. Upcott Gill, 1886.

Darwin, Charles. *The Correspondence of Charles Darwin*. Vol. 7, *1858–59*. New York: Cambridge University Press, 1985.

– *The Descent of Man, and Selection in Relation to Sex*. Amherst, NY: Prometheus Books, 1998.

Davie, Oliver. *Methods in the Art of Taxidermy*. London: H.T. Booth, 1894.

Davies, C.J. *Fancy Mice, Their Varieties and Management as Pets or for Show, Including the Latest Scientific Information as to Breeding for Colour*. 4th ed. London: L. Upcott Gill, 1912.

A Day in the Zoo, Realistic Pictures of the Birds, Beasts and Fishes. An Adaptation of an Antique Pop-up Book. Esslingen: J.F. Schreiber of Esslingen, 1890.

Dickens, Charles, Jr. *Dickens's Dictionary of London* 1879. Available from http:// www.victorianlondon.org/dickens/dickens-z.htm. Accessed 20 December 2007.

Dickens, Monica. *The Fancy*. Harmondsworth: Penguin Books, 1964.

Ditchfield's Little Wonder Book. No. 4. The General Management of Pond and Aquarium. London: Frank Ditchfield, Pet Specialist, n.d.

Doré, Gustave, and Blanchard Jerrold. *London: A Pilgrimage*. London: Grant and Co., 1872.

Finlayson, George. *The Mission to Siam and Hue, 1821–22*. Singapore: Oxford University Press, 1988.

Fitzgerald, William. "Animal" Furniture." *Strand Magazine* (July 1896): 273–80.

– "Dandy Dogs." *Strand Magazine* (January 1896): 538–50.

Fur Coats and Feathered Frocks [short stories of animals, with coloured illustrations]. London: E. Nister, 1892.

Galsworthy, John. *The White Monkey*. London: William Heinemann, 1928.

Garnett, David. *A Man in the Zoo*. London: Chatto and Windus, 1924.

Graham, W.A. *Siam: A Handbook of Practical, Commercial, and Political Information*. Chicago: F.G. Browne and Co., 1913.

Greene, W.T. *Birds I Have Kept in Years Gone By. With Original Anecdotes and Full Directions for Keeping Them Successfully*. London: L. Upcott Gill, 1885.

Grossmith, David, and Wheedon Grossmith. *Diary of a Nobody*. Bristol: J.W. Arrowsmith, Printer, Quay Street, 1910.

Hart, Edward. *An Annotated List of the Birds and Animals*. Bournemouth: Sydney J. Mate, 1913.

Hart-Scott, P.N. *True Stories of the London Zoo from the Westminster Gazette*. London: Claude Stacy, 1927.

Hibbard, Shirley. *Rustic Adornments for Homes of Taste*. London: Groombridge and Sons, 1870.

Hornaday, William Temple, and William Jacob Holland. *Taxidermy and Zoological Collecting*. New York: Charles Scribner's Sons, 1891.

Hudson, W.H. *The Book of a Naturalist*. 2nd ed. London: Hodder and Stoughton, 1920.

Huxley, Julian S. *Official Guide to the Gardens and Aquarium of the Zoological Society of London*. London: Offices of the Zoological Society of London, 1938.

Jaquet, Edward William. *The Kennel Club: A History Record of Its Works. With Numerous Portraits and Other Illustrations*. London: Kennel Club Gazette, 1905.

Jardine, John, and Nicholas Wiseman, eds. *The Burmese Empire a Hundred Years Ago As Described by Father Sangermano*. London: A. Constable and Co., 1893.

Jennings, John. *Domestic and Fancy Cats: A Practical Treatise on Their Varieties, Breeding, Management, and Diseases*. 2nd ed. London: L. Upcott Gill, 1906.

Kearton, Richard. "The Zoological Gardens." In *Living London: Its Work and Its Play, Its Humour and Its Pathos, Its Sights and Its Scenes*, ed. George Simms, vol. 1, section 2, 344–50. London: Cassell, 1901.

Lane, C.H. *Rabbits, Cats and Cavies: Descriptive Sketches of All Recognised Exhibition Varieties with Many Original Anecdotes ... With over 100 Illustrations from Life Studies of Prize Winners by Rosa Bebb*. London: J.M. Dent and Co., 1903.

Lee, Mrs R. *Taxidermy: or the Art of Collecting, Preparing and Mounting Objects of Natural History for the Use of Museums and Travellers*. London: Longman, Huist, Rees, Orme, and Brown, 1820.

Leigh, Major Egerton. *Pets a Paper. Dedicated to All Who Do Not Spell Pets – PESTS. Read at the Mechanics' Institution at the Music Hall, Chester*. London: Longman, Brown, Green, Longmans and Roberts, 1859.

Leonowens, Anna Harriette. *The English Governess at the Siamese Court: Being Six Years in the Royal Palace at Bangkok*. Boston: J.R. Osgood and Co., 1873.

Lyell, James C. *Fancy Pigeons: Containing Full Directions for Their Breeding and Management, with Descriptions of Every Known Variety and All Other Information of Interest or Use to Pigeon Fanciers*. London: L. Upcott Gill, 1887.

Lytton, Judith Neville. *Toy Dogs and Their Ancestors. Including the History and Management of Toy Spaniels, Pekingese, Japanese and Pomeranians*. London: Duckworth and Co., 1911.

MacGregor, Forbes. *Greyfriars Bobby: The Real Story at Last*. London and Edinburgh: Steve Savage, 2003.

Maxey, W. *Fancy Mice and Rats, How to Breed and Exhibit*. Idle, Bradford:
   Printed and Published at the Offices of *Fur and Feather*, 1920.
Mayhew, Henry. *London Labour and the London Poor by Henry Mayhew with a New
   Introduction by John D. Rosenberg*. Vol. 1. New York: Dover Publications, 1968.
– *London Labour and the London Poor Poor by Henry Mayhew with a New
   Introduction by John D. Rosenberg*. Vol. 2. New York: Dover Publications, 1968.
Mitchell, Peter Chalmers. *Centenary History of the Zoological Society of London*.
   London: Zoological Society, 1929.
– *Guide to the Gardens of the Zoological Society*. London: Bradbury and Evans,
   1853.
– *Official Guide to the Gardens of the Zoological Society of London*. 6th ed.
   London: Zoological Society of London, 1908
– *Official Guide to the Gardens of the Zoological Society of London*. 13th ed.
   London: Zoological Society of London, 1915.
– *Official Guide to the Gardens of the Zoological Society of London*. 24th ed.
   London: Zoological Society of London, 1926.
*The National Cat Club Stud Book and Register [This is the First Stud Book concern-
   ing the Cat that has been yet attempted, and contains the entries, &c., sent into the
   N.C.C. from July 31st, 1890, to the close of 1892]*. Bromley, Kent: E. Clarke and
   Son, 1893.
Neale, Frederick Arthur. *Narrative of a Residence at the Capital of the Kingdom
   of Siam, with a Description of the Manners, Customs and Laws of the Modern
   Siamese*. London: National Illustrated Library, 1852.
North, Franklin H. "The Taxidermal Art." *The Century: A Popular Quarterly* 25,
   no. 2 (1882): 230–40.
*Parrots and Monkeys by the Author of "The Knights of the Frozen Sea," Etc., with
   Twenty-Six Illustrations*. London: Seeley, Jackson and Halliday, 1879.
Patterson, Arthur. *Notes on Pet Monkeys and How to Manage Them*. London: L.
   Upcott Gill, 1888.
*Picturesque Guide to Regent's Park; with Accurate Descriptions of the Colosseum,
   the Diorama, and the Zoological Gardens. Illustrated with Upwards of Thirty
   Engravings*. London: John Limbird, 1829.
Pollock, Walter Herries. *Animals That Have Owned Us*. London: John Murray,
   1904.
*Potter's Museum of Curiosity, 6 High Street, Arundel Sussex [Text by Walter Potter,
   James Courtland and the "Saturday Book"]*. Derby: English Life Publications,
   1977.
Russ, Karl. *The Speaking Parrots: A Scientific Manual*. London: L. Upcott Gill, 1884.
Sanderson, G.P. *Thirteen Years among the Wild Beasts of India*. London: Wm. H.
   Allen and Co., 1878.

Scherren, Henry. "Bird-Land and Pet-Land in London." In *Living London: Its Work and Its Play, Its Humour and Its Pathos, Its Sights and Its Scenes*, ed. George Simms, vol. 2, section 2, 324–9. London: Cassell, 1901.
– *The Zoological Society of London: A Sketch of Its Foundation and Development, and the Story of Its Farm, Museum, Gardens and Menagerie*. London: Cassell, 1905.
Sclater, Philip Lutley. *Guide to the Gardens of the Zoological Society of London*. 6th ed. London: Bradbury and Evans, 1860.
– *Guide to the Gardens of the Zoological Society of London*. 13th ed. London: Bradbury and Evans, 1863.
Shaw, Bernard. *Pygmalion: A Romance in Five Acts*. London and New York: Penguin Books, 2000.
Simmonds, Peter Lund. *The Curiosities of Food; or the Dainties and Delicacies of Different Nations Obtained from the Animal Kingdom*. London: Richard Bentley, 1859.
Simms, George, ed. *Living London: Its Work and Its Play, Its Humour and Its Pathos, Its Sights and Its Scenes*. London: Cassell, 1901.
Simpson, Frances. "Cat and Dog London." In *Living London: Its Work and Its Play, Its Humour and Its Pathos, Its Sights and Its Scenes*, ed. George Simms, vol. 1, section 2, 254–60. London: Cassell, 1901.
Smith, Rev. Francis. *The Canary: Its Varieties, Management, and Breeding*. London: Groombridge and Sons, 1868.
Smith, Thomas Southwood. "A Lecture Delivered over the Remains of Jeremy Bentham, Esq. (1832)." Bristol, 1832. Reprinted in *The "Auto-Icon" of Jeremy Bentham and Related Writings*, ed. James E. Crimmins. Bristol: Thoemmes Press, 2002.
Spicer, Muriel Handley. *Toy Dogs: How to Breed and Rear Them Being the Life of a Griffon Bruxellois*. London: Adam and Charles Black, 1902.
Stables, William Gordon. *"Cats" Their Points and Characteristics, with Curiosities of Cat Life, and Chapter on Feline Ailments*. London: Dean and Son, 1876.
– *The Domestic Cat*. London: George Routledge and Sons, 1876.
– *Our Friend the Dog*. London: Dean and Son, 1903.
– *Sable and White: The Autobiography of a Show Dog*. London: Jarrold and Sons, 1893.
Stillman, W.J. "Billy and Hans: A True History." *Century Illustrated Monthly Magazine* (November 1896–April 1897): 619–26.
Stonehenge. *The Dog in Health and Disease. Comprising the Various Modes of Breaking and Using Him for Hunting, Coursing, Shooting, Etc., and Including the Points or Characteristics of Toy Dogs*. London: Longman, Green, Longman, and Roberts, 1859.

Swainson, William. *Taxidermy: With the Biography of Zoologists and Notice of Their Works.* London: Longman, 1840.

Travers, P.L. *Mary Poppins.* Orlando: Harcourt, 1997.

Trimmer, Sarah. *The History of the Robins: For the Instruction of Children on Their Treatment of Animals.* London: Griffith and Farran, 1869.

Veblen, Thorstein. *Theory of the Leisure Class: An Economic Study of Institutions.* New York: Macmillan Co., 1899.

Vincent, Frank. *The Land of the White Elephant: Sights and Scenes in South-East Asia, 1871–72.* Singapore: Oxford University Press, 1988.

Wallace, Alfred Russel. "Museums for the People." *Macmillan's Magazine* 19 (1869).

Wallace, Robert L. *The Canary Book.* London: "The Country Office," 1875.

Ward, Rowland. *The Sportsman's Handbook to Practical Collecting, Preserving, and Artistic Setting-up of Trophies and Specimens to Which Is Added a Synoptical Guide to the Hunting Grounds of the World.* 3rd ed. London: Rowland Ward, 1883.

Waterton, Charles. *Wanderings in South America, the North-West of the United States, and the Antilles, in the Years 1812, 1816, 1820 and 1824 with Original Instructions for the Perfect Preservation of Birds and for Cabinets of Natural History.* London: Oxford University Press, 1973.

Williams, C. *The Zoological Gardens Regent's Park.* London: C. Title, 1838.

Williams, Mrs Leslie. *A Manual of Toy Dogs: How to Breed, Rear, and Feed Them.* 3rd ed. London: Edward Arnold, 1910.

Winslow, Helen M. *Concerning Cats: My Own and Some Others.* London: David Nutt, 1903.

Winston, W.R. *Four Years in Upper Burma.* London: C.H. Kelly, 1892.

Wood, J.G. *Man and Beast: Here and Hereafter.* New York: Harper and Brothers, 1875.

Yule, Sir Henry. *Narrative of the Mission Sent by the Governor-General of India to the Court of Ava in 1855.* Kuala Lumpur and New York: Oxford University Press, 1968.

The Zoological Gardens: A Description of the Gardens and Menageries of the Royal Zoological Society. London: H.G. Clarke and Co., 1852.

Secondary Sources

Adams, Bluford. *E Pluribus Barnum: The Great Showman and the Making of U.S. Popular Culture.* Minneapolis: University of Minnesota Press, 1997.

Åkerberg, Sofia. "Knowledge and Pleasure at Regent's Park: The Gardens of the Zoological Society of London during the Nineteenth Century." PhD. diss., Dept. of Historical Studies, Umeå University, 2001.

Akin, Marjorie. "Passionate Possession: The Formation of Private Collections." In *Learning from Things: Method and Theory of Material Culture Studies*, ed. W. David Kingery, 102–29. Washington and London: Smithsonian Institution Press, 1996.

Alberti, Samuel J.M.M. "Placing Nature: Natural History Collections and Their Owners in Nineteenth-Century Provincial England." *British Journal of the History of Science* 35, no. 126 (2002): 291–311.

Alberti, Samuel J.M.M., ed. *The Afterlives of Animals: A Museum Menagerie*. Charlottesville: University of Virginia Press, 2011.

Alderton, David. *The Cat: The Most Complete, Illustrated Practical Guide to Cats and Their World*. London: Chartwell Books, 1983.

Allen, David Elliston. *The Naturalist in Britain: A Social History*. London: Allen Lane, 1976.

– "Tastes and Crazes." In *Cultures of Natural History*, ed. Nicholas Jardine, James A. Secord, and Emma Spary, 394–407. Cambridge: Cambridge University Press, 1996.

– *The Victorian Fern Craze*. London: Hutchison, 1969.

Altick, Richard D. *The Shows of London*. Cambridge, MA: Belknap Press of Harvard University Press, 1978.

Amato, Sarah. "The Quai Branly Museum: Representing France after the Loss of Empire." *Race and Class* 47, no. 4 (2006): 46–65.

Ames, Kenneth L. *Death in the Dining Room and Other Tales of Victorian Culture*. Philadelphia: Temple University Press, 1992.

Ames, Michael. *Cannibal Tours and Glass Boxes: The Anthropology of Museums*. Vancouver: University of British Columbia Press, 1992.

Anderson, Warwick. "Climates of Opinion: Acclimatization in Nineteenth-Century France and England." *Victorian Studies* 35, no. 2 (Winter 1992): 135–57.

Appadurai, Arjun, ed. *The Social Life of Things: Commodities in Cultural Perspective*. Cambridge: Cambridge University Press, 1986.

Assael, Brenda. *The Circus in Victorian Society*. Charlottesville: University of Virginia Press, 2005.

Asma, Stephen T. *Stuffed Animals and Pickled Heads: The Culture and Evolution of Natural History Museums*. Oxford: Oxford University Press, 2001.

Atterbury, Paul, and Suzanne Fagance Cooper. *Victorians at Home and Abroad*. London: V & A Publications, 2001.

Auerbach, Jeffrey. *The Great Exhibition of 1851: A Nation on Display*. New Haven: Yale University Press, 1999.

Auslander, Leora. "Beyond Words." *American Historical Review* (October 2005): 1015–45.

Baddeley, Jon. "Mr. Potter's Museum of Curiosities." In *The Contents of Mr. Potter's Museum of Curiosities*. Auction Catalogue. London: Bonhams, 2003.

Bagwell, Philip S. *The Transport Revolution*. London: Routledge, 1988.

Bailey, Peter. *Leisure and Class in Victorian England: Rational Recreation and the Contest for Control, 1830–1885*. London: Routledge, 1987.

Baker, Steve. *Picturing the Beast: Animals, Identity, and Representations*. Manchester: Manchester University Press, 1993.

Bakhtin, Mikhail. *Rabelais and His World*. Translated by Helene Iswolsky. Bloomington and Indianapolis: Indiana University Press, 1984.

Ballantyne, Tony, and Antionette Burton, eds. *Moving Subjects: Gender, Mobility and Intimacy in an Age of Global Empire*. Urbana: University of Illinois Press, 2009.

Barringer, Tim, and Tom Flynn. *Colonialism and the Object: Empire, Material Culture and the Museum*. London: Routledge, 1998.

Bartely, Mary M. "Darwin and Domestication: Studies on Inheritance." *Journal of the History of Biology* 25, no. 2 (1992): 302–33.

Beaver, Patrick. *The Crystal Palace, 1851–1936: A Portrait of Victorian Enterprise*. London: H. Evelyn, 1970.

Belk, Russel W. *Collecting in a Consumer Society*. London and New York: Routledge, 1995.

Belk, Russel W., Melanie Wallendorf, John Sherry, Morris Holbrook, and Scott Roberts. "Collectors and Collecting." *Advances in Consumer Research* 15 (1988): 27–32.

Bennett, Tony. *The Birth of the Museum: History, Theory, Politics*. London: Routledge, 1995.

Benson, John. *The Rise of Consumer Society in Britain, 1880–1990*. London: Longman, 1993.

Benson, John, and Laura Ugolini, eds. *Cultures of Selling: Perspectives on Consumption and Society since 1700*. Aldershot: Ashgate, 2006.

Berger, John. *About Looking*. London: Writers and Readers, 1980.

Blount, Margaret. *Animal Land: The Creatures of Children's Fiction*. London: Hutchinson and Co., 1974.

Blanchard, Pascal, Nicolas Bancel, Gilles Boetsch, Eric Deroo, Sandrine Lemaire, and Charles Forsdick, eds. *Human Zoos: Science and Spectacle in the Age of Colonial Empires*. Liverpool: Liverpool University Press, 2008.

Blunt, Wilfred. *The Ark in the Park: The Zoo in the Nineteenth Century*. London: Hamish Hamilton, 1976.

Boussahba-Bravard, Myriam, ed. *Suffrage Outside Suffragism: Women's Vote in Britain, 1880–1914*. Houndsmills: Palgrave Macmillan, 2007.

Bowler, Peter. *The Non-Darwinian Revolution: Reinterpreting a Historical Myth*. Baltimore: Johns Hopkins University Press, 1988.

Boyer, Deborah Deacon. "Picturing the Other: Images of Burmans in Imperial Britain." *Victorian Periodicals Review* 35, no. 3 (2002): 214–26.

Brantlinger, Patrick. "Victorians and Africans: The Genealogy of the Myth of
the Dark Continent." *Critical Inquiry* 12, no. 1 (1985): 166–203.

Branz, Dorthee., ed. *Beastly Natures: Animals, Humans and the Study of History.*
Charlottesville: University of Virginia Press, 2010.

Brewer, John, and Roy Porter, eds. *Consumption and the World of Goods.* London
and New York: Routledge, 1993.

Briggs, Asa. *Victorian Things.* Chicago: University of Chicago Press, 1988.

Bronner, Simon J., ed. *Consuming Visions: Accumulation and Display of Goods in
America 1880–1920.* New York and London: W.W. Norton and Co., 1989.

Brower, Matthew. *Developing Animals.: Wildlife and American Photography.*
Minneapolis and London: University of Minnesota Press, 2011.

– *"Take Only Photographs": Animal Photography's Construction of Nature Love.*
2005. Available from http://www.rochester.edu/in_visible_culture/
Issue_9/issue9_brower.pdf. Accessed 19 March 2007.

Brown, Laura. *Fables of Modernity: Literature and Culture in the English
Eighteenth Century.* Ithaca: Cornell University Press, 2001.

Brown, Penelope, and L.J. Jordanova. "Oppressive Dichotomies: The Nature/
Culture Debate." In *Women in Society: Interdisciplinary Essays*, ed. Cambridge
Women's Studies Group, 224–42. London: Virago Press, 1981.

Browne, E. Janet. *Charles Darwin: A Biography.* Vol. 2, *The Power of Place.* New
York: Knopf, 2002.

Bruce, Helen. "The White Elephant." *History Today* no. 21 (1971): 14–21.

Burt, Jonathan. "Violent Health and the Moving Image: The London Zoo."
In *Animals in Human Histories: The Mirror of Nature and Culture*, ed. Mary J.
Henninger-Voss, 258–95. Rochester: University of Rochester Press, 2002.

Burton, Antoinette. *The Burdens of History: British Feminists, Indian Women and
Imperial Culture, 1865–1914.* Chapel Hill: University of North Carolina Press,
1994.

– "Making a Spectacle of Empire: Indian Travellers in Fin-De-Siècle London."
History Workshop Journal 42 (1996): 127–46.

Butler, Judith. "Performative Acts and Gender Constitution: An Essay in
Phenomenology and Feminist Theory." In *Performing Feminisms: Feminist
Critical Theory and Theatre*, ed. Sue-Ellen Case, 270–82. Baltimore: Johns
Hopkins University Press, 1990.

Buzard, James, Joseph W. Childers, and Eileen Gillooly, eds. *Victorian Prism:
Refractions of the Crystal Palace.* Charlottesville: University of Virginia Press,
2007.

Caine, Barbara. *English Feminism, 1780–1980.* Oxford: Oxford University Press,
1997.

Calder, Jennifer. *The Victorian Home.* London: B.T. Batsford, 1977.

Cannadine, David. "War and Death, Grief and Mourning in Modern Britain."

In *Mirrors of Mortality: Studies in the Social History of Death*, ed. Joachim
Whaley, 187–242. London: Europa Publications, 1981.

Carpenter, Humphrey. *Secret Gardens: A Study of the Golden Age of Children's
Literature*. Boston: Houghton Mifflin Co., 1985.

Carrol, Victoria. "The Natural History of Visiting: Responses to Charles
Waterton and Walton Hall." *Studies in the History and Philosophy of Biological
and Biomedical Sciences* 35 (2004): 31–64.

Cheang, Sarah. "Women, Pets and Imperialism: The British Pekingese Dog
and Nostalgia for Old China." *Journal of British Studies* 45, no. 2 (2006):
359–86.

Clifford, James. "On Collecting Art and Culture." In *The Predicament of Culture,
Twentieth-Century Ethnography, Literature and Art*. Cambridge, MA: Harvard
University Press, 1988.

Cohen, Deborah. *Household Gods: The British and Their Possessions*. New Haven:
Yale University Press, 2006.

Connolly, Paula T. "The Marketing of Romantic Childhood: Milne, Disney,
and a Very Popular Stuffed Bear." In *Literature and the Child: Romantic
Continuations, Postmodern Contestations*, ed. James Holt McGavran. Iowa
City: University of Iowa Press, 1999.

The Contents of Mr. Potter's Museum of Curiosities. Auction Catalogue. London:
Bonhams, 2003.

Cook, James W. *The Arts of Deception: Playing with Fraud in the Age of Barnum*.
Cambridge, MA: Harvard University Press, 2001.

Cook, Jenny. "Bringing the Outside In: Women and the Transformation of the
Middle-Class Maritime Canadian Interior, 1830-60." *Material History Review*
38 (Fall 1993): 36–49.

Coombes, Annie E. *Reinventing Africa: Museums, Material Culture and Popular
Imagination in Late Victorian and Edwardian England*. New Haven and
London: Yale University Press, 1994.

Coombes, Annie E., and Avtar Brah. "Introduction: The Conundrum of
'Mixing.'" In *Hybridity and Its Discontents: Politics, Science, Culture*, 1–17.
London and New York: Routledge, 2000.

Cosslett, Tess. "Child's Place in Nature: Talking Animals in Victorian's
Children Fiction." *Nineteenth-Century Contexts: An Interdisciplinary Journal*
23, no. 4 (2002): 475–97.

– *Talking Animals in British Children's Fiction, 1786–1914*. Aldershot: Ashgate,
2006.

Coysh, A.W. *The Dictionary of Picture Postcards in Britain, 1894–1939*.
Woodbridge, Suffolk: Antique Collectors' Club, 1984.

Cowling, Mary. *The Artist as Anthropologist: The Representation of Types and
Character in Victorian Art*. Cambridge: Cambridge University Press, 1989.

Craik, Jennifer. "The Cultural Politics of the Uniform." *Fashion Theory* 7, no. 2 (2003): 127–48.

Crimmins, James E., ed. *Bentham's Auto-Icon and Related Writings*. Bristol: Thoemmes Press, 2002.

Crossick, Geoffrey, and Serge Jauman, eds. *Cathedrals of Consumption: The European Department Store, 1850–1939*. Aldershot: Ashgate, 1999.

Csikszentmihalyi, Mihaly. "Why We Need Things." In *History from Things: Essays on Material Culture*, ed. Steven Lubar and W. David Kingery, 20–9. Washington and London: Smithsonian Institution Press, 1993.

Curtis, L. Perry, Jr. *Apes and Angels: The Irishman in Victorian Caricature*. Revised ed. Washington: Smithsonian Institution Press, 1997.

Darnton, Robert. "Workers Revolt: The Great Cat Massacre of the Rue St. Séverin." In *Rethinking Popular Culture: Contemporary Perspectives in Cultural Studies*, ed. Chandra Mukerji and Michael Schudson, 97–120. Berkeley: University of California Press, 1991.

Daston, Lorraine, and Gregg Mitman. *Thinking with Animals: New Perspectives on Anthropomorphism*. New York: Columbia University Press, 2005.

David, Robert G. *The Arctic in the British Imagination: 1818–1914*. Manchester: Manchester University Press, 2000.

Davidoff, Leonore, and Catherine Hall. *Family Fortunes: Men and Women of the English Middle Class, 1780–1850*. London: Hutchinson, 1987.

Davies, Douglas J. *Death, Ritual and Belief: The Rhetoric of Funerary Rites*. 2nd ed. London: Continuum, 2002.

Davis, Tracy C. "Sex in Public Places: The Zaeo Aquarium Scandal and the Victorian Moral Majority." *Theatre History Studies* 10 (1990): 1–13.

de Grazia, Victoria, and Ellen Furlough, eds. *The Sex of Things: Gender and Consumption in Historical Perspective*. Berkeley: University of California Press, 1996.

de Groot, Joanna. "Metropolitan Desires and Colonial Connections: Reflections on Consumption and Empire." In *At Home with the Empire: Metropolitan Culture and the Imperial World*, ed. Sonya Rose and Catherine Hall, 166–90. Cambridge: Cambridge University Press, 2006.

Dennett, Andrea Stulman. *Weird and Wonderful: The Dime Museum in America*. New York and London: New York University Press, 1997.

Derry, Margaret Elsinor. *Horses in Society: A Story of Animal Breeding and Marketing, 1800–1920*. Toronto: University of Toronto Press, 2006.

Desmond, Adrian. "The Making of Institutional Zoology in London, 1822-1836, Parts I and II." *History of Science* 23, nos. 2 and 3 (1985): 153–85, 223–50.

Desmond, Adrian, and James Moore. *Darwin*. London: Michael Joseph, 1991.

Desmond, Jane. "Displaying Death, Animating Life: Changing Fictions of 'Liveness' from Taxidermy to Animatronics." In *Representing Animals*, ed. Nigel Rothfels, 159–79. Bloomington: Indiana University Press, 2002.

Dix, Harwood. *Love for Animals and How It Developed in Great Britain*. 1928. Reprint Lewiston, NY: Edwin Mellen Press, 2002.

Donald, Diana. "'Beastly Sights': The Treatment of Animals a Moral Theme in Representations of London, C. 1820–1850." *Art History* 22, no. 4 (1999): 514–44.

– *Picturing Animals in Britain, 1750–1850*. New Haven: Yale University Press, 2007.

Donald, Diana, and Jane Munro, eds. *Endless Forms: Charles Darwin, Natural Science, and the Visual Arts*. New Haven: Yale University Press, 2009.

Donald, Moira, and Linda Hurcombe, eds. *Gender and Material Culture in Historical Perspective*. New York: St Martin's Press, 2000.

Douglas, Mary. "Jokes." In *Rethinking Popular Culture: Contemporary Perspectives in Cultural Studies*, ed. Chandra Mukerji and Michael Schudson, 291–310. Berkeley: University of California Press, 1991.

Douglas, Mary, and Baron Isherwood. *The World of Goods: Towards an Anthropology of Consumption*. London: A. Lane, 1979.

Durant, Alice, and John Durant. *Pictorial History of the American Circus*. New York: A.S. Barnes and Co., 1957.

Durbach, Nadja. *Spectacle of Deformity: Freak Shows and Modern British Culture*. Berkeley: University of California Press, 2010.

Edwards, John. *London Zoo from Old Photographs, 1852–1914*. London: J. Edwards, 1996.

– "The Value of Old Photographs of Zoological Collections." In *New Worlds, New Animals: From Menagerie to Zoological Park in the Nineteenth Century*, ed. William A. Deiss, 141–50. Baltimore: Johns Hopkins University Press, 1996.

Elsner, John, and Roger Cardinal, eds. *The Cultures of Collecting*. Cambridge, MA: Harvard University Press, 1994.

Endersby, Jim. *A Guinea Pig's History of Biology*. Cambridge. MA: Harvard University Press, 2007.

Evans, L.T. "Darwin's Use of Analogy between Artificial and Natural Selection." *Journal of the History of Biology* 17 (1984): 113–40.

Farber, Paul Lawrence. "The Development of Taxidermy and the History of Ornithology." *Isis* 68, no. 4 (1977): 550–66.

Feldman, Shoshana. "Turning the Screw of Interpretation." *Yale French Studies* 55/6 (1977): 94–207.

Ferguson, Moira. *Animal Advocacy and Englishwomen, 1780–1900: Patriots, Nation, Empire*. Ann Arbor: University of Michigan Press, 1996.

Finley, Gregg. "The Gothic Revival and the Victorian Church in New
    Brunswick: Toward a Strategy for Material Culture Research." *Material
    History Bulletin* 32 (1990): 1–16.
Finn, Margot. "Men's Things: Masculine Possession in the Consumer
    Revolution, *Social History* 25, no. 2 (May 2000): 133–55.
Fitzsimons, Raymund. *Barnum in London*. London: Geoffrey Bles, 1969.
Flanders, Judith. *Consuming Passions: Leisure and Pleasure in Victorian Britain*.
    London: Harper Press, 2006.
Flemming, E. McClung. "Artifact Study: A Proposed Model." *Winterthur
    Portfolio* 9 (1974): 153–73.
Forty, Adrian. *Objects of Desire: Design and Society, 1750–1980*. London: Thames
    and Hudson, 1986.
French, Richard D. *Antivivisection and Medical Science in Victorian Society*.
    Princeton: Princeton University Press, 1975.
Frost, Christopher. *History of British Taxidermy*. Sudbury: C. Frost, 1987.
Fudge, Erika. *Animal*. London: Reaktion Books, 2002.
– *Animals, Rationality, and Humanity in Early Modern England*. Ithaca: Cornell
    University Press, 2006.
– *The History of Animals* [H-Animal]. 2006. Available from http://www.h-net
    .org/~animal/ruminations_fudge.html. Accessed 15 November 2007.
– *Perceiving Animals: Humans and Beasts in Early Modern English Culture*.
    New York: St Martin's Press, 2000.
Gates, Barbara T. *Kindred Nature: Victorian and Edwardian Women Embrace the
    Living World*. Chicago and London: University of Chicago Press, 1998.
Gibson, Robin. *The Face in the Corner: Animals in Portraits from the Collections
    of the National Portrait Gallery*. London: National Portrait Gallery, 1998.
Gillis, John R. *A World of Their Own Making*. Cambridge, MA: Harvard
    University Press, 1996.
Gowans, Alan. "The Case for Kitsch: Popular/Commercial Arts as a Resevoir
    of Traditional Culture and Humane Values." In *Living in a Material World*,
    ed. Gerald L. Pocius. St. John's, NL: Institute of Social and Economic
    Research, 1991.
Greenberg, Clement. *Avant-Garde and Kitsch*. 1939. Available from http://
    www.sharecom.ca/greenberg/kitsch.html. Accessed 13 October 2004.
Grice, Samantha. "Stuff, Things and Stuffed Things." *National Post*, 24 Septem-
    ber 2003, AL12.
Grier, Katherine C. *At Home with Animals: People and Pets in America*.
    Columbia, SC: McKissick Museum, University of South Carolina, 2005.
– "Material Culture as Rhetoric: 'Animal Artifacts' as a Case Study." In
    American Material Culture: The Shape of the Field, ed. Ann Smart Martin

and J. Ritchie Garrison, 65–104. Winterthur, DE: Henry Francis du Pont Winterthur Museum, 1997.

– *Pets in America: A History.* Chapel Hill: University of North Carolina Press, 2006.

– "The Material Culture of Pet Keeping." In *Routledge Handbook of Human-Animal Studies,* ed. Garry Marvin and Susan McHugh, 124–38. Abingdon: Routledge, 2014.

Guillery, Peter. *The Buildings of the London Zoo.* London: Royal Commission on the Historical Monuments of England, 1993.

Hall, Catherine, and Sonya Rose. "Introduction: Being at Home with the Empire." In *At Home with the Empire: Metropolitan Culture and the Imperial World,* ed. Catherine Hall and Sonya Rose, 1–31. Cambridge: Cambridge University Press, 2006.

Halttunen, Karen. "From Parlor to Living Room: Domestic Space, Interior Decoration, and the Culture of Personality." In *Consuming Visions: Accumulation and Display of Goods in America, 1880–1920,* ed. Simon J. Bronner, 157–90. New York and London: W.W. Norton and Co., 1989.

Haraway, Donna. "Teddy Bear Patriarchy: Taxidermy in the Garden of Eden, New York City, 1908–1936." In *Culture/Power/History: A Reader in Contemporary Social Theory,* ed. Nicholas B. Dirks, Geoff Eley, and Sherry B. Ortner, 49–95. Princeton: Princeton University Press, 1994.

Harding, Les. *Elephant Story: Jumbo and P.T. Barnum under the Big Top.* Jefferson, NC, and London: McFarland and Co., Publishers, 2000.

Harley, J.B. "Maps, Knowledge and Power." In *The New Nature of Maps: Essays in the History of Cartography,* ed. Paul Laxton, 51–83. Baltimore and London: Johns Hopkins University Press, 2001.

Harris, Neil. *Humbug: The Art of P.T. Barnum.* Boston and Toronto: Little, Brown and Co., 1973.

Harrison, Brian. "Animals and the State in Nineteenth-Century England." *English Historical Review* 88, no. 3 (1973): 786–82.

Harrison, Carole E. "Citizens and Scientists: Towards a Gendered History of Scientific Practice in Post-Revolutionary France." *Gender and History* 13, no. 3 (2001): 444–80.

Hauser, Kitty. "Coming Apart at the Seams: Taxidermy and Contemporary Photography." *Make (U.K.),* no. 82 (December 1998–February 1999): 8–11.

Henning, Michelle. "Anthropomorphic Taxidermy and the Death of Nature: The Curious Art of Hermann Ploucquet, Walter Potter, and Charles Waterton." *Victorian Literature and Culture* 35 (2007): 663–78.

Henninger-Voss, Mary J., ed. *Animals in Human Histories: The Mirror of Nature and Culture.* Rochester: University of Rochester Press, 2002.

Herriott, Sue. *British Taxidermists: A Historical Directory.* Leicester: Leicester
    Museums, 1968.
Hicks, Dan, and Mary C. Beaudry. *The Oxford Handbook of Material Culture
    Studies.* Oxford: Oxford University Press, 2010.
Higonnet, Anne. *Pictures of Innocence: The History and Crisis of Ideal Childhood.*
    New York: Thames and Hudson, 1998.
Hindley, Diana, and Geoffrey Hindley. *Advertising in Victorian England:
    1837–1901.* London: Wayland Publishers, 1972.
Hoage, R.J., and William A. Deiss, eds. *New Worlds, New Animals: From
    Menagerie to Zoological Park in the Nineteenth Century.* Baltimore: Johns
    Hopkins University Press, 1996.
Hoage, R.J., Anne Roskell, and Jane Mansour. "Menageries and Zoos to
    1900." In *New Worlds, New Animals: From Menagerie to Zoological Park in
    the Nineteenth Century*, ed. William A. Deiss. Baltimore: Johns Hopkins
    University Press, 1996.
Hochadel, Oliver. "Darwin in the Monkey Cage: The Zoological Garden as a
    Medium of Evolutionary Theory." In *Beastly Natures: Animals, Humans and
    the Study of History*, ed. Dorthee Brantz, 81–107. Charlottesville: University
    of Virginia Press, 2010.
Honeycombe, Gordon. *Selfridges: Seventy-Five Years the Story of the Store,
    1909–1984.* London: Park Lane Press, 1984.
Hood, Adrienne D. "Material Culture – The Object." *History beyond the Text:
    A Student's Guide to Approaching Alternative Sources*, ed. Sarah Barber and
    Corinna Peniston-Bird, 176–98. London: Routledge, 2009.
Hopkins, Eric. *Childhood Transformed: Working-Class Children in Nineteenth-
    Century England.* Manchester and New York: Manchester University Press,
    1994.
Horn, Pamela. *Pleasures and Pastimes in Victorian Britain.* Phoenix Mill: Sutton
    Publishing, 1999.
Howell, Philip. "Flush and the Banditti: Dog-Stealing in Victorian London."
    In *Animal Spaces, Beastly Places: New Geographies of Human-Animal Relations*,
    ed. Chris Philo and Chris Wilbert, 35–55. New York: Routledge, 2001.
– "A Place for the Animal Dead: Pets, Pet Cemeteries and Animal Ethics in
    Late Victorian Britain." *Ethics, Place and Environment* 5, no. 1 (2002): 5–22.
Huff, Cynthia. "Victorian Exhibitionism and Eugenics: The Case of Francis
    Galton and the 1899 Crystal Palace Dog Show." *Victorian Review* 28, no. 2
    (2002): 1–20.
Jalland, Pat. "Death, Grief, and Mourning in the Upper-Class Family, 1860-
    1914." In *Death, Ritual and Bereavement*, ed. Ralph Houlbrooke, 171–87.
    London and New York: Routledge, 1989.

– "Victorian Death and Its Decline: 1850–1918." In *Death in England: An Illustrated History*, ed. Peter C. Jupp and Clare Gittings, 230–55. Manchester: Manchester University Press, 1999.

Janasoff, Maya. "Collectors of Empire: Objects, Conquests and Imperial Self-Fashionings." *Past and Present* 184 (August 2004): 109–36.

Jenner, Mark S.R. "The Great Dog Massacre." In *Fear in Early Modern Society*, ed. William G. Naphy and Penny Roberts, 44–61. Manchester: Manchester University Press, 1997.

Johnson, Paul. "Conspicuous Consumption and Working-Class Culture in Late Victorian and Edwardian Britain." *Transactions of the Royal Historical Society* 38 (1988): 27–42.

Jolly, W.P. *Jumbo*. London: Constable, 1976.

Jones, Aled. "The Press and the Printed Word." In *A Companion to Nineteenth-Century Britain*, ed. Chris Williams, 369–80. Malden, MA: Blackwell Publishing, 2004.

Jones, Gareth Stedman. *Outcast London: A Study in the Relationship between Classes in Victorian Society*. Oxford: Clarendon Press, 1971.

Jones, Robert W. "The Sight of Creatures Strange to Our Clime: London Zoo and Consumption of the Exotic." *Journal of Victorian Culture* 2, no. 1 (1997): 1–26.

Kaloff, Linda, and Amy Fitzgerald. "Reading the Trophy: Exploring the Display of Dead Animals in Hunting Magazines." *Visual Studies* 18, no. 2 (2003): 112–22.

Kean, Hilda. *Animal Rights: Political and Social Change in Britain since 1800*. London: Reaktion Books, 1998.

– "Traces and Representations: Animal Pasts in London's Present." *London Journal* 36, no. 1 (2011): 54–71.

Kennedy, Dane Keith. *The Magic Mountains: Hill Stations and the British Raj*. Berkeley: University of California Press, 1996.

Kent, Susan Kingsley. *Gender and Power in Britain, 1640–1990*. London and New York: Routledge, 1999.

Kete, Kathleen. *The Beast in the Boudoir: Petkeeping in Nineteenth-Century Paris*. Berkeley: University of California Press, 1994.

Kete, Kathleen, ed. *A Cultural History of Animals: Animals in the Age of Empire*. New York: Berg, 2007.

Kidd, Alan, and David Nicholls, eds. *Gender, Civic Culture and Consumerism: Middle Class Identity in Britain, 1800–1940*. Manchester: Manchester University Press, 1999.

King, Geoff. *Mapping Reality: An Exploration of Cultural Cartographies*. New York: St Martin's Press, 1996.

Klamkin, Marian. *Picture Postcards*. New York: Dodd, Mead and Co., 1974.

Kopytoff, Igor. "The Cultural Biography of Things: Commoditization as Process." In *The Social Life of Things: Commodities in Cultural Perspective*, ed. Arjun Appadurai, 64–94. Cambridge: Cambridge University Press, 1986.

Koven, Seth. *Slumming: Sexual and Social Politics in Victorian London*. Princeton: Princeton University Press, 2006.

Kriegel, Lara. *Grand Designs: Labor, Empire and the Museum in Victorian Culture*. Durham, NC: Duke University Press, 2007.

Kunhardt, Philip B., Jr, Philip B. Kunhardt, III, and Peter W. Kunhardt. *P.T. Barnum: America's Greatest Showman*. New York: Alfred A. Knopf, 1995.

Lanci-Altomare, Michele. *Good-Bye My Friend: Pet Cemeteries, Memorials and Other Ways to Remember*. Irvine: Bowtie Press, 2000.

Landes, Joan B., Paula Young Lee, and Paul Youngquist, eds. *Gorgeous Beasts: Animal Bodies in Historical Perspectives*. University Park: Pennsylvania University Press, 2012.

Lansbury, Coral. *The Old Brown Dog: Women, Workers and Vivisection in Edwardian England*. Madison: University of Wisconsin Press, 1985.

Laqueur, Thomas. "Bodies, Death and Pauper Funerals." *Representations* 1, no. 1 (1983): 109–31.

– *Making Sex: Body and Gender from the Greeks to Freud*. Cambridge, MA: Harvard University Press, 1990.

– "Orgasm, Generation, and the Politics of Reproductive Biology." In *The Making of the Modern Body: Sexuality and Society in the Nineteenth Century*, ed. Catherine Gallagher and Thomas Laqueur, 1–41. Berkeley: University of California Press, 1987.

Larson, Anne. "Equipment for the Field." In *Cultures of Natural History*, ed. Nicholas Jardine, Jim Secord, and Emma Spary, 358–77. Cambridge: Cambridge University Press, 1996.

Leach, William. "Strategists of Display and the Production of Desire." In *Consuming Visions: Accumulation and Display of Goods in America, 1880–1920*, ed. Simon J. Bronner, 99–132. New York and London: W.W. Norton and Co., 1989.

Lemire, Beverly. *The Business of Everyday Life: Gender, Practice and Social Politics in England, C. 1600–1900*. Manchester: Manchester University Press, 2005.

– "Shifting Currency: The Culture and Economy of the Secondhand Trade in England, c. 1600-1850." In *Old Clothes, New Looks: Secondhand Fashion*, ed. Alexandra Palmer and Hazel Clark, 29–47. Oxford: Berg Publishers, 2004.

Levine, Philippa. *The British Empire: Sunrise to Sunset*. Harlow: Pearson Education, 2007.

– *Prostitution, Race and Politics: Policing Venereal Disease in the British Empire.* New York: Routledge, 2003.

Lightman, Bernard. "'The Voices of Nature': Popularizing Victorian Science." In *Victorian Science in Context*, ed. Bernard Lightman, 187–211. Chicago: University of Chicago Press, 1997.

Linkman, Audrey. *The Victorians: Photographic Portraits.* London: Tauris Parke Books, 1993.

Lippencott, Louise, and Andreas Bluhm. *Fierce Friends: Artists and Animals, 1750–1900.* London and New York: Merrell Publishers, 2005.

Loeb, Lori Anne. *Consuming Angels: Advertising and Victorian Women.* Oxford: Oxford University Press, 1994.

Logan, Thad. *The Victorian Parlour.* Cambridge: Cambridge University Press, 2001.

MacInnes, Ian. "Mastiffs and Spaniels: Gender and Nation in the English Dog." *Textual Practice* 17, no. 1 (2003): 21–40.

MacKenzie, John M. *The Empire of Nature: Hunting, Conservation and British Imperialism.* Manchester: Manchester University Press, 1988.

– "The Imperial Exhibitions of Great Britain." In *Human Zoos: Science and Spectacle in the Age of Colonial Empires*, ed. Pascal Blanchard, Nicolas Bancel, Gilles Boetsch, Eric Deroo, Sandrine Lemaire, and Charles Forsdick. Liverpool: Liverpool University Press, 2008.

MacKenzie, John M., ed. *Imperialism and Popular Culture.* Manchester: Manchester University Press, 1986.

Magnum, Teresa. "Animal Angst: Victorians Memorialize Their Pets." In *Victorian Animal Dreams: Representations of Animals in Victorian Literature and Culture*, ed. Deborah Denenholz Morse and Martin A. Danahay, 15–34. Aldershot: Ashgate, 2007.

Marmoy, C.F.A. "The 'Auto-Icon' of Jeremy Bentham at University College, London." *Medical History* 2, no. 2 (1958): 77–85.

Marshall, Cynthia. "Bodies and Pleasures in the Wind in the Willows." *Children's Literature Association Quarterly* 22 (1994): 58–69.

Martin, Charles D. *The White African American Body: A Cultural and Literary Exploration.* New Brunswick, NJ: Rutgers University Press, 2002.

McClintock, Anne. *Imperial Leather: Race, Gender, and Sexuality in the Colonial Contest.* New York: Routledge, 1995.

– "Soft-Soaping Empire: Commodity Racism and Imperial Advertising." In *Travellers' Tales: Narratives of Home and Displacement*, ed. George Robertson, Melinda Mash, Lisa Tickner, Jon Bird, Barry Curtis, and Tim Putnam, 131–54. London: Routledge, 1997.

McCracken, Grant. *Culture and Consumption: New Approaches to the Symbolic Character of Consumer Goods and Activities.* Bloomington and Indianapolis: Indiana University Press, 1988.

McKendrick, Neil, John Brewer, and J.H. Plumb. *The Birth of a Consumer Society: The Commercialization of Eighteenth-Century England.* London: Europa Publications, 1982.

Merish, Lori. "Cuteness and Commodity Aesthetics: Tom Thumb and Shirley Temple." In *Freakery: Cultural Spectacles of the Extraordinary Body*, ed. Rosemarie Garland Thomson, 185–206. New York: New York University Press, 1996.

Meskell, Lynn. *Object Worlds in Ancient Egypt: Material Biographies Past and Present.* Oxford: Berg, 2004.

Milgrom, Melissa. *Still Life: Adventures in Taxidermy.* Boston: Houghton Mifflin Harcourt, 2010.

Millard, Charles. "Images of Nature: A Photo Essay." In *Nature and the Victorian Imagination*, ed. U.C. Knoepflmacher and G.B. Tennyson, 3–28. Berkeley: University of California Press, 1977.

Miller, Daniel. *The Comfort of Things:* Cambridge: Polity Press, 2008.

– *Material Culture and Mass Consumption.* Oxford: Blackwell, 1987.

Miller, Daniel, ed. *Materiality.* Durham, NC: Duke University Press, 2005.

Miller, Michael B. *The Bon Marché: Bourgeois Culture and the Department Store, 1869–1920.* Princeton: Princeton University Press, 1981.

Morris, P.A. *Walter Potter's Curious World of Taxidermy.* London: Constable and Robinson, 2013.

Morse, Deborah Denenholz, and Martin A. Danahay, eds. *Victorian Animal Dreams: Representations of Animals in Victorian Literature and Culture.* Aldershot: Ashgate Publishing Co., 2007.

Murray, Narisara. "Lives of the Zoo: Charismatic Animals in the Social Worlds of the Zoological Gardens of London." PhD diss., Indiana University, 2004.

Myers, Greg. "Science for Women and Children: The Dialogue of Popular Science in the Nineteenth Century." In *Nature Transfigured: Science and Literature, 1700–1900*, ed. John Christie and Sally Shuttleworth, 171–200. Manchester and New York: Manchester University Press, 1989.

Myint-U, Thant. *The Making of Modern Burma.* Cambridge: Cambridge University Press, 2001.

Nava, Mica. "Modernity's Disavowal: Women, the City and the Department Store." In *Modern Times: Reflections on a Century of English Modernity*, ed. Mica Nava and Alan O'Shea, 38–76. London: Routledge, 1996.

Neil, Timothy. "White Wings and Six-Legged Muttons: The Freakish Animal."
    In *Victorian Freaks: The Social Context of Freakery in Britain*, ed. Marlene
    Tromp, 60–75. Columbus: Ohio State University Press, 2008.
Nicks, Trudy. "Dr. Oronhyatekha's History Lessons: Reading Museum
    Collections as Texts." In *Reading Beyond Words: Contexts for Native
    History*, ed. Jennifer S.H. Brown and Elizabeth Vibert. Peterborough, ON:
    Broadview Press, 2003.
Paul, Lissa. "Beatrix Potter and John Everett Millais: Reproductive
    Technologies and Coolhunting." In *Beatrix Potter's Peter Rabbit: A Children's
    Classic at 100*, ed. Margaret Mackey, 53–77. Lanham, MD and London:
    Children's Literature Association and Scarecrow Press, 2002.
Peacock, Shane. *The Great Farini: The High-Wire Life of William Hunt*. Toronto:
    Viking, 1995.
Pearce, Susan M. "Thinking about Things." In *Interpreting Objects and
    Collections*, ed. Susan M. Pearce, 125–32. London: Routledge, 1994.
Pearce, Susan M., ed. *Interpreting Objects and Collections*. London: Routledge,
    1994.
Pearl, Sharrona. *About Faces: Physiognomy in Nineteenth-Century Britain*.
    Cambridge, MA: Harvard University Press, 2010.
Pearson, Susan J., and Mary Weismantel. "Does the Animal Exist? Towards
    a Theory of Social Life with Animals." In *Beastly Natures: Animals,
    Humans and the Study of History*, ed. Dorthee Branz, 17–37. Charlottesville:
    University of Virginia Press, 2010.
Peleggi, Maurizio. *Thailand: The Worldly Kingdom*. London: Reaktion Books, 2007.
Pemberton, Neil, and Michael Worboys. *Mad Dogs and Englishmen: Rabies in
    Britain, 1830–2000*. Basingstoke: Palgrave Macmillan, 2007.
Perkin, Harold. *Origins of Modern English Society*. London: Routledge, 1994.
Perkins, David. *Romanticism and Animal Rights*. Cambridge: Cambridge
    University Press, 2003.
Perren, Richard. *The Meat Trade in Britain, 1840–1914*. London: Routledge and
    Kegan Paul, 1978.
Philo, Chris, and Chris Wilbert. *Animal Spaces, Beastly Places: New Geographies
    of Human-Animal Relations*. London: Routledge, 2000.
Pick, Daniel. *Faces of Degeneration: A European Disorder c. 1848–c. 1918*.
    Cambridge: Cambridge University Press, 1989.
Pieterse, Jan Nederveen. *White on Black: Images of African and Blacks in Western
    Popular Culture*. New Haven: Yale University Press, 1992.
Poliquin, Rachel. *The Breathless Zoo: Taxidermy and the Cultures of Longing*.
    Pennsylvania State University Press, 2012.

Pollak, Oliver B. *Empires in Collision: Anglo-Burmese Relations in the Mid-Nineteenth Century*. Westport, CT: Greenwood Press, 1979.

Pratt, Mary Louise. *Imperial Eyes: Travel Writing and Transculturation*. London: Routledge, 1992.

Price, Jennifer. *Flight Maps: Adventures with Nature in Modern America*. New York: Basic Books, 1999.

Prodger, Phillip. *Darwin's Camera: Art and Photography in the Theory of Evolution*. Oxford: Oxford University Press, 2009.

Prown, Jules David. "Mind in Matter: An Introduction to Material Culture Theory and Method." *Winterthur Portfolio* 17, no. 1 (1982): 1–19.

Qureshi, Sadiah. "Displaying Sara Baartman, the Hottentot Venus." *History of Science* 9, no. 3 (2004): 236–8.

– *Peoples on Parade: Exhibitions, Empire and Anthropology in Nineteenth-Century Britain*. Chicago: University of Chicago Press, 2012.

Ramamurthy, Anandi. *Imperial Persuaders: Images of Africa and Asia in British Advertising*. Ed. John M. MacKenzie. Studies in Imperialism. Manchester: Manchester University Press, 2003.

Rappaport, Erika. *Shopping for Pleasure: Women and the Making of London's West End*. Princeton: Princeton University Press, 2000.

Ray, Romita. "The Beast in a Box: Playing with Empire in Early Nineteenth-Century Britain." *Visual Resources: An International Journal of Documentation* 22, no. 1 (2006): 7–32.

Reiss, Benjamin. *The Showman and the Slave: Race, Death, and Memory in Barnum's America*. Cambridge, MA: Harvard University Press, 2001.

Richards, Eveleen. "Darwin and the Descent of Women." In *The Wider Domain of Evolutionary Thought*, ed. David Oldroyd and Ian Langham, 57–111. London: D. Reidel Publishing Co., 1983.

– "Redrawing the Boundaries: Victorian Science and Victorian Women Intellectuals." In *Victorian Science in Context*, ed. Bernard Lightman, 119–42. Chicago: University of Chicago Press, 1997.

Richards, Thomas. *The Commodity Culture of Victorian England: Advertising and Spectacle, 1851–1914*. Stanford: Stanford University Press, 1990.

– "The Image of Victoria in the Year of the Jubilee." *Victorian Studies* 31, no. 1 (1987): 7–32.

Richardson, Ruth. "Bentham and Bodies for Dissection." *Bentham Newsletter* 10 (1986): 22–33.

– *Death, Dissection and the Destitute*. London: Routledge and Kegan Paul, 1987.

– "Why Was Death So Big in Victorian Britain?" In *Death, Ritual and Bereavement*, ed. Ralph Houlbrooke, 105–17. New York and London: Routledge, 1989.

Richardson, Ruth, and Brian Hurwitz. "Jeremy Bentham's Self Image: An Exemplary Bequest for Dissection." *British Medical Journal* 295 (1987): 195–8.

Ridell, Jonathan. *By Underground to the Zoo: London Transport Posters 1913 to the Present*. London: Studio Vista, 1995.

Riello, Giorgio. "Things That Shape History: Material Culture and Historical Narratives." In *History and Material Culture: A Student's Guide to Approaching Alternative Sources*, ed. Karen Harvey, 24–46. London: Routledge, 2009.

Ringis, Rita. *Elephants of Thailand in Myth, Art and Reality*. New York: Oxford University Press, 1996.

Ritvo, Harriet. *The Animal Estate: The English and Other Creatures in the Victorian Age*. Cambridge, MA: Harvard University Press, 1987.

– "The Emergence of Modern Pet-Keeping." In *Animals and People Sharing Their World*, ed. Andrew N. Rowan, 13–31. Hanover, NH: University Press of New England, 1988.

– "Learning from Animals: Natural History for Children in the Eighteenth and Nineteenth Centuries." *Children's Literature* 13, no. 1 (1985): 72–93.

– "On the Animal Turn." *Daedalus* 136, no. 4 (2007): 118–22.

– "The Order of Nature: Constructing the Collections of Victorian Zoos." In *New Worlds, New Animals: From Menagerie to Zoological Park in the Nineteenth Century*, ed. William A. Deiss, 43–50. Baltimore: Johns Hopkins University Press, 1996.

– *The Platypus and the Mermaid and Other Figments of the Classifying Imagination*. Cambridge, MA: Harvard University Press, 1997.

– "Pride and Pedigree: The Evolution of the Victorian Dog Fancy." *Victorian Studies* 29, no. 2 (1986): 227–53.

– "Sex and the Single Animal." *Grand Street* 7, no. 3 (1988): 124–39.

– "Zoological Nomenclature and the Empire of Victorian Science." In *Victorian Science in Context*, ed. Bernard V. Lightman, 334–53. Chicago: University of Chicago Press, 1997.

Robbins, Louise E. *Elephant Slaves and Pampered Parrots: Exotic Animals in Eighteenth-Century Paris*. Baltimore: Johns Hopkins University Press, 2002.

Roediger, David R. *Wages of Whiteness: Race and the Making of the American Working Class*. London and New York: Verso, 1999.

Rosenblum, Robert. *The Dog in Art: From Rococo to Post-Modernism*. New York: Harry N. Abrams, 1988.

Ross, Ellen. *Love and Toil: Motherhood in Outcast London*. Oxford: Oxford University Press, 1993.

Rothfels, Nigel. "Catching Animals: The Mirror of Nature and Culture." In *Animals in Human Histories: The Mirror of Nature and Culture*, ed. Mary J.

Henninger-Voss, 182–231. Rochester: University of Rochester Press, 2002.
– *Savages and Beasts: The Birth of the Modern Zoo.* Baltimore: Johns Hopkins University Press, 2002.
– "Touching Animals: The Search for a Deeper Understanding of Animals." In *Beastly Natures: Animals, Humans and the Study of History,* ed. Dorthee Branz. Charlottesville: University of Virginia Press, 2010.
Rothfels, Nigel, ed. *Representing Animals.* Bloomington: Indiana University Press, 2002.
Rowan, Andrew N., ed. *Animals and People Sharing the World.* Hanover: University Press of New England, 1988.
Rowold, Katharina, ed. *Gender and Science: Late Nineteenth-Century Debates on the Female Mind and Body.* Bristol: Thoemmes Press, 1996.
Rubin, James H. *Impressionist Cats and Dogs: Pets in the Painting of Modern Life.* New Haven: Yale University Press, 2003.
Rugg, Julie. "From Reason to Regulation: 1760–1850." In *Death in England: An Illustrated History,* ed. Peter C. Jupp and Clare Gittings, 202–29. Manchester: Manchester University Press, 1999.
Ryan, James R. *Picturing Empire: Photography and the Visualization of the British Empire.* London: Reaktion Books, 1997.
Ryder, Richard. *Animal Revolution: Changing Attitudes towards Speciesism.* Oxford: Basil Blackwell, 1989.
Saxon, A.H. *P.T. Barnum: The Legend and the Man.* New York: Columbia University Press, 1989.
Scanlon, Jennifer, ed. *The Gender and Consumer Culture Reader.* New York: New York University Press, 2000.
Schlereth, Thomas J., ed. *Material Culture Studies in America.* Walnut Creek, CA: AltaMira Press, 1999.
Schneer, Jonathan. *London 1900: The Imperial Metropolis.* New Haven and London: Yale University Press, 1999.
Schudson, Michael. "Historical Roots of Consumer Culture." In *Readings in Advertising, Society and Consumer Culture,* ed. Roxanne Hovland, Joyce Wolburg, and Eric Haley, 61–81. Armonk, NY: M.E. Sharpe, 2007.
Scott, Carole. "Clothed in Nature or Nature Clothed: Dress as Metaphor in the Illustrations of Beatrix Potter and C.M. Barker." *Children's Literature Association Quarterly* 22 (1994): 70–89.
Scott, Joan Wallach. *Gender and the Politics of History: Revised Edition.* New York: Columbia University Press, 1999.
Secord, Anne. "Science in the Pub: Artisan Botanists in Early Nineteenth-Century Lancashire." *History of Science* 32 (1994): 269–315.

Secord, James A. "Darwin and the Breeders: A Social History." In *The Darwinian Heritage*, ed. David A. Kohn, 519–42. Princeton: Princeton University Press, 1985.

– "Nature's Fancy: Charles Darwin and the Breeding of Pigeons." *Isis* 72 (1981): 162–86.

– *Victorian Sensation: The Extraordinary Publication, Reception, and Secret Authorship of Vestiges of the Natural History of Creation.* Chicago: University of Chicago Press, 2000.

Secord, William. *Dog Painting 1840–1940: A Social History of the Dog in Art.* Woodbridge, Suffolk: Antique Collectors' Club, 1992.

– *Dog Painting: The European Breeds.* Woodbridge, Suffolk: Antique Collectors' Club, 2000.

Sheets-Pyenson, Susan. *Cathedrals of Science: The Development of Colonial Natural History Museums during the Late Nineteenth Century.* Montreal and Kingston: McGill-Queen's University Press, 1988.

Shivelbusch, Wolfgang. *The Railway Journey: The Industrialization of Time and Space in the 19th Century.* Leamington Spa: Berg, 1986.

Smart Martin, Ann. "Makers, Buyers, Users: Consumerism as a Material Culture Framework." *Winterthur Portfolio* 22, no. 2/3 (1993): 141–57.

Spang, Rebecca L. "'And They Ate the Zoo': Relating Gastronomic Exoticism in the Siege of Paris." *MLN* 107 (1992): 752–73.

Stallybrass, Peter. "Marx's Coat." In *Border Fetishisms: Material Objects in Unstable Places*, ed. Patricia Spyer, 183–207. London and New York: Routledge, 1998.

Stearn, William T. *The Natural History Museum at South Kensington: A History of the British Museum (Natural History), 1753–1980.* London: Heinemann, 1981.

Stearns, Peter N. *Childhood in World History.* New York and London: Routledge, 2006.

– "Stages of Consumerism: Recent Work on the Issues of Periodization." *Journal of Modern History* 69 (1997): 102–17.

Steedman, Carolyn. *Strange Dislocations: Childhood and the Idea of Human Interiority, 1780–1930.* Cambridge, MA: Harvard University Press, 1995.

Stewart, Susan. *On Longing: Narratives of the Miniature, the Gigantic, the Souvenir, the Collection.* Durham, NC: Duke University Press, 1993.

Strange, Julie-Marie. *Death, Grief and Poverty in Britain, 1870–1914.* Cambridge: Cambridge University Press, 2005.

Swart, Sandra. "'The World the Horses Made': A South African Case Study of Writing Animals into Social History." *International Review of Social History* 55 (2010): 241–63.

Tagliacozzo, Eric. "Ambiguous Commodities, Unstable Frontiers: The Case of Burma, Siam and Imperial Britain, 1800–1900." *Comparative Studies in Society and History* 46, no. 2 (April 2004): 354–77.

Taylor, Basil. *Animal Painting in England: From Barlow to Landseer.* Harmondsworth: Penguin Books, 1955.

Tebbutt, Melanie. *Making Ends Meet: Pawnbroking and Working-Class Credit.* New York: St Martin's Press, 1983.

Thomas, Keith. *Man and the Natural World: A History of the Modern Sensibility.* New York: Pantheon Books, 1983.

Thompson, Andrew. *The Empire Strikes Back? Impact of Imperialism in Britain from the Mid-Nineteenth Century.* Harlow: Pearson Longman, 2005.

Thwaite, Ann. *A.A. Milne: His Life.* London: Faber, 1990.

– *The Brilliant Career of Winnie-the-Pooh: The Story of A.A. Milne and His Writing for Children.* London: Methuen, 1992.

Tickner, Lisa. *The Spectacle of Women: Imagery of the Suffrage Campaign, 1907–1914.* Chicago: University of Chicago Press, 1998.

Tolini, Michelle. "'Beetle Abominations' and Birds on Bonnets: Zoological Fantasy in Late-Nineteenth-Century Dress." *Nineteenth-Century Art Worldwide: A Journal of Nineteenth-Century Visual Culture* 1, no. 1 (2002): http://www.19thc-artworldwide.org/index.php/spring02/206-qbeetle-abominationsq-and-birds-on-bonnets-zoological-fantasy-in-late-nineteenth-century-dress.

Tosh, John. *Manliness and Masculinities in Nineteenth-Century Britain: Essays on Gender, Family and Empire.* Harlow: Pearson Education, 2005.

– "Masculinities in Industrializing Society: Britain 1800–1914." *Journal of British Studies* 44, no. 2 (2005): 330–42.

Tosh, John, and Michael Roper, eds. *Manful Assertions: Masculinities in Britain since 1800.* London and New York: Routledge, 1991.

Trentman, Frank. "Materiality in the Future of History: Things, Practices and Politics." *Journal of British Studies* 48 (April 2009): 283–307.

Tuan, Yi-Fu, *Dominance and Affection: The Making of Pets.* New Haven and London: Yale University Press, 1984.

Turner, E.S. *All Heaven in a Rage.* London: Michael Joseph, 1964.

Turner, James. *Reckoning with the Beast.* Baltimore: Johns Hopkins University Press, 1980.

Turner, John M. *Victorian Arena: A Dictionary of British Circus Biography.* Formby: Lingdales Press, 1995.

UCL Bentham Project. *The Auto-Icon.* Available from http://www.ucl.ac.uk/Bentham-Project/info/auto-iconhtm.htm. Accessed 27 September 2007.

Veltre, Thomas. "Menageries, Metaphors and Meanings." In *New Worlds, New Animals: From Menagerie to Zoological Park in the Nineteenth Century*, ed. William A. Deiss, 19–31. Baltimore: Johns Hopkins University Press, 1996.

Vickery, Amanda. *Behind Closed Doors: At Home in Georgian England*. New Haven: Yale University Press, 2009.

Victoria and Albert Museum. "Bubbles: A Child's World." http://collections.vam.ac.uk/item/O75697/ bubbles-a-childs-world-print-millais-john-everett/

Victorian Christmas Cards from the Seddon Collection. Stockport: Stockport Gallery, 1980.

Vogel, Susan. "Always True to the Object in Our Fashion." In *The Poetics and Politics of Museum Display*, ed. Ivan Karp and Steven D. Levine, 191–204. Washington: Smithsonian Institution Press, 1990.

Wahrman, Dror. *The Making of the Modern Self: Identity and Culture in Eighteenth-Century England*. New Haven: Yale University Press, 2004.

Walkowitz, Judith. *City of Dreadful Delight: Narratives of Sexual Danger in Late-Victorian London*. Chicago: University of Chicago Press, 1992.

– *Prostitution and Victorian Society: Women, Class and the State*. Cambridge: Cambridge University Press, 1980.

Wallace, Irving. *The Fabulous Showman: The Life and Times of P.T. Barnum*. New York: Alfred A. Knopf, 1959.

Walvin, James. *Leisure and Society: 1830–1950*. London and New York: Longman, 1978.

Weiner, Martin J. *English Culture and the Decline of the Industrial Spirit, 1850–1980*. Harmondsworth: Penguin Books, 1981.

Wenzel, Jennifer. "Literacy and Futurity: Millennial Dreaming on the Nineteenth-Century Southern African Frontier." In *Utopia/Dystopia: Conditions of Historical Possibility*, ed. Michael D. Gordin, Helen Tilley, and Gyan Prakash. Princeton: Princeton University Press, 2010.

Werner, M.R. *Barnum*. New York: Harcourt, Brace and Co., 1923.

White, Allon. "Pigs and Pierrots: The Politics of Transgression in Modern Fiction." *Raritan* 2 (1982): 51–70.

White, Allon, and Peter Stallybrass. *The Politics and Poetics of Transgression*. Ithaca: Cornell University Press, 1986.

Willis, Susan. "Looking at the Zoo." *South Atlantic Quarterly* 98, no. 4 (1999): 669–87.

Wilson, A.N. *The Victorians*. London: Hutchinson, 2002.

Wilson, Mark. *Nanoq: Flat Life and Bluesome: A Cultural History of Polar Bears*. London: Black Dog Publishing, 2006.

Winichakul, Thongchai. *Siam Mapped: A History of the Geo-Body of a Nation.*
   Honolulu: University of Hawaii Press, 1994.
Wirtz, Patrick H. "Zoo City: Bourgeois Values and Scientific Culture in the
   Industrial Landscape." *Journal of Urban Design* 2, no. 1 (1997): 1–16.
Wonders, Karen. *Habitat Dioramas: Illusions of Wilderness in Museums of Natural
   History.* Uppsala: Uppsala University, 1993.
Yanni, Carla. *Nature's Museums: Victorian Science and the Architecture of Display.*
   London: Athlone Press, 1999.
Young, Lola. "Hybridity's Discontents: Rereading Science and 'Race.'" In
   Hybridity and Its Discontents: Politics, Science, Culture, ed. Annie E. Coombes
   and Avtar Brah, 154–71. London and New York: Routledge, 2000.
Young, Robert M. *Darwin's Metaphor: Nature's Place in Victorian Culture.*
   Cambridge: Cambridge University Press, 1985.